Pfeiffer Country

Pfeiffer Country

The Tenant Farms and Business Activities
of Paul Pfeiffer in Clay County, Arkansas: 1902-1954

Sherry Laymon

BUTLER
CENTER

BOOKS

Little Rock, Arkansas

BUTLER
CENTER

BOOKS

The Butler Center for Arkansas Studies
Central Arkansas Library System
100 Rock Street
Little Rock, Arkansas 72201

First Edition, 2009

ISBN (hardcover) 978-0-9800897-6-9
10-digit ISBN (hardcover) 0-9800897-6-X
Hardcover printing: 10 9 8 7 6 5 4 3 2 1

ISBN (paperback) 978-0-9800897-7-6
10-digit ISBN (paperback) 0-9800897-7-8
Paperback printing: 10 9 8 7 6 5 4 3 2 1

Acquired for Butler Center Books by David Stricklin
Project manager: Ted Parkhurst
Book design and cover design: H. K. Stewart
Proofreader: Rod Lorenzen
Cover photograph: Arkansas Photo Archive, Butler Center for
    Arkansas Studies
The photographs and illustrations used in this book were secured
    by the author.

Library of Congress Catalog Card Number: 2008927765

Printed in the United States of America

This book is printed on archival-quality paper that meets requirements of the American National Standard for Information Sciences, Permanence of Paper, Printed Library Materials, ANSI Z39.48-1984.

Contents

Foreword

The history of agriculture in the American South seems oversupplied with stories of tragedy and failure. In Arkansas, numerous families recall hard times of poverty and displacement, especially during the Great Depression of the 1930s and the "Great Depopulation" of the countryside that accelerated during the 1950s. In northeast Arkansas's Clay County, one man, Paul Pfeiffer, took a different approach to the development of the land he owned and toward the tenant families who worked his fields. He often provided two-story homes, large barns, corn cribs, and other buildings at a single farmstead. He wanted his tenants to succeed and planned to sell them the land they worked at an accommodating price with reasonable financial arrangements. Pfeiffer did not try to trap his farmers in a cycle of endless debt and unremitting exploitation. Surprisingly his most active decade for these enlightened policies, 1925 to 1935, coincided with some of the worst years for American agriculture in the twentieth century. One hundred twenty-nine farm families worked for him during this time, and he did not alter his benevolent philosophy as the national economy spiraled downward.

Sherry Laymon applies her multiple talents as a scholar, writer, and artist in examining Paul Pfeiffer and his contributions to Clay County. She knows the old buildings, especially the houses and barns, that Pfeiffer placed on his farms. With the aid of former tenants, she has sketched these structures and recreated their floor plans. She also has examined the financial records of Pfeiffer's enterprises and found a remarkable story of business acumen and humane generosity in hundreds of warranty deeds, sales documents, and other transactions. She has done numerous interviews, read dusty newspapers, and compiled statistical evidence. Most tellingly, she knows the story of this land and how it became a place for extensive farming only after its swamps were drained and its timber cut. Paul Pfeiffer accelerated this process when he began purchasing Clay County acreage in 1902. Here was a midwestern businessman, fresh from St. Louis, who saw the possibilities of raising crops on previously untilled soil. A new man in a new place looking for economic opportunity, he had not come to some far western locale, but to the northern reach of the Mississippi Delta. After a few years, he brought his wife, Mary, and their children to the small town of Piggott. They had relocated to a remote, underdeveloped region down river from St. Louis that for some could still be called a frontier.

One daughter, Pauline, only lived in Piggott for two years before going off to college in 1915. She corresponded often with her mother and when Pauline lived in Paris later on, she became Ernest Hemingway's second wife. The famous American author regularly visited the Pfeiffer home in Piggott. Throughout the 1930s, Hemingway spent many weeks with his in-laws. Local families remember these sojourns, but their occasional sightings of the great writer have not obscured their even brighter memories of his father-in-law. Paul Pfeiffer did not join Hemingway for hunting trips out west and only fished with him once off the Florida Keys. By remaining in Piggott during the depths of the Great Depression, Pfeiffer's generous acts helped numerous individuals in these hardest of times. For example, one story has him hiring men to paint his home time and time again to provide some form of useful work. The layers of paint uncovered in the later restoration of the family home as a museum indicates the truth of this legend.

Sherry Laymon well understands both Paul Pfeiffer and Clay County where he remains so well respected. When a scholar of Laymon's ability looks so closely at a life, the results do not always match the public reputation. Yet after her examinations, Paul Pfeiffer remains a good man who did many good deeds. This excellent study is an appropriate recognition of a very fine life. Readers will benefit greatly from learning about Paul Pfeiffer and his vision for improving one part of Arkansas in the first half of the twentieth century.

Clyde A. Milner II
Arkansas State University

I. Introduction

The Civil War and the Thirteenth Amendment to the United States Constitution ended slavery, but it did not end the South's agricultural economy. Although greatly reduced in profitability, Southern plantations would rise again utilizing the labor of black and white sharecroppers and tenant farmers.

Paul Pfeiffer, a transplanted Midwesterner to northeastern Arkansas, owned extensive acreage in Clay County that he farmed with tenant farmers, but his agricultural operations were not the same as the new plantation of the post-Civil War South. In many ways, Paul Pfeiffer seemed to have been a land developer who set out to improve both the agricultural lands and the economic livelihoods of tenant farmers.

The significance of Paul Pfeiffer's tenant farming operation in Clay County, Arkansas, cannot be appreciated until the reader understands how it contrasted with similar systems in the Mississippi River Delta region. Pfeiffer provided excellent living arrangements for his tenants. He did not operate a commissary where he required them to purchase needed items. He allowed his tenants to grow a large garden of fruits and vegetables for their family and five to 10 acres to grow hay and corn to feed their livestock. Pfeiffer provided quality houses for his tenant farmers. Each farmstead contained a set of outbuildings to shelter farm activities and livestock. Furthermore, Pfeiffer's tenant farmers prospered, and they often hired seasonal laborers or their own tenants to assist with planting, cultivating, and harvesting the crops.

During the first half of the twentieth century when Pfeiffer began farming in northeastern Arkansas, sharecropper and tenant farmers provided the labor for most of the cotton farms in the Delta region. Although many sharecropper and tenant farming systems existed in the Mississippi River Delta during the early twentieth century, all planters did not conform to the infamous stereotypes that became largely publicized. Pfeiffer's farming operation in Clay County became overshadowed by the national attention focused on the violence and mistreatment of poor sharecroppers elsewhere in the Delta. The plight of the croppers cannot be discounted; however, it is necessary to present a counter model that accentuated the positive relationship between landlord and tenant farmers.

Many scholarly books and articles discuss the dismal living arrangements that the sharecropper and tenant farmers endured during this period. The authors examine the inadequate living conditions, poor diets, disease, and high mortality rates associated with the croppers' lifestyles. The writers explore the operations of prominent planters in the Delta and described the horrendous actions taken against the farm laborers when they united to obtain better pay and benefits from the planters. Surprisingly, Paul Pfeiffer's tenant farming arrangement, one of the largest operations in eastern Arkansas, escaped scholarly study.

In 1932, during the bleakest period of the Depression years, a three-year surplus of cotton had accumulated, and the price plunged to 6.5¢ per pound. Although Roosevelt created the Agricultural Adjustment Administration to assist croppers and tenants in surviving the financial difficulties that they faced, internal problems within the organization resulted in little being accomplished on their behalf. After Roosevelt's New Deal programs and the mechanization of agriculture decreased the demand for their labor, the sharecroppers and tenant farmers fought to maintain their meager lifestyles and the job security they associated with working the land.

Arkansas's geography contributed to the diverse economies, demographics, and politics that developed in different regions of the state. The Mississippi River, the major transportation route in the South, played an important role in the old South culture becoming prominent in southeast Arkansas. Meanwhile, northeast Arkansas, where the future Clay County would be created in 1873, remained sparsely populated because of the swampy terrain and impassable rivers.

The coming of the railroads into northeast Arkansas during the post-Civil War period attracted logging companies, sawmills, stave mills and other industries that processed the timber from the virgin forests. The railroads brought a new migration of settlers, primarily from the Mid-western states, to the area.

The merging of the diverse cultures and backgrounds of the new settlers in Clay County resulted in it developing its own social atmosphere. Soon after Paul Pfeiffer began purchasing property in Clay County in 1902, his impact on the area became evident. As one of the local leaders, he contributed to the economy, agronomy, culture, modernization, and development of the county.

Pfeiffer's tenant farming arrangement in Clay County, Arkansas, is important because of the many ways it contrasted with the majority of similar systems in the Delta. During its most active period [1925-1935], Pfeiffer's farming operation consisted of 129 farmsteads occupied by individual farm families. Pfeiffer avoided conflicts with tenants that other large planters encountered because he treated his farmers humanely and provided excellent living arrangements for them.

Paul Pfeiffer recruited good farmers who seldom moved from their farms. Although the children of most sharecroppers and tenant farmers in the Delta did not attend school regularly and remained in a cycle of poverty, many of the children of Pfeiffer's farmers graduated high school and attended college. Pfeiffer also did not run a company commissary where he could have required the farmers to shop for overpriced goods.

Pfeiffer did not hold his tenants in a never-ending cycle of poverty, but he preferred for them to prosper from the crops they raised. Furthermore, he assisted them in following an upwardly mobile economic path. When Pfeiffer began liquidating his farms in the 1940s, he sold most of them to his tenants. Pfeiffer priced his farms reasonably and often allowed the buyers to suggest a payment plan that suited their financial abilities. When some farmers struggled with the payments, Pfeiffer worked with them until their financial situation improved. Many of these former tenants eventually accumulated more acreage and hired their own tenants to farm for them. Elsewhere in the Delta, many of the sharecroppers also aspired to own their own farms one day. Few ever did.

The sharecroppers and tenant farmers throughout most of the Delta primarily resided in shotgun shanties during the early twentieth century. Pfeiffer's workmen built shotgun houses and bungalows for seasonal labor, but they erected quality two-story houses that the tenant families occupied.

Only a few relics of Paul Pfeiffer's farming operation remain 60 years after he sold his farmsteads. Of the remaining farm structures still in existence most have been substantially altered or have deteriorated to a point beyond repair. Using photographs of existing Pfeiffer farm structures and drawing upon the memories of former Pfeiffer farmers, sketches of the Pfeiffer houses, floor plans, farm buildings, and farmsteads were developed.

The four elevations of each building, the upstairs and downstairs floor plans of the houses, the various floor plans of the farm structures, and the layout of the farmsteads are shown. Two views are included of buildings, such as the shotgun house and mule barn, where the opposite elevations of the buildings were identical.

The method used to create the sketches involved the trial and error technique. After initial drawings were made from photographs, the experts who lived on Pfeiffer farmsteads—W. F. "Dub" and Marguerite Smart, Alfred and Louise Smith, Jim and Roma Richardson, Jim Poole, and Rodney Rouse—reviewed them for accuracy. Using their personal knowledge of the Pfeiffer houses, barns, and farms, they offered suggestions for revisions and/or additions to the drawings. In some cases they produced their own sketches, which proved to be most helpful.

Changes to the drawings were made several times and the ones that appear in this work emerged from the final critiquing process. Some of the Pfeiffer houses and barns strongly resembled others in the neighborhood of the same design, but due to the desire of the farm family, availability of building materials, or other reasons, some of the buildings varied from the standard floor plans.

The measurements of the structures, when given, are only approximate. Although some measurements were taken of existing Pfeiffer structures, a few were altered to fit into the floorplan sketches. These drawings are mere images of the real structures that existed more than half a century ago. They were designed to present a glimpse into the past history of Paul Pfeiffer's tenant farming operation in northeastern Arkansas.

To examine the extent of Pfeiffer's impact on the local economy in Clay County and the differences between his farming operation and others in the Delta, data taken before, during, and after Pfeiffer's entrance into Clay County agriculture has been examined. The author produced all statistics, percentages, and tables presented throughout the text. The agricultural data for Clay County represent numbers published in the United States censuses, the United State agricultural census, or by the Clay County Extension Agency for the respective years.

Many hours spent studying the seemingly endless stacks of deeds emanating from Pfeiffer's land deals in Clay County revealed the business philosophy of a kind and generous man. He consistently sold farms to tenants on terms they could afford, regardless of their financial situation. Many times he allowed them to set their own payment terms. When a perspective landowner encountered financial difficulties and could not make the scheduled payment, Pfeiffer allowed him to work the farm as a tenant until such time that the farmer could resume his payments. On those occasions Pfeiffer did not punish the tenant by adding late fees, penalties, or additional interest to the delinquent amount. The tenant simply resumed payments on the balance he owed.

The following chapters contain an extended profile of Paul Pfeiffer, his family, farm structures, farming operation, and business activities in Clay County. Hardly any of Pfeiffer's personal documentation of his tenant farming operation exists. Consequently, the conclusions cited in the dissertation are based upon the physical evidence remaining from Pfeiffer's activities in northeast Arkansas, such as the architecture in his farm structures, the layout of the farmsteads, work spheres, patterns of interaction, and male and female roles of the tenant farmers.

The first chapter begins with a brief background of the Arkansas Delta that allows the reader to better understand the demographics of the region. The Indians, Spaniards, and French who traversed the Mississippi Valley left their cultural imprints on the land. The physical evidence resulting from the New Madrid earthquakes of 1811-1812 and frequent onslaughts of the Mississippi, St. Francis, Tyronza, and Little Rivers caused such massive devastation that pioneers bypassed northeastern Arkansas to settle in other areas until the late nineteenth century. The Mississippi River and railroad networks provided important transportation routes that played a major role in the settlement of Clay County.

Life for the early settlers in Clay County was filled with hardships and loneliness. Most of the inhabitants lived in crude shelters located miles away from their closest neighbors. Once the population of Clay County grew and townships formed, the local people established several Protestant churches. Churches not only provided a place for the local people to worship, but they also served as centers for social activities. Even though the geography of Clay County made travel by a horse or mule drawn wagon difficult, it seldom prevented avid churchgoers from assembling together every Sunday.

The town of Piggott was still young and underdeveloped when Paul Pfeiffer began purchasing land in Clay County in 1902. A native Midwesterner, he eventually moved to Piggott after living in St. Louis for several years. Although he joined his brothers, Henry and Gus, as business partners in the Pfeiffer Chemical Company in St. Louis, Pfeiffer's love for agriculture influenced him to focus upon building a tenant farming operation in Clay County. Pfeiffer immediately invigorated the economy in the area when he began draining the swampy terrain for cultivation.

Pfeiffer's wife, Mary, found the transition from the big city of St. Louis to the rural logging town of Piggott difficult. Although her daily routine changed drastically after the Pfeiffer family moved to Piggott, Mary Pfeiffer eventually became involved with the local people and community activities. She initially occupied her time by practicing her Catholic faith, reading many books, and corresponding systematically with family members. The frequent letters she exchanged with her daughter Pauline provided important information in documenting the Pfeiffers' life in Clay County.

Paul Pfeiffer owned one of the largest farming operations in the Delta that contained a portion of the most fertile soil in the world. Although he invested in the land to make a profit, he preferred for others to regard him as a decent human being more than a firm businessman. He based his business deals and land transactions on the word and goodwill of the parties involved instead of written contracts.

Pfeiffer's farming operation diverged from others in the Delta during the early twentieth century in several ways. He provided quality homes, spacious residential areas, and adequate farm structures for his tenants. Most of his farmers prospered from the arrangement. Perhaps an arrangement such as Pfeiffer's may have been intended when the sharecropping system was implemented. Possibly the best rationale to explain the differences between Pfeiffer's farming operation and the sharecropper system is the fact that Paul Pfeiffer implemented a management style that focused on land development and did not insist on maximum income for him from his tenant farmers.

II. Clay County—
Arkansas's Frontier

*Not to know what has been transacted in former times is to
continue always a child. If no use is made of the labor of
past ages, the world must remain always in the infancy of
knowledge.*

—Cicero

While traveling through Clay County, Arkansas, on a train, Paul
Pfeiffer, a St. Louis businessman, realized an incredible
opportunity. In 1902 he began purchasing land and eventually
accumulated approximately 63,000[1] acres. Timber companies had
harvested much of the hardwood trees in the area before Pfeiffer's
initial purchase, leaving stumps in the swampy terrain. He
dramatically improved the land by draining it and converting it into
fields for crops, and then he divided his acreage into small farmsteads.

During the period from 1901 to 1945 these small sharecropping and
tenant farms dominated Arkansas's agricultural system. Pfeiffer did
lease his farms to tenants, but the system he employed and his
relationships with his tenant farmers differed greatly from comparable
arrangements utilized by other planters throughout the Arkansas Delta.

Cotton agriculture prevailed in the Delta economy of the early
twentieth century, but the culture of northeast Arkansas where
Pfeiffer settled contrasted significantly from that of the remaining
Arkansas Delta region. The differences existed not only in the farming
practices implemented by Pfeiffer, but also in the politics and
demographics of the area.

The influence that the planters in the southeast Arkansas Delta[2]
maintained with state legislators spread racist attitudes throughout
other sections of the state; however, changes in the state's

transportation system brought a new population[3] of immigrants to northeastern Arkansas. As a result, the attitudes and customs that rooted in this portion of the state diverged from the Old South mindset associated with the Delta elite.

With the exception of the geographic region known as Crowley's Ridge, the Arkansas Delta covers approximately the eastern one-third of the state. The Lower Mississippi River Valley includes the Arkansas Delta and comprises a vital part of the American landscape stretching from southern Illinois to the southeastern tip of Louisiana. Spanning approximately 35,000 square miles, it covers more than 90,000 miles of rivers and streams, more than three million acres of land, and portions of seven states. The rich, black, alluvial soil deposited by the Mississippi River over many centuries dictated much of the region's social development as well as its landscape and land use.[4]

Geographic regions of Arkansas[5]

Both human and natural resources contributed to the cultural makeup of the Lower Mississippi River Valley. The fluctuation in the human relations of Delta inhabitants mirrored that of the natural environment—sometimes harmonic, sometimes traumatic. Although human-engineered measures controlled the flow of the Mississippi River to an extent, they failed to deter all its sporadic onslaughts. Similarly, the cultural differences birthed from the Delta soil occasionally raged out of control regardless of attempts made periodically to contain them.

Agriculture and "King Cotton" epitomized the Delta, yet converging cultures produced a complexity of history and ethnic expression. The literature, religion, music, politics, and economy reflect the assorted customs and traditions of the people who inhabited Arkansas's Delta. Throughout the centuries the various ethnic groups that settled there consisted of Native Americans, French, Arab, Spanish, African, German, English, Irish, Scots-Irish, Jewish, Italian, Chinese, Mexican, and Southeast Asian peoples. Often these groups intermingled, leaving new cultural imprints on the Delta landscape.

Native Americans in the Mississippi Valley

Many people already lived in the Lower Mississippi Valley when Columbus "discovered" America in 1492. Along with their skills in weaving, carving, sculpting, and painting, the Native Americans relied upon farming, fishing, hunting, and gathering to sustain the Mississippian[6] economies. Their society thrived primarily by hand-farming native plant crops such as maize [corn], a crop first domesticated by Native Americans in the semiarid lands of present-day Mexico.[7]

Farming corn allowed the Mississippians to produce food surpluses, a practice that gradually transformed their lifestyles socially, politically and economically. As they became more agricultural, they increasingly relied on a centralized authority and economic redistribution. The concentrated economic and communal controls required larger agricultural surpluses to support the social structure. They reorganized their settlements into hierarchical ranks that reflected a growing social distance between nobles and commoners.

The Native American groups used the high grounds in the area later known as Clay County, Arkansas, to negotiate peace agreements. One trail, later called Chalk Bluff and Pocahontas Trail, became a famous wilderness road used by early French explorers and pioneers who crossed the Black River. Native Americans grew corn, beans, squash, tobacco, and other crops in the fertile fields on the riverbank. Many years after the Native Americans left the area, mounds and fields yield a varied collection of arrows, stone axes, tomahawks, clay pots, and other artifacts.[8]

Spanish Imprints in the Future Arkansas Delta

Hernando de Soto's Spanish expedition made its way overland through the Southeast to the Mississippi River in 1541. They wandered around the territory later called Arkansas until the spring of 1542. Assuming the swampy lands and people held little value for Spain, they opted not to continue. After de Soto and approximately half the group died from exposure and disease, the survivors made their way to Mexico.[9]

The diseases the Europeans spread among the indigenous people devastated their population. The natives, lacking immunity for smallpox, malaria, typhoid fever, measles, syphilis, and tuberculosis, suffered an overwhelming loss of life when the various epidemics and fevers ravaged their community. The surviving remnants of the traditional mound builders formed new groups, including the Chickasaws, Seminoles, Cherokees, and Choctaws.[10]

The Spanish presence in the region, though limited, left its stamp on the Arkansas Delta. In 1795 the Spanish governor of Louisiana sent Benjamin Foy (Fooy) to Arkansas to serve as a Native American agent. That same year Foy established the first settlement in Crittenden County and the second one in Arkansas. Located on the west bank of the Mississippi River directly across from present day Memphis, the settlement became known as Foy's Point but changed to Campo de la Esperanza (Camp of Hope) in 1797. It adopted the English version of that name, Hopefield,[11] when the United States assumed ownership of the settlement with the Louisiana Purchase in 1803. Since the government of Spain gave much of the land lying in present day Crittenden County to individuals, the legal descriptions of the property still reflect Spanish grant numbers.[12]

French Culture in the Delta

Almost a century and a half passed after de Soto's journey before the next known group of Europeans arrived in Arkansas. In 1673 a small party of French explorers led by Louis Joliet and Jacques Marquette penetrated the hinterlands of the continent. Joliet, a fur trader and amateur geographer, and Marquette, a Catholic missionary, canoed down the Mississippi from the Great Lakes seeking a route to the Pacific Ocean.

Around present day Helena, they encountered a village of Quapaws who confirmed that the river emptied into the Gulf of Mexico. They also warned the Frenchmen about the hostile people in the Spanish territory to the south. The explorers decided not to continue further because of the increased risks of capture by the unfriendly savages or death by the Spanish, whose relationship with the French was not very cordial during this period.[13]

In 1682 Rene Robert Cavelier, another Frenchman known as Sieur de LaSalle, came to America to make a name for himself. He desired to build a series of military bases, trading posts and settlements along the waterways. Rather than seeking riches through gold in the new lands, he thought the real wealth existed in the untapped natural resources. Even though King Louis XIV encouraged LaSalle and provided a little money for his adventure, the French monarch offered no sustained support.[14]

LaSalle led a group of Native Americans, soldiers, and frontiersmen down the Mississippi to its mouth, named the entire region "Louisiana" to honor his King, and claimed the territory for France. In 1686 a French settlement at Arkansas Post[15] became the region's first permanent white settlement. The French subsequently established a line of posts and settlements from present-day Mobile (Alabama), New Orleans (Louisiana), and Ste. Genevieve (Missouri) northeastward to Detroit.[16]

In 1800 a Frenchman named Peter LeMew located on and improved a tract of land where the little village of Brookings, Clay County, later developed. Other Frenchmen followed him and settled in the cleared areas left by the Native Americans and planted peach trees there. They called the settlement Petit Baril, a name it kept for many years until the English renamed it Peach Orchard.[17]

Transportation—River Travel

As the newcomers' settlements became established, Delta inhabitants used keelboats, rafts, and canoes to transport cotton, rice, sugar, tobacco, indigo, and whiskey down the Mississippi River to Natchez and New Orleans. The steamboat travel on the Mississippi River during the first half of the nineteenth century greatly influenced the Delta region's economy. Steamers began traversing the Mississippi River and its tributaries and many made regular stops at Arkansas River towns, such as Marion, Lake City, and Jacksonport. The population and trade of river settlements swelled as steamboat use increased. People who lived along the riverbanks benefited from the traffic by selling firewood and other necessities to the vessels.[18]

Steamboats eventually transported more cargo on the river than all the flatboats, barges, and other crafts combined. The St. Francis, White, and Black Rivers became Arkansas's lifeline to the rest of the world. Riverboats enabled Delta inhabitants to transport goods through New Orleans to the international markets.

Steamers that plied the rivers of eastern Arkansas often encountered various problems. The uncontrolled rivers frequently flooded the region causing banks to cave in and creating sandbars and snags of dead trees and brush. The currents, swirls, and eddys constantly altered the channel and thus generated navigational challenges for the pilots.

Earthquakes Create Sunk Lands and Enlarge the Swamp

The New Madrid earthquakes of 1811-1812, one of the most remarkable natural catastrophes to occur in North America, created Arkansas's sunken lands. On December 16, 1811, several shocks occurred throughout the region of western Tennessee, southeast Missouri, and northeast Arkansas. The ground rose and fell like the ocean, tilting trees, creating deep crevices in the earth, and sweeping large masses of land down hillsides and bluffs. The Mississippi River's current engulfed trees and boats and destroyed everything in its path.[19]

Three people rafting down the river below New Madrid when the first tremors occurred related a graphic account of experiencing the quake. The powerful current carried the helpless rafters upstream for two days. The heaving and undulating banks offered no place for them to land.

The banks of the river started to move about, sand and sulphur smoke were spewed up from what a moment before had seemed solid earth. Then the river current turned back on itself and the raft began to float upstream. The banks rose and fell; there was the gurgling of water and subterranean booming. Whole forests along the river disappeared but for the tips of the tallest trees, and water filled in where the forests had been.[20]

Shocks continued to be felt for several days at short intervals and then gradually diminished in intensity. On January 23, 1812, a second severe quake occurred, followed by another large tremor on February 7, 1812. The earth remained in motion for a full year afterwards. When the tremors ended, the extensive destruction became known. Thousands of square miles of terrain had been permanently transformed.[21]

The earthquake altered the course of the St. Francis westward several miles and created the "sunk lands" in eastern Arkansas. Large landmasses fell in some places 30 feet below their prior elevations, and the depressions filled with water from the St. Francis River. Other sections of the sunk lands rose above their previous level to form domes. Water immediately flowed into the voids, creating lakes and enlarging swamps.

The rushing waters carried topsoil, trees, and brush downstream and deposited them at the mouth of the St. Francis River. The river debris accumulated over time and blocked the natural drainage of the area. The backlog of water caused the Cache and Black Rivers in Clay County to overflow their banks and flood northeast Arkansas.

The Black River and the Cache River, only a few miles apart, run diagonally northeast to southwest across the northeastern corner of Arkansas. During the rainy seasons these streams formed a solid sea of water eight to ten miles wide, impassable except by boat. Furthermore, the vast Mingo Swamp west of Dexter, Missouri, emptied slowly into the St. Francis River and kept its banks full until the annual June floods subsided.[22]

The fertile lowlands, unable to shed the excess water, remained flooded from the Mississippi River west to the higher elevation of

Crowley's Ridge. The entire Arkansas Delta region became a swampy bog from the Missouri border in the north to Helena in the south. Few people inhabited northeastern Arkansas during the period after the New Madrid earthquakes, and the swampy conditions further retarded settlement for another 80 years.

Elias McNabb, one of the earliest settlers to brave the dangers of the swamp, emigrated from Kentucky in 1840. He settled just north of Buckskull [Current View] and later described the region for his grandson, Jake McNabb:

> Buckskull…had only one or two families and a few old vacant log business houses…There were no farms between Current and Little Black Rivers…Bears, panthers, wildcats, wolves and many other fur-bearing animals there made that wilderness a hunter's paradise…My parents…homesteaded 160 acres of land…cleared a farm and built a log house moving into it in 1852. At that time a trading post was located where Corning now stands; it was called Colony…Those roads, during winter and rainy seasons were all but impassable, logs laid crosswise through swamps…In those virgin forests was water everywhere during rainy seasons…[23]

Religion—Clay County

A strong Protestant religious culture developed in what became Clay County. Often early Christian settlers erected churches before building shelters for their own families. In 1842 they established Salem Missionary Baptist Church near Boydsville and New Hope Missionary Baptist Church close to Pollard in 1846. At least eight additional Baptist and Methodist churches appeared as more people moved into the area.[24]

During this period, people often lived at least five miles from their closest neighbors. They attended church on Sundays not only to hear the preachers' sermons but also to socialize with everyone present, thereby learning the latest news and strengthening friendships. Well-attended summer camp meetings also served as social gatherings, a pleasant time that the people usually neglected during the long working days required to keep apace with the farming tasks. In his 1933 history of Clay County, Robert T. Webb illustrated Sunday reunions of early northeast Arkansas residents:

> On Sundays people would hitch up teams or yoke of oxen early and come the long miles over the faint hill trails to the church. Before they reached it those already there would hear the creaking protest of the homemade wagons being echoed down the valleys and about the hills…people were glad to see other people and there were shouted greetings, much laughter, and joking before church took up. The sermons were long and afterward there would be an intermission before church in the evening. The men would gather to exchange talk and strong tobacco and discuss farming and hunting. The women had the growth and merits of their children to compare, and clothes and housekeeping. Friendliness and sentiment, not dissipated by contact with many people, was allowed to flower full and the many friendships formed by these weekly or monthly contacts was lasting and of remarkable sincerity and strength.[25]

A steady flow of settlers, usually single men, from Kentucky and Tennessee entered Clay County until the Civil War. They spent their time building shelters or dugouts, hunting, trapping, fishing, and raising a little corn. When they accumulated a surplus of corn or furs, they made a trip to the trading post at Pocahontas or Cape Girardeau, Missouri, to exchange those items for shot, powder, and food. Some eventually went back to their former home states, returned to the area with a wife and sometimes a family, and established homes on the ridge.[26]

These early settlers cleared small areas for a garden and grew corn, tobacco, potatoes, and wheat for food, and they used the timber cut from the clearing to erect cabins. They only raised enough cotton to make clothes for themselves. Some brought a few hogs, cattle, and chickens with them. Occasionally a hog would stray away, become wild, and be hunted for food by other settlers in the area. They supplemented their diets with the abundant game from the forest, including bear, turkey, deer, raccoon, squirrel, and rabbit.[27]

Creation of Clay County

Clay County first had the name Clayton County. In 1873, the state government formed it out of portions of Randolph and Greene Counties, and named it for Powell Clayton, the Republican Governor of Arkansas following the Civil War.[28] The governor appointed the first county officials to serve until a county government could be formed. The town of Corning sprang up that same year and became the county seat. Two years later the county's name changed to Clay in honor of Henry Clay, the former Kentucky Senator. The renaming happened because of the unpopularity of Powell Clayton in Arkansas.

Clay County's geography created problems among the residents. Crowley's Ridge runs north and south through Clay County and divides it into two sections. Corning rests on the western side of the ridge, but the majority of the residents lived in the eastern section. Crossing over the ridge and through the bottoms by horseback to reach the county seat created hardships for most of the people. Within the year that Corning became the county seat, many wanted a more suitable site.

In June 1874 an election held to decide the issue revealed that the majority of the residents preferred to move it to the Bradshaw field, a more centralized location; however, those on the western side of the ridge opposed the change and prevented the county records from being taken away. Meanwhile, Corning remained the county seat. A second election held in May 1877 resulted in the same outcome as the first one, but with a larger majority.

Two residents named Taylor and Boyd donated a total of 25 acres for the creation of the new county seat, and called it Boydsville.[29] Despite a crowd assembled to hinder the move, a group loaded the county records into ox carts and hauled them across the swamp to the new location. Changing the location did not solve the problem; it just shifted the difficulty of crossing the bottoms to the people living on the western side of the ridge. The discontentment continued over the county seat location until 1881. J. C. Hawthorne, a state senator, influenced the Arkansas legislature to pass an act that divided the county into an eastern and a western district, each having a separate seat of government. The county hired drivers to move the records by oxcarts between the county seats during court terms.

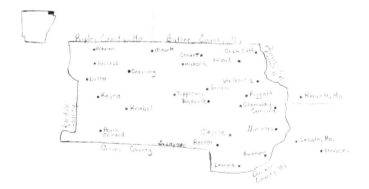

Towns in Clay County, Arkansas

Johnnie Harris, one of the drivers, related the details of one of the trips.

> The ox wagons carrying the records followed a series of trails that led to the final destination. Many sloughs had to be avoided or forded at the shallowest places. Occasionally the trail twisted about so that the creaking of the wagon in front was heard [by the driver] a quarter of a mile behind; or [when one looked] through the woods on either side [he] saw the cart preceding him going back in the direction it had come

from while avoiding large trees and covering bog holes with small trees and saplings so the wagons could continue.[30]

Even with the division of the county and each section receiving a separate county seat, the people living in the eastern district continued to protest. They found the location of Boydsville inconvenient and petitioned to have the eastern seat moved to Greenway. When voters rejected the petition in September 1888, much political manipulation resulted in the selection of Piggott as the county seat of the eastern district.[31]

The county seat issue created an intense political atmosphere in Clay County until it had been settled; however, the county elections aroused little excitement afterwards. John Morrows, an early resident of Boydsville, described the first political contest held in the small community.

> On Election Day the crowd met in a grove. Nominations were made, usually only two. A line was drawn; those favoring one candidate stood on one side, those favoring the other stood on the opposite side. This was repeated until all offices were filled. Later the court room was used. A hat was passed and a vote was dropped in for a favorite candidate. A dozen men held all the important county offices for a number of years, alternating at election time. Within a few years this convention form was abandoned, and primary elections adopted.[32]

By the time Clay County had settled the dispute over its eastern county seat, the railroads had entered the state.

Railroad Debut in Northeast Arkansas

Railroad companies first laid track in northeast Arkansas in 1873 and construction peaked by 1879 and continued until the late 1880s. By 1897, Clay County had the core of a great transportation network that linked the previously isolated region to national and international markets for locally produced timber and farm goods. The railroad industry also stimulated the area's economic growth.

Clay County contained four notable towns—Boydsville, Scatterville, Hamburg, and Clayville—when the railroad debuted. Because of differences with the local leadership, the railroad bypassed these towns and they rapidly declined, while other towns, including Piggott, blossomed.[33] Scatterville became Rector; Hamburg and Clayville combined to form Greenway; and Boydsville dwindled away.[34]

The coming of the railroad opened up a new logging era because for the first time vast stands of timber far removed from waterways could be cut. Railroads made it profitable to process the timber along the rights-of-way; therefore, the process of floating logs down the rivers to market gradually decreased as timber companies began shipping them to the sawmills and manufacturing plants by rail. Railroads also offered greater flexibility by building tram roads to haul logs from the cutting areas to the loading skids.[35]

Harvesting the large trees became the predominant industry, and it provided a stable source of income for many Clay County residents. The untapped forests presented an illusion of unlimited development of permanent resources. As the timber companies cleared the land and moved their cutting sites deeper into the forests, they left a vast amount of cutover swampland covered with small trees and saplings.

Around the turn of the century, several large timber mills operated in Clay County, including the Southwestern Lumber Company, the Myers Lumber Company, Chapman and Dewey, the Henry Quallmalz Lumber and Manufacturing Company,[36] the Campbell Lumber Company, and the B. D. Williams Stave Mill.[37] Aside from the few local residents who operated saw mills at various locations and sawed custom house and barn patterns for new settlers who moved into the area, Clay County did not reap much profit from its timber harvest. The large timber companies hauled most of the logs to Poplar Bluff or Campbell, Missouri, for processing.

Some of Clay County's wood products went overseas. One local account recalled that an agent of the Proctor and Gamble Company of England named Frazier came to Clay County to "work out" the black walnut timber around the Vincent Community. Frazier employed local boys to carve wooden pegs and paid a cent each for all they produced. When this method proved unsuccessful, he acquired a portable saw mill and moved it from place to place as he worked the timber out. He left the sawed lumber stacked at the cutting site until the dry season when he shipped it to England to be made into wine casks.[38]

The lifestyle of the Clay County residents changed immediately after the lumber companies began operations. A local resident related the following description of the hustle and bustle they generated among the quiet towns.

> There was no sleep past six o'clock in the morning. At that time each mill whistle, all different tones, gave forth two long blasts, getting up time. At five minutes before seven one long blast from each gave warning that the starting toot was just five minutes away. A long blast at 12, a short toot at one, a long blast at six would signal the end of a 10-hour day. Most workers earned 10 cents an hour, a few were upgraded to 15, 'head sawyer' and filer got 20, millwright 25.[39]

Second Migration to Clay County

Toward the end of the nineteenth century the timber and railroad companies had removed most of the valuable trees and combined efforts to entice new people to the area with the advertisements of farmland at bargain prices. Seeking to divide the land into small lots for sale to farmers and independent timber cutters, they promoted opportunities for them to acquire cheap land that abounded along the tracks of the railroad. They sent thousands of brochures publicizing land for sale at "colonists' rates" to the National Land Congress in Chicago hoping to entice immigrants to northeastern Arkansas. Many people responded to the ads and flocked to Piggott, most coming by train from the Midwestern states of Illinois, Native Americana, and Missouri.[40]

O. L. Dalton recounted the following description of the second migration to Clay County:

> A host...would cross the broad Mississippi and the swift flowing St. Francis Rivers into this wilderness of paradise now called Clay County. [They] would 'send word back' to friends and relatives of wonderful forests on fertile ridges, lowlands abounding in wild game in abundance where in stern reality there was never heard a discouraging word. After a few years of development, they again sent word back of a new country where there was no sleep after early dawn of account of the awakening toots from the whistles of timber mills and the noise from busy saws and hammers of home builders.[41]

Robert Webb, whose parents came to Piggott in 1889, described the makeup of early Clay County residents and the mixing of their cultures as his family knew them:

> The local people took over some of the habits of those that came in [from the North] and the latter took over some of the Southern social ideals. And over this durable philosophy of the north and the romantic one of the south was cast the influence of the frontier; its buoyancy, breeziness, large gestures and optimism, generated, as they were, by the unlimited resources and places for expansion, the rapidly changing conditions and the elbow rubbing of many people.[42]

The railroads also encouraged immigration into the newly-opened areas by offering special immigrant rates to settlers. They hired land agents who negotiated real estate deals with prospective settlers and enticed businessmen and investors into the area. Railroad conductors and engineers even stopped trains at any point on the line to discharge passengers who responded to their advertisements.[43]

The efforts of the timber and railroad companies to attract new settlers generated a tremendous response, which spurred an increase in the value of the "fine farming country." Soon lumber companies that owned the cutover areas began selling them to settlers and speculators. R. W. Balch advertised "A Half-Million Acres of Timber and Farm Lands for Sale—large and small tracts. Land for the rich and the poor—the farmer, the sawmill man, stave men and tie makers. Finely timbered with oak, ash, cypress and cottonwood."[44]

Until 1895 the plentiful timberwork provided the chief means of livelihood for Clay County residents.[45] By the end of the nineteenth century, several small farms began emerging, and the land in northeast Arkansas gradually fell more and more into the hands of small landowners. The timber companies subdivided their holdings, and real estate agents advertised cheap land for sale in plots of 10, 20, or 40 acres. This land sold for a discounted price since it no longer contained the valuable hardwood. Many people who could not afford to purchase land beforehand now found the price within their means.

Although most timber companies opted to sell the cutover land, some put it into agriculture production and used tenant farmers to work the land. As soon as the Henry Quallmalz Lumber and Manufacturing Company removed the timber from a sizable piece of ground, it converted the cutover wilderness into farmland. At one time it owned 27,000 acres and operated five cotton gins. The company built houses and barns for the tenants, dug ditches to drain the land of excess water, and laid out roads on their property.[46]

The number of small farms established and amount of agricultural goods produced in northeast Arkansas increased significantly as the population increased. The 1880 census[47] taken after the formation of

Clay County and the entrance of rail service to the area revealed a total population of 7,213, most who resided on 960 farms. The total farm acreage equaled 87,131 acres of which only 27,132 [31%] had been improved. The value of an acre of farmland equaled $5.08.[48] [See Table 2.1 below]

Table 2.1 Agricultural Data for Clay County, 1880-1910[49]

Year	Total farms	Avg # of farm acres	# of tenant farms	Total # acres in farms	Acres of improved farmland	Value of land acre	Total pop.
1880	960	91	219	87,131	27,132	$5.08	7213
1890	1418	88	201	124,426	51,937	$8.16	12,200
1900	1985	79	810	157,209	80,350	$7.37	15,886
1910	2,943	90	1,526	186,195	111,713	$29.24	23,690

Rail transportation and the timber industry greatly stimulated the growth of the population and farming operations in the region, a trend that continued for several decades. The 1890 census data reflected remarkable increases in population—69%, number of farms—48%, improved land in farms—91%, total acreage in farms—43%, and value of farmland—61%.[50] Most farmers owned farms of approximately 90 acres and produced the agricultural goods themselves. Although some larger farms employed tenants or sharecroppers to assist in farm production, they only worked on 23% of the farms in 1880. That number decreased somewhat in 1890 to 14% as more croppers purchased cutover land and became owners themselves.

The growth of population and production of farm goods in Clay County continued according to the 1900 census information; however, the Depression of 1893 slowed the rapid pace to some extent. Local farmers needing cash to meet their mortgage debt increased output. The rapid expansion of farming operations across the nation during this decade propelled the output of staples to new highs. Furthermore, fierce competition by foreign countries flooded the world markets with cotton, grain, and corn,[51] the major crops produced in Clay County.

As a result, farmers received smaller profits for their crops, but most still owed mortgage payments on their farms. The lack of cash limited the farmers' ability to hire laborers and purchase farm implements, livestock, seed, and fertilizers. Production of farm crops and demand for farm equipment declined as early as 1891, and the number of foreclosures of farm mortgages and amount of farmland forfeited for back taxes increased.[52]

During the 1890s, the growth rate of the previous decade in Clay County slowed by 39%; however, the percentage of improved acreage in farmland increased by 9%, and the number of farms employing day laborers skyrocketed by 303%. The huge increase in temporary workers included people "from the hills"[53] and farm owners who forfeited their land for back taxes who then assisted with the labor-intensive tasks of cultivating and harvesting the crops during peak seasons.

Regardless of the sluggish economy throughout the nation, land speculators from northeast Arkansas presented their region as the "Land of Opportunity"[54] to prospective immigrants. Farmers from the Midwest who struggled financially responded in great numbers to the advertisements, bringing another wave of new people to Clay County. The 1910 census reflected a 49% increase in population, a 48% increase in new farms, and an 88% increase in tenant farmers. Edwin Reed, whose family moved to Clay County in 1909 from a southern Illinois farm, recalled years later

> ...the struggle my parents were having trying to eke out a meager survival for their small family. My Dad, along with several other families, decided to move just a little farther west. Some decided to make the trip by covered wagons, taking what belongings they could load on and still have room for their family, including their dog...Dad thought the grass

was a little greener west of the Mississippi River. It didn't take Mother long to decide that the covered wagon trip was out, and we would sell out lock-stock-and-barrel, so to speak, and make the trip by train…Dad had heard of a big boom in Arkansas…such as cutting timber, land clearing, logging, and building…where we knew some friends.[55]

Clay County Homesteads in the Early Twentieth Century

Most of the new settlers rejected the swampy, yet fertile river bottoms and opted to settle on the higher ground that Crowley's Ridge provided. In a pattern similar to frontier farming in the early decades of the nineteenth century, the newcomers erected log cabins as shelters for their families and began the laborious task of clearing the land for farming purposes.[56] They used the best timber for their cabins and farm structures, cut and burned the smaller growth, and killed the remaining trees by chopping or sawing a ring around the trunk. After the dead timber decayed or fell during a strong storm, they removed it.[57]

The survival of the immigrants in the Arkansas wilderness depended upon their ability to provide for their own needs. The average man built a house, constructed rail fences, and made his own ash-hopper, plows, churns, and shoes, including the pegs that held the footwear together. Additionally he hunted, fished, and collected tannin from tree bark to tan hides. His wife made clothes for the entire family after spinning and weaving cotton and flax into cloth. Furthermore, she quilted, made soap and candles, and used herbs to treat illnesses that threatened the household. She also assisted her husband with farming tasks such as cultivating and harvesting the crops, feeding the livestock and chickens, and milking cows.[58] Some referred to these experiences as "hard barefooted times."[59]

Usually neighbors assisted each other with the cumbersome tasks of "house raising and barn raisings." One old-timer recalled the frequent occurrences when a new family picked out a commanding eminence overlooking the surrounding valley and erected the famous old log cabins of the pioneer days "without the use of a nail." The general custom for these functions required the host family to provide the laborers with a barbeque or dinner with all the trimmings. Men did the major construction on the buildings while the women assisted in food preparation.[60] Young men carried cut logs from the woods by slipping strong "carrying sticks underneath the logs and hauling them pall bearer style" to the building site.[61]

The day consisted of social activities for those who desired to participate in log rolling, corn husking, and lumberjack competitions. Women exchanged recipes; quilt patterns, and stories about their children. People came from miles away in oxcarts, on horseback, and on foot to attend these gatherings. Food and an opportunity to socialize remained the primary drawing cards when someone planned a house or barn raising. The front porch offered the famous southern hospitality and a genuine welcome to all who attended.[62]

Although the pioneers' homes consisted of a simple cabin, they regarded it as "a castle in a wide domain of freedom." The settlers' homes contained a puncheon[63] floor, roughly hewn, but kept "sparkling clean and glistening" from its regular scrubbing with a home-made broom, lye soap, and water carried from a distant spring or drawn from a nearby well. The tabletops and cupboard shelves reflected the same immaculate radiance. Homemade bedding consisted of "ticks," a cloth case filled with corn shucks or oak leaves until straw and feathers became plentiful. Men folks wore homespun overalls, and most had beards because of the scarcity of razors. The women dressed in home woven linsey, a rough wool-like material usually dyed a dull gray that resembled closely woven burlap.[64]

Settlers placed an ash-hopper in one corner of the yard to collect fireplace ashes. They covered this V-shaped wooden device with boards to keep the ashes dry until they used them to make soap. On the appointed day they poured water over the top sparingly and allowed it to trickle down through the ashes into a trough attached to the bottom that caught the water. After the water passed through the ashes, it turned an amber color and became toxic. The potent solution, called lye, could "eat the barbs off a feather leaving only the quill intact." By boiling lye and "soap grease" together in an iron kettle they eventually produced soap.[65]

Most settlers erected a smokehouse close to the kitchen where they cured and kept game they killed during hunting trips until they consumed it. Jim Matheny of Greenway built a one-room log house with a clapboard lean-to attached. After he learned that a game trail ran near this spot, he sat in his front yard with his rifle and shot anything edible that passed. One winter day he shot an elk but did not kill it. The crippled animal swam the river to Buck Horn. Payne pursued the elk to the river where he shed part of his clothes, swam the stream, and finished the kill. He then walked a mile downstream to a cabin, where he found a neighbor to help him dress it in exchange for part of the meat.[66]

The local settlers fished and hunted for food as well as sport, and many groups found Buck Horn Landing a favorite fishing spot. After farm families had crops "laid by,"[67] groups of six, eight, or more wagon loads of families and friends gathered at Buck Horn to spend the day fishing and socializing. This favorite fishing ground became a memory of the past in 1920 when the St. Francis Drainage District dredged out Middle Slough.[68]

When Paul Pfeiffer first traveled through Clay County, the frontier atmosphere and rural countryside of the Arkansas Delta enthralled him. On one trip when high water over the railroad tracks resulted in a lengthy layover there for the passengers, Pfeiffer walked around Greenway and visited with local residents. They considered the cutover swamp land in no better shape for agriculture production than it had been before the timber companies came. Since the logging industry slowed down, the economic outlook for Clay County appeared bleak. Pfeiffer knew from his farming experience in Parkersburg, Iowa, that an opportunity existed in the area. With his knowledge of agriculture and his vision to drain the swampy bogs and uncover the fertile soil for cultivation, he drastically shaped the economy and culture of Clay County and northeastern Arkansas.

III. Cotton Fields in Clay County

Where there is no vision, the people perish.
—Proverbs 29:18
King James Version

Paul Mark Pfeiffer's parents, Heinrich and Barbara Kluftinger Pfeiffer, immigrated to America immediately following their marriage on April 13, 1856, in Kempton, Bavaria, Germany.[69] They participated in the sizable mid-century exodus from Germany, Switzerland, and Scandinavia—a movement that played an important role in the building of the Midwestern part of the United States. When Heinrich asked Barbara to marry him, she replied, "Yes, if you will take me to America."[70] After their arrival, they lived briefly in Lewiston, Pennsylvania, before moving to Dubuque, Iowa in 1858.[71] The following year they settled on a farm near the Iowa prairie town of Cedar Falls where they raised eight boys and two girls. Barbara gave birth to Paul, the seventh of the Pfeiffer's 10 children, on February 15, 1868.

The Pfeiffer family attended the Methodist Church in Cedar Falls. Harris Franklin Rall, whose father served as pastor of the church, knew them well. According to Rall, to understand the high character and unselfish service of the Pfeiffer children, one must consider the "simple and devout home" in which their parents reared them. His recollection of Heinrich and Barbara Pfeiffer follows:

> [Barbara's] strength was matched by a spirit of love and good will…her eight strapping sons [and] two daughters all looked up to her and [appreciated] her influence while she lived and long after she was gone. Her husband, a man of highest character…too felt the influence of her spirit and faith.[72]

As Paul Pfieffer grew up on the family farm, he readily accepted responsibility around his home. His parents taught him to be independent and to solve his problems by confronting them. By performing daily chores on the farm, he developed an appreciation for cultivating crops at an early age. Although he made remarkable achievements in other vocations, his deep-rooted love for agriculture brought him the most satisfaction during his lifetime. His wife, Mary Pfeiffer, called him a "veritable child of nature—needs only the sun to make him happy."[73]

Paul demonstrated "fine business judgment" as a youth. His mother recognized this trait in his character and sent him to market to barter and exchange surplus produce from their farm for other items. Because of his ability to negotiate a good price for the products, his brothers referred to him as "his mother's agent."[74] He obtained his first job away from the farm in a bookstore where he "read continuously" on a variety of subjects. As a result, he learned to carry on "enlightening conversation on nearly all subjects of discussion."[75] After a period of selling books, he followed his brother Henry's example and obtained a job working in a drug store in Parkersburg, Iowa. Through careful management and hard work, he eventually purchased the store and operated it until a fire destroyed it in the summer of 1893. He rebuilt the store and reopened it under the name Pfeiffer Drug Company. He later hired his younger brother Gustavus, also called Gus, who had attended the Illinois College of Pharmacy,[76] to manage the drug store while he pursued yet another career at the Bank of Parkersburg.[77]

Paul's financial situation improved, and soon he became able to support a family. He married Mary Downey, daughter of Irish Catholic immigrants Daniel and Katherine Byrnes Downey, on October 8, 1894, at St. Patrick's Catholic Church in Parkersburg.[78] Mary devoutly practiced the Catholic religion at the time of their marriage, but Paul, like his father, did not attend church regularly; however, he respected

Mary's devotion to her faith and supported her desire to instill its doctrines in their children and grandchildren.

Although Paul realized financial success early in life in the drug store and banking businesses, he could not ignore his love for farming and agriculture. In October 1895 he purchased 136 acres in Butler County, Iowa, from A. P. and R. L. Everest for $5,200, the first of over 1,100 land transactions that he made during his lifetime.[79] [See Appendix I, page 223]

Gus obviously shared Paul's interest in real estate because they jointly bought, sold, or exchanged several tracts of land in Butler County for the next few years. [See Appendix II, page 223] Although Paul possessed a passion for agriculture, he and Gus learned how to earn a quick profit from their land purchases.

Paul's business relationships with his older brother Henry and younger brother Gus resulted in a strong bond between their families. Paul, Gus, and Henry reflected their mother's strength, humility, spirit of love, and good will toward others. Each of them became very wealthy[80] during their lifetimes, and they continue to be remembered across the nation for their generosity to many people.

Henry, the oldest child of Heinrich and Barbara Pfeiffer, began his first job as a youth in Miner's Flour Mill in Cedar Falls. The dust that Henry encountered daily agitated his allergies, and he soon "shook the dust from his feet" and served as an apprentice to Anton Sartoria, owner of The Corner Drug Store in Cedar Falls for three years. Pfeiffer earned a salary of $100 the first year, $200 the second year, and $300 the third year, minus charges deducted for room and board while working for Sartoria. At the end of the third year, Henry passed the state examination and earned a certificate that allowed him to fill prescriptions and operate the drug store. The following year Sartoria moved to western Iowa and sold the store to the 23-year-old Pfeiffer.[81]

Shortly after Pfeiffer purchased the store he married his childhood sweetheart. He met Annie Merner at the Methodist church in Cedar

Falls where both families attended. Born in Ontario, Canada, to Swiss immigrants John and Maria Merner, Annie moved to Cedar Falls, Iowa, at an early age with her parents. Annie and Henry became engaged, but before they married on March 7, 1882,[82] she secured a promise from him that he would leave Cedar Falls for a city offering more opportunities.[83] They kept house in the rooms above the store and lived frugally until Henry eventually saved enough money to keep his promise to Annie.

As a young entrepreneur, Pfeiffer used various methods to stimulate the local people's curiosity and increase his sales. Instead of buying stick licorice candy in the standard five-pound box, he purchased it by the barrel, thus starting the wholesale druggist business. He placed the barrel of candy in the window and soon the entire contents sold and he repeated the process.[84]

Pfeiffer became the first businessman in Cedar Falls to purchase a full-page advertisement in the local paper. He ran catchy rhymes such as "Pfeiffer pays his chinks for the printer's ink that brings trade to his store." His innovative ideas kept the public interested, increased his business profits, and left his competitors "amazed and dumbfounded."[85]

The owner of the building, aware of Pfeiffer's success as a local businessman, decided to increase Pfeiffer's rent. Pfeiffer stunned the landlord when he bought the lots that surrounded the corner and built the largest store in the town. Henry continued in the retail drug business until 1891 when he sold the store and, keeping his promise to Annie, moved to St. Louis, Missouri. He formed a partnership with a man named Allan, and together they founded the Allan Pfeiffer Chemical Company.[86]

Pfeiffer and Allan struggled financially while trying to turn the young company into a profitable business; however, their efforts proved unproductive and it appeared to be a complete failure. In a final effort to revive the business, Allan and Pfeiffer used their meager funds to hire a clerk to run the office and they became salesmen. They had no money to pay for railroad tickets, but persuaded a ticket broker to provide them with mileage books for their sales trips based upon their word to pay him for the tickets used upon their return. The company struggled for a period, but soon it became successful and remained so for 10 years.[87] In 1901 Allan and Pfeiffer opted to pursue separate interests. Allan withdrew from the business and Pfeiffer named the new company the Pfeiffer Chemical Company.[88]

The Pfeiffer Chemical Company in St. Louis had little working capital and many notes receivable when Henry contacted his brothers, Paul and Gus, to join him in the business. Henry sold Paul and Gus the majority of the shares in the business even though they did not have the money to pay for them at the time. After a lengthy discussion among the three brothers, Paul and Gus decided to sell the remainder of their real estate in Butler County, Iowa, and move their families to St. Louis.

Gus signed his interest in the property over to Paul and immediately relocated to St. Louis. Paul moved his family to St. Louis after he sold most of the land that he owned in Parkersburg, Iowa; however, he still owned 935 acres of which he eventually sold 320 acres in 1903 and 190 acres in 1907. He kept the other 425 acres and allowed one of his brothers, who still resided in Butler County, to farm it for him.[89]

The end of 1901 found the three Pfeiffer brothers as partners in the Pfeiffer Chemical Company; however, Paul Pfeiffer's interest in agriculture ultimately influenced his decision to reject further pursuit of the pharmaceutical business. In 1902, the same year that he made his first land purchase in Clay County, Arkansas, he sold his interest in the Pfeiffer Chemical Company back to Henry.[90] Although Paul Pfeiffer pursued a different vocation than his brothers for the remainder of his life, he showed the same commitment to social benevolence in Clay County that they demonstrated in the national and international arenas.

Under Henry's leadership, the Pfeiffer Chemical Company became prosperous. In 1908 Pfeiffer's business bought control of William R. Warner and Company (founded in 1856) that owned a large manufacturing plant in Philadelphia, Pennsylvania. Annie and Henry Pfeiffer subsequently moved to Philadelphia and lived there until they purchased the Richard Hudnut Perfumery Company in 1916. They then moved to New York City where they retained the company headquarters and principal manufacturing plant.

Their financial situation greatly changed after they moved to New York City; however, they maintained a simple Spartan lifestyle far below their means. A modest-sized and simply furnished apartment on Riverside Drive overlooking the Hudson River replaced the rooms over the village drugstore. Although their business operations spanned three continents, they never owned a summer home in the mountains or a winter residence in the South. They remained unchanged and retained their early habits of industry and thrift.[91]

Harris Rall, who knew Henry and Annie as young people, remembered Henry as a hard working and daring man who demonstrated great enterprising skills and business insight. Although he wanted his business to grow, he did not pursue money to enrich himself, but to improve the lives of others. For example, Henry Pfeiffer rode the subway to work every day instead of having a chauffeur drive him. When asked about his choice of transportation, he replied, "I will have that much more to give."[92]

Henry and Annie Pfeiffer never had children of their own, so they poured their "great love" out on relatives and friends. According to their nephew and beneficiary, Dr. Robert Henry Pfeiffer,[93] Annie treated Gus Pfeiffer, 12 years her junior, and the Merner and Pfeiffer nephews and nieces, as though they belonged to her. He further described her relationship with them.

Her dry humor and common sense prevented her love from ever becoming sentimental or embarrassingly effusive, but those she loved were always aware of its depth and sincerity. They knew they could always depend on her counsel, her comfort, her help, whatever happened.[94]

Even though Henry and Annie struggled financially early in their marriage, they developed an interest in helping others, especially the sick, aged, and orphans, and donated monetary gifts to those with special needs.[95] They eventually devoted themselves to schools and colleges. Their interest in education puzzled Robert Henry Pfeiffer since they regarded the time spent obtaining a college education as a "waste of time, if not as a breeder of worthless highbrow idlers."[96]

Henry Pfeiffer credited the struggles and hard work he experienced in his early business endeavors as the reason for his success. Consequently, he discouraged the pampering of young people and considered a college education a dangerous luxury. Through his business dealings he came to realize the need for trained leaders and understood the mental discipline necessary to obtain a college education. He subsequently financed the education of several young relatives and donated much of his wealth to educational institutions, particularly those conducted under the auspices of the Methodist Episcopal Church.[97]

In 1911 Henry and Annie Pfeiffer promised to pay Robert Henry Pfeiffer $50 a month to attend the theological school at the University of Geneva, Switzerland, while he prepared for the ministry. At that time in Europe, he not only lived well on $600 a year but "had enough money left to start his professional library."[98]

Although Henry and Annie Pfeiffer knew great financial success, they did not live a life of luxury. Their personal frugality contrasted sharply with their generosity toward others. They occasionally traveled abroad, not as tourists, but to visit places that needed schools, churches, or hospitals. They regularly contributed funds to selected locations for those purposes. Rather than creating a foundation to administer her philanthropy, Annie oversaw it herself. She visited and inspected institutions that requested her charity, and she attended board meetings until her health confined her to her home. Between 1919 and 1946 Henry and Annie Pfeiffer contributed more than $15,000,000 to over 60 schools, colleges, hospitals, religious groups, and charitable institutions in America and abroad, many of which bear their names.[99]

Gus and Louise Foote Pfeiffer left St. Louis and moved to New York City about the same time as Henry and Annie. They eventually owned homes in Connecticut and Florida, as well; however, they displayed the same generosity for which Henry and Annie became well known. Dr. Robert Henry Pfeiffer eulogized Gus by saying:

> He was daring without being reckless, firm without being stubborn, imaginative without being quixotic, practical without being an unrealistic theorist, idealistic without being inefficient…All…with whom he came in contact have been helped and enriched by…his…boundless generosity.[100]

Although Gus experienced life from the same humble beginnings as Paul and Henry, success came much easier for him after his older brothers established themselves as leading businessmen in Parkersburg and Cedar Falls, Iowa. He often related to others that the success he enjoyed resulted from his brothers' support as well as his ability to recognize an opportunity and seize it immediately. Even though he worked as diligently as Henry and Paul, he used intuition to make "brilliant and daring decisions" about possibilities of further achievements in the business world. His "rare type of mind" focused on insignificant details as well as those requiring profound thought.[101]

Gus and Louise's only child died an infant. Like Henry and Annie, perhaps for emotional compensation, they doted on their many nieces and nephews. Dr. Robert Henry Pfeiffer knew well the generosity of his uncles Henry and Gus. Not only did they fund his educational expenses, but during 1928 and 1929 when he took a sabbatical from his teaching duties at Harvard to direct an archaeological dig in Nuzi, Iraq, Gus insisted on paying his and Matilde's, his wife, expenses. In a letter Gus wrote Robert dated February 20, 1929, he stated:

> ...I wish to carry out the arrangement to pay all of your expenses until you return to Cambridge. Not knowing how much these are, or whether you need additional funds at this time, I am depending upon you to make request. Please do not hesitate to make this, because doing so will only be carrying out the arrangement made. Therefore, if you need additional funds either now or later, let me know.

Gus, unlike his stoic brothers, enjoyed entertaining youngsters during his frequent visits with them. Dr. E. T. Jaynes, whose father lived next door to Gus and Paul Pfeiffer in Cedar Falls, remembered how Gus delighted children with his "stumblebum" act. He "staggered about, coming perilously close to falling down over and over again." After his performance he encouraged them to avoid becoming a stumblebum like him.[102]

Jaynes also recalled the many times he observed Gus play croquet with such "intensity—almost ferocity"—that he never displayed at any other time.[103] Gus conceded that sometimes his desire to win "warped his hasty judgment." In a letter written to Robert Henry Pfeiffer, he apologized for his behavior during a croquet game with Robert and his young nephew, George. Gus stated, "...besides not being good sportsmanship it was not a good example to George...Frankly, my conscience bothered me after we separated."[104]

Gus's quick mind and sense of humor often afforded him the ability to turn an awkward situation into a comical one. His wife, Louise, shared a particular incident that occurred while she and Gus toured a church in a small German town. Gus could not resist the urge to give the bell rope a small tug. To his surprise, it tolled so loud that the local people assembled in the church. Determined to ensure they did not leave empty handed, Gus delivered a sermon for them—in fluent German![105]

Because of Gus's ability to entertain, those around the Pfeiffer families obviously enjoyed some memorable times while they lived in St. Louis. The city afforded more cultural activities and modern conveniences than the small towns of Cedar Falls and Parkersburg offered. Karl Pfeiffer recalled his father taking him to see every Shakespearean play that came to St. Louis.[106] Furthermore, St. Louis hosted the event of the new century, the World's Fair, in 1904. The Pfeiffer families attended the exhibition and also took other children on occasion. One such guest, the 14-year-old Ethel Ferguson, carried her memory of attending the World's Fair for the remainder of her life.[107]

Although the Pfeiffer family enjoyed their life in St. Louis around the turn of the century, Paul Pfeiffer began focusing on his land purchases in Clay County, Arkansas. The exact circumstances that originally brought Pfeiffer to Clay County became obscure with the passage of time, but the plausible facts can be gleaned from a mixture of accounts still in existence.

According to Karl Pfeiffer, his father had been on a fishing trip in Texas. The train Pfeiffer boarded on his way back to St. Louis stopped for several days in Greenway "for some repairs." During the layover, Pfeiffer surveyed the surroundings and "fell in love" with this part of the country. He returned many times to buy land "by the gallon,"[108] until he eventually owned around 63,000 acres of Clay County real estate, most of which he bought at the rate of one dollar or less per acre. His initial purchase on July 1, 1902, consisted of 220 acres in St. Francis, Arkansas, from Charles and Mary Wing of Cincinnati, Ohio, for eight dollars per acre.[109]

Karl's wife, Matilda, provided some additional details about her father-in-law's introduction to Clay County. Pfeiffer, returning with "some buddies" from a fishing trip near New Orleans, boarded the Cotton Belt train for St. Louis. Recent rains flooded the tracks in Clay County and the train could not continue. As a result Pfeiffer stayed over, most likely at the Greenway Hotel,[110] for three days until the water receded. While in the area he walked around and noted the exceptional fertility of the soil.

Henry Pfeiffer   *Annie Pfeiffer*
Reproduced from Bostonia Magazine, *April, 1942, Robert Henry Pfeiffer Collection, Harvard School of Divinity Archives, Andover, Massachusetts.*

Paul and Mary Pfeiffer   *Gus Pfeiffer*
Courtesy of Hemingway-Pfeiffer Museum and Educational Center

After talking to the local people and asking questions about the land, he learned that they considered the cutover land no more suitable for cultivation than before the timber companies arrived in the area. Even though the economic outlook for Clay County appeared bleak, Pfeiffer began buying tracts that he planned to clear and convert into farmland.[111]

Although Pfeiffer's first visit to Clay County appeared to be accidental, another version of events suggested that Pfeiffer may have planned a stopover there. On the train Pfeiffer met Doctor S. P. Weigart,[112] a land speculator from Rector who spoke well of the region and aroused Pfeiffer's interest in the place. Pfeiffer's curiosity, coupled with a nasal problem that became irritated during the lengthy trip in the smoke filled railcar, convinced him to disembark at Greenway. After looking over the "jungle and cutover land in the St. Francis Valley,"[113] he realized the potential for developing agriculture in the area. Pfeiffer, who suffered from allergies, liked the town because "he felt good here…he could breathe here."[114]

After Pfeiffer made his initial land purchase in Clay County, he hired 200 men[115] who cleared it of trees and underbrush with "a misery whip" [cross-cut saw].[116] Afterwards they dug an incredible ditch to drain the area—a feat many called "impossible."[117] He subsequently planted the acreage in cotton and placed tenant farmers on it to care for the crops. Pfeiffer's daughter-in-law, Matilda, stated that he attracted the best tenants by providing the best farming operation for them. Before he hired anyone to work his land, he "made sure they knew the farming business."[118]

Pfeiffer made frequent trips by train to Clay County to oversee the progress of the cotton. Since local residents only grew a limited amount of the finicky staple, he remained unsure of its success in the area. Pfeiffer's efforts in growing the fiber proved fruitful, earning him approximately $1,442 in 1903.[119]

Even though Pfeiffer lived in St. Louis he continued to grow cotton on his Arkansas property for the next few years and prospered from it. His success in cotton farming in Clay County influenced other farmers in the area to follow suit and soon it became the source of greatest income in Clay County.[120] In fact, their desire to grow cotton became so intense that they often raised it instead of other crops that produced greater yields. The 1910 Agricultural Census reflected an increase in cotton production by 239% over the 1900 numbers, while the output of wheat decreased by 88% and corn by 65%. [See Appendix III, page 224]

In December 1908, Pfeiffer purchased two additional pieces of land in Clay County that totaled 1,700 acres,[121] divided it into farmsteads of 40 and 80 acres, and recruited tenant farmers from as far away as Iowa and Illinois to cultivate his crops.[122] Because of Pfeiffer's agricultural ingenuity and knowledge of supply and demand economics, he grew crops of corn, wheat, and soybeans in addition to cotton. The improvements Pfeiffer made to his land and the success he realized from his crops increased the value of the real estate in the region significantly.

Pfeiffer more than doubled his Clay County land holdings in 1909 by acquiring 5,310 more acres at the average cost of $15.19 per acre, of which he sold 459 for approximately $27.53 per acre.[123] He realized an attractive return on his investment when he harvested his cotton. The price per pound reached a record high of $13.42,[124] earning Pfeiffer approximately $27,327 on his 1909 crop.

Land speculators used the recent success of cotton farming in Clay County to encourage others to relocate to the area. Although Paul Pfeiffer appeared to be a willing candidate, Mary Pfeiffer needed more persuasion to exchange the grand scale of shopping, libraries, museums, and entertainment readily available to her for a "content to live where life began"[125] existence. Furthermore, she greatly valued her Catholic church and the Catholic education her children received at the Academy of the Visitation in St. Louis.[126]

The decision to relocate to Piggott became easier for her after the lifestyle she became familiar with in St. Louis began to change. In 1908, Pfeiffer's brothers and former business partners in the Pfeiffer Chemical Company, Henry and Gus, expanded their business operations and moved from St. Louis to Philadelphia and New York City, respectively. Also, Paul Pfeiffer's widowed mother, Barbara, died in February 1908, followed by the death of Mary's mother in October 1909.[127] The void she realized when the Pfeiffer brothers moved, compounded by the loneliness she felt from the loss of her and Paul's mothers, undoubtedly caused Mary Pfeiffer to ponder the thought that a change of scenery might be a good idea. She became less resistant to the idea of moving to Piggott, Arkansas.

Pfeiffer, supported by Mary's consideration of relocating to Clay County and encouraged by record high cotton prices, continued to accumulate property in the St. Francis River Valley. In 1910, he added another 1,277 acres for approximately $17.43 an acre and sold 207.6 acres for an average of $23.85 per acre. His real estate holdings in Clay County at the end of the decade totaled 5,920 acres. The price of cotton that year reached 13.96¢ per pound, surpassing the record set the previous year. Pfeiffer's share of his tenants' cotton crops alone equaled about $34,434.[128]

The weather of 1911 affected production for some farmers in Clay County. A drought delayed cotton from coming up on schedule.[129] When a cold front moved through the area in early June, the high temperatures caused by the drought created stormy conditions. The heavy rains and hail resulting from the storm did considerable damage to the cotton crop. James Parrish, a tenant on the Brown farm in the northern section of the county, reported that half of his cotton had been beaten down by the hail.[130]

Due in part to the damaged cotton crops earlier in the year, prices remained high enough during the fall of 1911 that C. P. Mabry came to town and purchased cotton bolls that failed to open. He owned a threshing machine and "will thresh and has baled more than 100 bales of cotton that would have been an entire loss to the growers, had it not been for his machine."[131] Mabry received from seven to 12 cents per pound for the lint, depending upon its grade.

Pfeiffer's cotton operations ended with good profits in 1911, but he encountered problems with one of his tenants that almost cost him his life when the enraged tenant attacked him with a knife over a disagreement about a land transaction. On November 23, 1911, Pfeiffer entered into a tenant contract with George M. Jackson, a 71-year-old[132] Socialist leader in Clay County.[133]

According to the terms of the contract, Jackson conveyed his interest in approximately 1,400 acres that he owned in the Eastern District of Clay County to Pfeiffer in exchange for $800 cash and a "life estate" consisting of 360 acres that Pfeiffer owned in the same area. Jackson maintained that as part of the "life estate," Pfeiffer agreed to the following:

> ...to erect a substantial barn yard fence to be constructed of wire, to erect a substantial shingle roof barn not to be less than 24 feet by 40 feet and to reshingle the dwelling house and to otherwise repair the same so as to render it tenantable...on or before May 15, 1912.[134]

Acting upon the agreement of Pfeiffer to repair the house, Jackson immediately moved into it, although he called the shape of it at that time "in a very low state of repair." He further described it as:

> ...wholly unfit for habitation, the roof was old and rotton [sic], the chimneys and flews [sic] were in dangerous condition and the walls and floors were such that the exposure occassioned [sic] thereby was dangerous to health...[135]

As time progressed, Pfeiffer failed to make the repairs to the house. Jackson, a man of many moods,[136] became enraged after he repeatedly requested that Pfeiffer make the improvements. In a forthcoming legal case, Jackson complained that Pfeiffer "willfully, carelessly and negligently" allowed the house to deteriorate to a point that Jackson "contracted rheumatism, bladder trouble, and a seveare [sic] lung trouble." He further suffered "great bodily pain and mental anguish" that required him to spend $10,000 for medical attention and nursing care.[137]

Although Pfeiffer and Jackson signed the aforementioned contract, the legal transfer of the property never occurred. Pfeiffer, well acquainted with Jackson's history of dealing with local businessmen, refused to make the improvements until they legally finalized the land transaction.

George M. and Fanny C. Jackson moved to St. Francis, Clay County, from Fort Jefferson, Kentucky,[138] in the early 1890s. Fanny exchanged some land that she owned in Ft. Jefferson for 1,406 acres of heavily timbered land in St. Francis.[139] While processing the legal transactions on the properties, the land speculator "transferred and combined" the title of the Arkansas lands with those at Ft. Jefferson,[140] resulting in a "mixture of the titles."[141] Her mortgage on the Clay County property burned in the fire that destroyed the Clay County courthouse in 1893,[142] and thus, created a legal quagmire for her because she had no mortgage to show for the Arkansas lands.

W. S. Bryan, an author and publisher in St. Louis, created a fake mortgage for her to protect her interest in the Arkansas property. In a letter to her in July 1894, he stated:

> …I thought it a good thing to tie up the Arkansas lands as much as possible so that if any trouble came up at Fort Jefferson no one would care to undertake to do anything with the Arkansas lands…by holding the mortgage I was in a good position to protect this interest.[143]

In January 1887, the Jacksons and Bryan hired J. M. Myers, a saw mill owner in Clay County, to harvest the timber off their 1,400 acres and cut it into merchantable lumber. They agreed that Jackson and Bryan together receive 50% of the proceeds from the lumber sales and Myers get the remaining half.[144] After Fanny died around 1895 or 1896, George moved to St. Louis where he resided for approximately 10 years.[145]

When Jackson and Bryan decided to settle on their share of the timber proceeds, they disagreed with Myers over the accounting details and filed a lawsuit against him. The particulars of the court documents reflected several dishonest actions and statements by Jackson and revealed his intent to undermine the integrity of the court.

Pfeiffer, who completed several land transactions with J. M. Myers, undoubtedly became familiar with the deception of Jackson during the course of the trial. Jackson consistently exaggerated the truth, twisted the facts, and omitted important information when it suited his purpose. The defense in *Jackson v. Myers* labeled Jackson's exaggerations as "wild." For example, Jackson stated that he only received "about $1,500 worth of lumber which was used in fencing the place." At that time, as the defense pointed out, lumber valued at $1,500 would "make about 15 miles of fence,"[146] an extraordinary amount that greatly surpassed Jackson's fencing needs.

Jackson engaged in many frivolous lawsuits[147] seeking damages or taking advantage of several property owners in Clay County. Most of the lawsuits resulted in a dismissal of the charges and all costs for the proceedings charged to Jackson. The court found Jackson in *State of Arkansas v. George M. Jackson* guilty of perjury. One noteworthy case, *C. E. Blackshare, et. al. v. G. M. Jackson*, demonstrated Jackson's tenacity.

On December 27, 1911, Jackson petitioned the Clay County Circuit Court–Eastern District to establish a new road 30 feet wide running north/south connecting the Boydsville/Piggott road to the Crockett/Piggott road. The court appointed J. J. Walls, E. W. Roddery, and G. L. Lorance as "viewers" to meet, view, and lay out the road on or about February 15, 1912. On August 15, 1912, the court "by its order established and laid out" the road as requested with "some change as to the location."[148]

Although the establishment of the road appeared a good thing for all concerned, Blackshare, et. al. became furious when Jackson proceeded without informing them of his intentions. Of the four plaintiffs in the case, only one resided in Clay County. Jackson took advantage of their absence by having a road laid out that took "part of their most valuable land without practically any compensation."[149] On April 8, 1913, W. J. Driver, the Circuit Judge, issued a temporary restraining order that prevented the work on the road from continuing until the matter could be heard in court. The judge also assessed Jackson with a fine of $250.[150]

Jackson's dishonest and fraudulent behavior during his lawsuits and dealings with the local people damaged his reputation in Clay County. He also eroded any friendships he and Fanny made while they lived on her property in St. Francis during the 1890s. Moreover, the fines and court fees assessed to Jackson resulting from his many frivolous lawsuits left him penniless. Jackson alluded to this fact himself when he filed a lawsuit against Pfeiffer in October 1912. He stated that at the time he moved into the unsafe house he needed "a proper home where he could be cared for during his old age" because:

> …[he] was old, without friends or relatives to whom he could go in the time of need, without funds to provide himself a proper home or to provide himself with proper assistance…[151]

Pfeiffer allowed Jackson to move into the home but procrastinated about making the repairs on the house until the legal exchange of titles to the properties had been made. Pfeiffer never received clear title to the 1,400 acres Jackson owned most likely because of the "mixture of the titles" with that of the Ft. Jefferson property. The matter became more complex when Bryan "tie[d] up the Arkansas lands as much as possible" when he created the fake mortgage for it. After Fanny Jackson died, George Jackson never officially owned the land, and he could not present Pfeiffer with a Warranty Deed to it. Consequently, the tenant contract between Jackson and Pfeiffer became void when Jackson could not meet the terms to which they had agreed.

Pfeiffer went to the house to discuss the issue with Jackson a few days after Jackson filed the lawsuit against him. Jackson demanded that the improvements be made, but Pfeiffer still refused. Jackson became angry, but Pfeiffer, "being used to dealing with Jackson[152] and knowing his moods,"[153] ignored him and started to leave the place. Jackson pursued Pfeiffer and stabbed him in the back with a knife. The weapon entered just below Pfeiffer's shoulder blade and pierced his lung. The physicians at the hospital in Paragould who treated Pfeiffer for his wounds stated that "Pfeiffer is in a dangerous condition, but may recover."[154]

In January 1913, a jury found Jackson guilty of assault with intent to kill for which he received a one-year sentence in the penitentiary.[155] Jackson filed a motion for a new trial and appealed the case to the Arkansas Supreme Court after paying a $2,500 bond.[156] For some unknown reason, but most likely related to Jackson's age or health, the Arkansas Supreme Court never heard the case. Nevertheless, his conviction ended Jackson's exploitation of local residents and the Clay County court system.

Despite the injury that Pfeiffer suffered from Jackson's attack, the continued prosperity of the tenant farming operation in Clay County made the eventual decision of the Pfeiffer family to move to Piggott inevitable. The younger Pfeiffer children—Karl, Virginia, and Max— could adapt to the change in lifestyle much easier than Pauline, a teenager at the time. By the time Pauline graduated from high school in June 1913,[157] most of the obstacles hindering their relocation to Piggott had been removed. Mary still had one final condition to be met before she finally committed. She devoutly practiced the Catholic faith but Piggott had no Catholic church for her to attend.[158] Therefore, Paul Pfeiffer promised to build a chapel in their home so a Catholic priest could regularly administer mass.

Once Mary agreed to move the family to Piggott, Pfeiffer began looking for an appropriate house on his many trips down from St. Louis. Meantime, he continued to buy and disperse farmland. In 1911, his sales exceeded his purchases by 254 acres. He added 743.81 acres at an average price of $24 per acre and sold 998.16 acres for approximately $34.92.[159] In 1912, he assumed another 4,209 acres at $17.30 each, but sold only 344 acres at the same price.[160] At the end of 1912 he had amassed 9,532 acres.

One of Pfeiffer's land sales in April 1912, consisted of a 40-acre farm to W. D. "Buck" and Mabel Templeton of Piggott for $1,050.[161] At the time of the purchase Templeton owned a large house outside the incorporated area but only eight blocks from the courthouse. Furthermore, it sat across the road from the Piggott School on West Cherry Street that the younger Pfeiffer children attended. When Pfeiffer first saw the house, he thought it perfect for his family and offered to buy it from Templeton, who had built it as well as many businesses and 45 additional houses in Piggott.[162]

Since Templeton erected the house for his own family, he installed several features that did not exist in many other residences. At first, he hesitated to sell it to Pfeiffer, but eventually they reached an agreement. Templeton basically exchanged the house for a comparable one that Pfeiffer owned on 20 acres outside the town limits.[163] Since Templeton's family consisted of 18 children (five more subsequently arrived) the extra land surrounding the house provided them with adequate space.[164]

Along with acquiring Templeton's house on May 21, 1913, Pfeiffer made other land transactions. He purchased 1,082 acres at an increased price of $40.41 per acre and sold 60.84 improved and commercial acres for an appealing $114.61 per acre.[165] He completed these transactions prior to his move to Piggott.

After finalizing the purchase of Templeton's house for his family, Pfeiffer kept his word to Mary and converted one of the rooms into a chapel, complete with altar.[166] He also arranged for a priest to travel frequently from Paragould to hold services for his family.[167]

On July 4, 1913, the Pfeiffers arrived in Piggott,[168] a young town that lacked the comforts they experienced during their 12 years in St. Louis. After settling his family in their new home, Pfeiffer bought an additional 320 acres for $37.61 per acre and sold another 414 acres for approximately $49.06 an acre.[169]

The year 1913 proved so special for Paul Pfeiffer that it remained in his memory throughout his remaining years. He survived a brush with death. The relocation of his family to the part of the country that he loved pleased him. Also, he prospered from the increased land values in Clay County as well as from the high profits his cotton produced. At year's end, Pfeiffer owned 10,459 acres and earned around $54,343 as his share of the cotton proceeds.[170]

IV. Pfeiffers in Piggott

This is a county upon which the Almighty has with His
most lavish hand bestowed His richest gifts. It is the most
beautiful portion of God's earth upon which feet have ever
trodden.[171]

At the turn of the century the *Piggott Banner* referred to the town
as "the greatest Emporium of northeast Arkansas" and Clay
County the "Eden of the South." The editors also stated that "these
lines are written without the Spirit of a fictitious boom, but truthful to
the duties of a 'Scribe' who is writing history."[172]

Approximately 200 people called the logging town of Piggott their
home when it incorporated on August 15, 1891.[173] Aside from the
sawmills, lumber yards, and stave factories located there, it contained
a railroad station that also housed the post office, two stores, the
courthouse, Clay County Bank—"the first brick building in Piggott,"[174]
a four-room schoolhouse, and several Protestant churches. After it
became the county seat of the Eastern District of Clay County, it
began to grow rapidly.[175]

Residents from other Clay County towns, including Boydsville,
Crockett, and Pollard, relocated to Piggott and many opened new
businesses there. New people, like the Pfeiffers, moved in from other
states. J. F. Davault, raised on a farm in Illinois, came to Piggott in
1891 and opened the Famous Store, an "exclusive hardware and
furniture establishment ... chocked full of ... dry goods, notions,
clothing, boots, shoes, and everything carried in a general store."[176] He
later operated an electric light plant and built the Electric Roller Mill,
a flour mill that operated by electricity.[177]

J. H. Parrish, known as a clever, sociable and successful hosteller,
opened the Parrish Hotel near the downtown area. It furnished "the

traveling public ... with good sample rooms, office, bedrooms, large dining room, all of which are well ventilated." Also in 1891, another prominent businessman, George A. Evans, started publishing the *Clay County Argus*, a local paper that later became *The Banner*.[178] The Bank of Piggott subsequently opened in 1905.[179]

By 1898 the economic decline caused by the Depression of 1893 abated and development in Clay County resumed. The number of farms, acres in farmland, and newcomers increased considerably. During the first decade of the new century, Clay County farmers produced a variety of crops including cereals, grains and seeds, hay and forage, vegetables, fruits and nuts, and cotton that totaled $2,179,762 in value.[180] In the fall of 1909 the local farmers and businessmen set aside a day for the residents to bring their farm products and display them in the town square. The idea excited the local people and the entire community turned out. Because of its success the community under the leadership of the County Agent, Dr. S. P. Weigert,[181] organized the first Clay County Fair to be held the following year on October 27-29, 1910.[182]

Business continued to boom in the area, and local residents prospered as well. As agricultural productivity increased, farmers shipped surplus goods by railroad to national and international markets via Memphis or St. Louis. They also hired additional labor to assist them with the farming tasks. The 1910 census reflected substantial increases since 1900 in population [49%], improved land placed into cultivation [60%], sharecropper labor [52%], and a startling 297% increase in land value per acre to $29.24 up from $7.36. Paul Pfeiffer entered Clay County at an opportune time to reap the benefits of deflated land values resulting from the depression of the 1890s and contribute to the agricultural growth and prosperity that dawned with the new century. By improving large sections of land and putting it into cotton production, he also helped boost its value.

Rumors circulated that Piggott contained an oil field and added to the escalation of construction there. In August 1910, Josh Dycus and Newt Cross, the postmaster of Nimmons, pulled a prank by pouring about six ounces of black oil into a pump behind the Webber and Dycus Store. When the people heard about it, they came from as far away as Kennett, Missouri, on 12 flat wagons rigged with homemade seats to experience the excitement. Many purchased property hoping that it contained an oil field. Land in the area sold at high prices as long as oil speculation continued.[183]

Although Piggott never produced oil, it contained other types of mineral wealth. The foothills of Crowley's Ridge near the St. Francis River contained a lead mine and the vicinity of "Dirt Mine Hills"[184] northwest of Piggott held a coal field near the earth's surface. Also, a good quality of potter's clay used for making stoneware existed in large quantities approximately one mile north of Piggott. John (Jeff) Pratt, a prominent builder around the turn of the century, operated a kiln at Rector that processed local clay into bricks. Piggott once served as a shipping point for ocher[185] because of the abundant supply of clay in the area. During World War II, the Hardy Sand Mill sold clay and sand from Piggott to war plants for molding purposes; however, in Clay County's fertile, black soil that produced some of the best crops in the world became the most important natural resource that sustained the local economy after its other resources became exhausted.[186]

The rural, humble lifestyles Clay County residents enjoyed did not match the culture and modern conveniences the Pfeiffers experienced in St. Louis. The Protestant religious beliefs and customs carried out by the local people differed from those familiar to the Pfeiffers as practicing Catholics. Local congregations did not follow the traditional Catholic baptism ceremony of sprinkling holy water on infants at the time of their christening. Instead, Baptists assembled around a nearby stream, slough, or bayou, sang *Shall We Gather at the*

River, and joined their pastor by wading out into the water completely clothed. Standing waist deep with his flock, the pastor recited the appropriate scriptures and fully immersed the new converts who confessed their belief in Jesus Christ.[187]

The slang used by native Arkansans often required interpretation for northern transplants to southern soil. The front page of the *Clay County Courier* used Southern dialect when it published an article entitled "Pounded the Preacher." The first paragraph went as follows:

> The good ladies of the Baptist church of this city pounded their new pastor, Rev. J. J. Mathis, last Friday night. The pounding was quite severe, but the good minister stood the punishment well, and is now ready for another round.[188]

The next paragraph clarified any misunderstandings that arose for the newcomers, such as the Pfeiffers, who recently moved to the South. It stated that the ladies carried "a quantity of meat, flour, lard, meal, baking powder, and everything needed in preparation of several good meals" to Mathis' residence to "show their appreciation" for him and his wife.[189]

Every July or August Baptist and Methodist churches in Clay County participated in another southern tradition—the annual brush arbor camp meetings. The congregations moved the two-week revival services outside because of the high temperatures and humidity during that time of year. Since thunderstorms frequently occurred on short notice, they erected a crude shelter of "brush" to protect the attendants from the elements.[190]

The religious practices of Clay County residents may have seemed strange to Mary Pfeiffer who had been raised in a Catholic home. On the other hand, Paul's mother, Barbara, had converted to the evangelical faith[191] and taught Protestant beliefs to her children. Therefore, Paul probably had been exposed to similar rituals while attending church in Cedar Falls, Iowa, as a child.

Although the local people embraced a religious culture different from the Pfeiffers, it did not prevent them from demonstrating goodwill to newcomers to their town W. E. Spence,[192] a descendant of one of the earliest families in Clay County, became one of Pfeiffer's first business acquaintances in Piggott. He purchased a 40-acre farm from Pfeiffer in February 1912.[193] Active in "everything from church to politics to education,"[194] he knew well when a new family arrived in town. Due to his strong belief in being good neighbors, Spence instructed his kids to contact the Pfeiffer children soon after they arrived in town. His daughter, Ayleene, befriended Virginia Pfeiffer and stayed in constant contact with her after they became adults. The Spence and Moore law firm handled all legal matters arising out of Pfeiffer's land transactions, and their families remained lifelong friends.

As time elapsed the Pfeiffers busied themselves and adjusted to the rustic surroundings of the Piggott community. Mary Pfeiffer spent ample time in the home chapel having daily devotions and attending mass one Sunday each month when the priest, Father Joseph M. Hoflinger,[195] arrived from Paragould. On days when the priest visited, he rode a train in the morning to Piggott and held a late morning mass in the Pfeiffer home. Afterwards he joined the family for the Sunday noontime meal. Hoflinger passed the afternoon playing pinochle with Paul Pfeiffer before boarding the return train back later in the day. Mary, accompanied by other members of the family, attended mass in Paragould or Rector[196] on other Sundays during the month. Otherwise, she passed the time reading books, tending to her family's needs, and writing letters to family members—especially daughter Pauline who attended the University of Missouri School of Journalism in Columbia after her graduation from high school in June 1913.[197]

Pfeiffer's interest in improving the rustic conditions in Clay County began before he became a permanent resident of Piggott. As an organizer and director of the Piggott Power Company in June 1913 he demonstrated his commitment to the new corporation by purchasing four times as much stock as its other 16 stockholders.[198] The Articles of Incorporation of the Piggott Power Company stated:

> The general nature of the business...to be transacted by this corporation is furnishing electric power for lights, fans, etc., manufacturing ice and furnishing power for a general water-works plant in the Town of Piggott, including the laying of mains, pipes, etc., necessary for a complete waterworks system, and selling gasoline and oils, and to perform any and all things necessary to be done in furnishing lights, water, and ice to the public.[199]

The effort to create facilities to provide electricity and public water to residents in Piggott during 1913 accentuated the vision Pfeiffer and his peers in the Piggott Power Company held for their community. During this period, less than six per cent of the population of Arkansas had electricity, and as late as 1940, those who did lived primarily in cities and large towns. In fact, many rural areas of the state, including Clay County, would not establish similar electrification programs until the Roosevelt Administration funded them during the 1930s.[200]

Pfeiffer remained proactive in efforts to improve the community while he continued clearing and draining his land, putting some into cultivation, selling other sections, building houses and barns, leasing farms to tenants, and establishing several businesses. Immediately after Pfeiffer first purchased real estate in Clay County until his death, the local residents benefited immensely from his generosity. Known as a man of endless talents who achieved success through hard work, perseverance and "fair and square dealing," like his brothers Henry and Gus, he received the greatest joy by demonstrating good will toward others.[201]

The year 1914 brought some trying times for cotton farmers across the nation, including Pfeiffer. The increased production produced a bumper crop. When it flooded the world market, prices plunged to

7.35 cents per pound, the lowest in 13 years. Probably as a precautionary step in case the downward trend continued, Pfeiffer began selling much of the land he had accumulated and only acquired a limited amount of new acreage the next few years. [See Appendix IV, page 224]

Many times Pfeiffer sold a parcel of land to a farmer who eventually encountered financial difficulties and could not make the scheduled payments. Instead of repossessing the property, Pfeiffer allowed them to occupy the farmstead as tenants until they could resume the payments on the property. Since he gave the buyers a Warranty Deed when they made the purchase, he purchased the land back for $1 and assumed legal title to the land during the meantime. When they resumed the payments, he transferred the deed back to them for $1.[202] A transaction of this nature is shown in Appendix IV regarding a tract of land that included 103.15 acres.

Pfeiffer presented George and Nellie Price with a Warranty Deed to the property when they originally purchased it from him in November 1917 for $7,725, or $74.89 per acre. After they found they could not make the payments, Pfeiffer "bought" the property back from them for $1 but allowed them to continue farming the land as tenants in return for 25% of the cotton crop and 33% of all other crops they produced.[203] For some reason, either their slack work habits or inability to assume the payments, Pfeiffer purchased the land back from them for $79.91 an acre in 1919.[204]

The deflated cotton prices of 1914 rebounded in 1915 to 11.22 cents per pound, largely due to heavy rains ruining the crop during harvest time. In the fall and winter of 1915 an enormous amount of rainfall caused several breaks in the St. Francis River levee near Nimmons. The bottomland south of Carryville and Nimmons contained "from two to four feet [of water] with…sand ridges sticking out."[205] The flooded conditions continued throughout the winter of 1915 and the spring of 1916. Residents frequently recalled how water often seeped into the wagon beds during funeral processions during that time.[206] Jerry Hendrick, a mail carrier on Greenway Route One for 28 years, stated that many times residents on his route pulled or pushed him out of the mud. He further described the soupy terrain.

> Road conditions were terrible. Lack of proper drainage and the St. Francis River water was pocketed in the bious [bayous]. Water would freeze making the roads impassable from the effects of thin ice. Frequently it was necessary to leave the regular line of travel and go through fields seeking higher ground so that complete mail service could be rendered…A lot of volunteer donation work was done on the trails called roads.[207]

Although visionaries like Paul Pfeiffer advanced ideas to modernize Clay County, the vast span of flooded land hindered efforts to develop them. The spring rains saturated areas that stayed inundated year-round. Individual landowners and large companies attempted to drain the land, but the task proved overwhelming for their isolated efforts. Meantime, the upward movement of cotton prices continued throughout this same period when Pfeiffer sold a large portion of his land. Cotton prices reached a new record each year until it peaked at 35.36 cents per pound in 1919. [See Appendix IV, page 224]

By the end of 1919, Pfeiffer owned 5,369 acres, approximately half the amount that he accumulated by 1913. Since he had cleared and drained most of the land and erected barns and houses on the land he sold, the average price per acre he received reflects the value of improvements he made to the property while he owned it.

The problems associated with the fickle cotton prices and certain flooding of farm land faded in comparison to the worldwide desolation caused by an unfamiliar epidemic called the "Spanish flu" of 1918.[208] Doctors knew very little about the disease except that it was very contagious. It appeared in Europe during World War I and killed approximately 21,642,274 people on every continent except Antarctica. From August 1918 until July 1919 over half a million Americans died from the illness.[209]

To curb the outbreak's spread many local governments closed down public gathering places such as theaters and churches. Some passed laws making it illegal to spit, cough, or sneeze in public. Many people only went outside when necessary and wore gauze masks that had been soaked in camphor over their nose and mouth. Those caring for the sick treated them with every possible therapy, including quinine, castor oil, morphine, aspirin, hot and cold baths, and expectorants of pine tar.[210] The Pfeiffer family suffered the effects of the flu when the epidemic arrived in Arkansas. Their youngest child, Max, died of the disease on November 5, 1918.[211]

Virginia, a peppy girl who enjoyed teasing those around her, often livened up the Pfeiffer household. Her mischief periodically lightened the gloomy house after Max's death. The hustle and bustle in the large house declined with only two children—Karl and Virginia—remaining. When Karl and Virginia attended school, the large house became very quiet, and most likely, lonely for Mary Pfeiffer. Furthermore, Pauline accepted a job working on the night desk of the *Cleveland Press* in Ohio in November 1918,[212] which limited her visits to Piggott.

Unquestionably Mary Pfeiffer depended upon her faith to endure the pain and grief known to a mother who lost a child to death. She became involved with the people of the community and began helping the less fortunate members of society. By operating a soup kitchen she fed "a steady stream of…railroad bums" who came to the side door of her house. She also sent them to the doctor if they needed medication.[213]

Mary Pfeiffer replicated locally the benevolence of her sisters-in-law, Annie and Louise Pfeiffer, by contributing liberally to all churches around in addition to the Catholic churches. She also gave to the child welfare program in Clay County "any amount" requested.

Because of her interest in reading and the arts, she later spearheaded a movement to establish a library in Piggott and donated many of the books from her personal collection to it.[214]

Mary became active on the social scene as well by joining a bridge club, and she frequently entertained her friends at cards. She enjoyed hosting these activities more than she did participating in them, especially since she did not play the game well. She also belonged to the Civic Club and helped beautify Piggott by creating flower beds around town and cleaning up the railroad depot.[215]

Paul Pfeiffer duplicated Mary's efforts by taking a lead in improving the community and the local landscape. Because of his success in draining flooded bottom lands and placing them into cultivation, he became an expert on the subject. Several leaders in Clay and Greene counties established the St. Francis Drainage District on May 5, 1905, to create a uniform effort to control the persistent flooding. In the initial meeting, the drainage district commissioners stated as its objective "to patrol and protect the levee on the west side of the St. Francis River;"[216] nevertheless, their efforts proved trivial during the 1915 inundation.

Drawing from Pfeiffer's example, the commissioners instituted a comprehensive system of primary and subsidiary ditches and channels to drain excess water off the land and accommodate runoff during rainy seasons. After the drainage plan became a reality, notable results occurred. Health conditions improved because the number of illnesses precipitated by mosquito bites declined. The number of adult men who died from pneumonia and exposure decreased because the standing water around the timber and in farmland where they worked eventually dispersed. Also, pumped water replaced slough water for drinking, cooking, and bathing purposes.[217]

Jake McNabb, an early resident of Clay County, moved to Ennis, Texas, but revisited the area 32 years later in 1924. He noted the improvements made there during his absence.

I was astonished at the progress and improvements: draining
ditches, good roads, improved farm homes; tilled land where
it was just a morass when I left there. . . We...drove over a
fine, hard surfaced road...crossed Current River on a fine
concrete bridge...I remember, in pioneer days that you were
lucky if you got through, having to ford or swim rivers...[218]

The close of the decade brought changes on many fronts—locally
in Clay County, across the nation, and overseas. The price of cotton
reached record highs, and sharecropper and tenant farmers began
purchasing farms for themselves. In June 1919, the signing of the
Treaty of Versailles brought an end to World War I. War-weary
Americans desired to return their lives to a normal routine. Even so,
social and political unrest in America affected the decade of the 1920s
in its infancy.

Northern factories experienced numerous labor strikes over
working conditions. The side effects of the prohibition movement led
to violent shootouts between gangsters on the streets of Chicago and
New York.[219] Many American intellectuals, including Ernest
Hemingway, tried to escape the postwar turmoil at home and
remained in Paris. In the South planters and political leaders
determined to keep African Americans in economic bondage,
regardless of their emancipation more than 50 years earlier.

Clay County remained on the fringes of the racial problems that
plagued the remaining Delta region, probably because the racism of
the local people discouraged African Americans from settling there.
Paul Pfeiffer, along with other business leaders in Piggott and Clay
County, issued an ad to attract "good white people...who believe in
education, morality, and the better things of life" to their region.
The advertisement placed in *The Arkansas Gazette* stated that Clay
County had "less crime...than in any county in the state of
Arkansas and Missouri [and] no Negroes in the county."[220] [See ad
on pages 76-77]

Although African Americans lived in Clay County from its inception, their numbers never totaled more than 50. [See Table 4.1 below] During the Civil War about 30 slaves lived with their owners in Clay County. Isolated accounts of racism exist regarding how white men spread "unrest among them—trying to get them to leave their owners,"[221] and at least one incident exists in which they succeeded.

Neal McNeil and his family lived near Scatterville with one slave. McNeil died before the war, leaving his widow and some small children. The slave continued to work on the McNeil's farm after the Civil War began. Two years before the war ended, two white men visited the McNeil farm and told the slave that he was a free man. The slave got his coat and told McNeil's widow he was leaving her. He left with the two men, who took him to Pocahontas and sold him on the slave block for $1,900.[222]

Table 4.1 African Americans in Clay County[223]

Year	Number
1880	22
1890	43
1900	9
1910	10
1920	3
1930	10

Two other accounts that explain why Clay remained a white county follow. During 1881, a prolonged drought created a difficult year for farming. The local people welcomed the opportunity to cut ties and lay track for the railroad companies once the construction work reached Clay County. When the tracks crossed the state line into Arkansas, contrary to the assumptions of the white population, the contractors did not discharge the black laborers and hire white ones. White residents of Clay County decided not to let the railroad companies upset their status quo.

O. L. Dalton recounted:

> The…construction contractors moved their colored laborers to the Arkansas side of the river and housed them in tents along the river bank. On the first night, as it became dark and the laborers in bed, (on loose straw piles), a group of white men, with lighted lanterns, marched single file past these tents, opened the tent flaps, passed their lanterns inside, just looked around and passed on. Came sunrise the tents were empty, the former occupants gathered on the Missouri side of the river and no persuasion could get them to re-enter Arkansas. Native white men were hired to fill their places. My father carried one of those lanterns.[224]

Bill Waddle,[225] who supervised a gang of African Americans working for the railroad companies laying track in Missouri, walked off the job and recruited some local people who armed themselves and returned to the construction site at St. Francis.[226] C. E. Jewell, whose father participated in the incident, recalled:

> W. A. (Uncle Bill) Waddle…led the shot gun parade…to the Missouri line at St. Francis in 1881 when the railroad was being built, and told the bosses and Negroes, who were doing the work, that was where the Negroes stopped and the whites would take over. My father was in the march but never helped build the road, neither did Uncle Bill, but white people did build it through Clay County, and the Negroes never inhabited Uncle Bill's County to this day.[227]

Although Pfeiffer had nothing to do initially with Clay County becoming an all white county, he maintained the status quo by not hiring black farmers as tenants on his property. Pfeiffer did not advocate racial prejudice, but he preferred to operate his farming system without the strife that afflicted other Delta planters. He focused on the local situation and opted to live in peace with his neighbors.

Pfeiffer continued buying land in a conservative manner until 1929,[228] largely because of the unpredictable cotton market. The years of deflated prices required him to spend more capital financing his tenants' crops and left less cash to invest in land purchases. [See Appendix V, page 224]

By the end of 1928 Pfeiffer's land holdings in Clay County totaled 7,839 acres. This number shows an increase from the amount he possessed in 1919, but it includes 3,271 acres that he previously sold after the record high cotton prices of 1919. The unusually profitable cotton crops of 1919 encouraged many farmers to invest heavily in cotton farming, but the 55% decline in the price the following year did not produce enough cash to cover their debt. As a result, Pfeiffer leased the farms to the same farmers as tenants, or resold them to other interested buyers.[229]

Some of the most remarkable increases in values of farm products from 1910 to 1920 include overall crops = 157%; cereal = 123%; grains and seeds = 272%; hay and forage = 287%; vegetables = 222%; cotton = 157%; and average price per acre of farmland = 179%. Related to this excessive growth is the 77% decline in sharecropper farms.[230]

The profits reaped from the 1919 cotton harvest not only resulted in many croppers purchasing their own farms but they also encouraged farmers to plant every available inch of farmland in the staple. They incorrectly assumed the trend would continue. Nevertheless, many who received loans to purchase farms could not maintain their mortgages when the price of cotton fell to less than half its value in 1920. As a result, the increase in sharecropper farms increased by a startling 681% from 1920 to 1930.

As the 1920s roared along, they brought many changes to the Pfeiffer family. With Gus's encouragement and assistance Pauline accepted a position in New York working for the *Daily Telegraph*, but she changed jobs soon afterwards and began working for *Vanity Fair* as a fashion reporter. In 1925 she accepted a position with *Vogue* magazine as an assistant to the Paris editor. While there, she met and eventually married Ernest Hemingway on May 10, 1927.[231]

Top half of ad appearing in the Arkansas Gazette *on 20 November 1919*

Bottom part of ad appearing in the Arkansas Gazette *20 November 1919*

After graduating from Piggott High School in 1918, Karl entered college at Notre Dame.[232] He later transferred to Harvard for two additional years before becoming employed by his uncles Henry and Gus as a salesman for the Richard Hudnut Company. He met Matilda Schmitt of New Jersey while working in New York and they married on December 9, 1922.[233]

Virginia Pfeiffer never married, but she enjoyed traveling with her friends and family members. After her graduation from Piggott High School in 1920 Paul Pfeiffer bought her a new Ford and instructed her to "get your friends…and take them on a little trip wherever you want to go."[234] Ayleene Spence later recalled the trips to Fayetteville and St. Louis they made with two other girls and a chaperone, as well as how they received a sendoff and welcome back for their trips at the Pfeiffer house in Piggott.

> The morning we were going to leave, we were going to meet up at Pfeiffers. They had breakfast for us. Mrs. Pfeiffer would have this gift—you know her brother-in-law owned Hudnut Cosmetics…so they would be pretty gold compacts from the Hudnut Company…When we came home, she had a meal for us.[235]

With the children out of the house and in different parts of the world, Paul and Mary Pfeiffer started a tradition of going to Tucson, Arizona, every year right after Christmas and staying until the first of March. Paul Pfeiffer suffered from asthma and the dry desert air allowed him to recuperate during their absence from the farming routine.[236]

Pauline returned to Piggott from October through December 1926. During her visit the townspeople became enthusiastic about the possibility of oil being struck in Piggott. Despite the 1910 hoax drillers located an oil well three miles west of Corning,[237] and the people remained hopeful.

In September 1926, the local people raised money to drill 1,200 feet for an oil well. When the efforts produced no oil, the people raised another $2,000, and the drilling continued. According to Pauline Pfeiffer, the whole town buzzed with excitement and anticipation.

> …practically all the men who are involved have given up their regular employment and hover about expecting

deliverance hourly. Piggott will be very funny if the oil does arrive. For not one person in town has more than $10 ahead. The poor cotton crop here combined with the price slump has reduced everything to a nominal basis. Yesterday the circus cancelled its engagement.[238]

The drilling continued, and the residents of Piggott raised more money to "case in the well" that in turn would "bring in the oil." Hopes remained alive since the engineer located a cavity containing gas, and "where's there's gas, there's oil."[239] The drillers who leased the land paid for it by selling shares at $10 each. As time passed, the drilling remained unproductive, and the local people became upset. Pauline stated:

> ...two other oil men are here trying to get leases. One is looking for potash, also, and Papa is FURIOUS at everyone, because they are giving leases. And they are furious at Papa because he isn't leasing his [land]. And if leases are mentioned Papa foams at the mouth. He says everyone is a fool and oil men are crooks, and if oil is found here everyone will have leased his land...[240]

The drillers completed their work on the well almost two months after they began the project. They poured the cement and waited a few days for it to dry. They decided to "pull the plug"[241] out of the well on December 4, 1926, at 7:30 in the morning. The enthusiasm and anticipation spread to surrounding towns, and the trains scheduled additional itineraries to accommodate the crowd of people gathered to observe a moment of history.

The excitement subsided, and the crowds dispersed when "the bottom dropped out."[242] In Pauline's letter to Ernest a week later, she summed up the outcome by simply writing, "no oil yet."[243] Gus Pfeiffer rekindled the prospect of discovering oil in Piggott when he intimated to Paul and Mary Pfeiffer that he might put down a test oil well.[244]

Interest continued to rise when a "reliable party from the El Dorado field" also considered making a test drill. Mary estimated the cost of doing so at "about 50,000."[245] The exorbitant expense and the huge risk involved, given the history of failed drilling for oil in Clay County, eventually extinguished any desire Gus and the group from El Dorado had to pursue it further.

Although the Pfeiffers became involved with the people and social activities of Piggott, Mary, Pauline, and Virginia Pfeiffer considered the local people quite peculiar. Mary Pfeiffer often referred to them as "natives" in her correspondence to family members.[246] Over time, though, the antipathy she first felt toward Piggott dissipated, and she found it a peaceful and serene place to live. She admitted that its small town atmosphere "irked" her for a while "but it…passed and now after periodic excursions into the outer world, I find it restful to return."[247] Mary later referenced her aversion to the big city.

> And so the life of the city is beginning to pall at times…I find I would not do for the city at all anymore. A couple of days greatly tires me, not physically but in the head, the weakest part.[248]

Virginia offered the following depiction of "that big hulking Audria," a typical Arkansas girl who assisted the Pfeiffers with housekeeping chores.

> She…doesn't know her place and is now whistling out on the front porch in her stocking feet while writing to her sweetie. Mother is along side looking her most formidable over Shaw's big book but she can't lock little Audria into the back part of the house. If ever a gent calls up for me she yells out, 'Vaginnie, your fella wants to make a date.' Otherwise she's a fine gal, makes swell food and gets untold amounts of work done in her stocking feet…[249]

Pauline Pfeiffer penned the following illustration of a local lady who followed another church tenet of spreading the gospel of Christ to those in prison.

> The only person who seems to be ambitious as usual is Mrs. Jones. She is a religious moron, and is at present putting pictures in the jail—or rather trying to. She bought a Good Shepherd and a Jesus in Gethsemane. She thinks they will be a good influence in the jail. Mrs. Potter thinks they will only be defaced in the jail. Mrs. Marshall feels that the kind of people who go to jail won't appreciate those pictures. She says a man with a lamb will be just a man with a lamb, and a lot of people in this part of the country won't even know it is a lamb.[250]

Paul Pfeiffer, content to be living in Piggott, broadened his involvement in community affairs. He joined the St. Francis Drainage District Board of Directors on January 4, 1927 and served until January 5, 1943. Upon Pfeiffer's appointment to the drainage district and until the end of his tenure, remarkable advancement came in draining the land. Local residents credited Pfeiffer for the establishment of Big Slough Ditch[251] on May 20, 1927, one of the most complete drainage subsidiaries of the St. Francis River.

The implementation of the drainage plan came none too soon. In June, 1928, Arkansas had "one rain after another—fully 13 inches." As a result, the St. Francis River surged to a record high, but with "much emergency work we saved all the Arkansas side levees."[252] Farmers on the Missouri side of the river suffered substantial losses to their crops when their levee broke in three places.[253]

During Pfeiffer's tenure as a commissioner of the drainage district, he oversaw many ditching activities, including the removal of trees and other debris, the filling of washed out areas, the sowing of grass seed to prevent erosion and the construction of fences, levees, and gravel roads.[254] Pfeiffer made the following reference to the progress being made.

Our new state hyway between Piggott-Corning will be completely hard surfaced with gravel in a few weeks. We drove it last Sunday in less than 50 minutes. This goes thru center of our Cache bottom lands. Also getting two more state hyways thru these lands, so will be well provided with hyways. No direct tax on lands…[255]

The other directors of the St. Francis Drainage District stated that while he served as a commissioner, Pfeiffer "rendered a conspicuous and unselfish service…prompted by no consideration other than the district's and its people's welfare." His colleagues on the drainage district knew him as a citizen who never compromised with wrong, but stood for what he deemed right "without fear or favor."[256]

Pfeiffer established other businesses in Clay County that supported the local economy including the Piggott Custom Gin Company in March 1923, and the Piggott Land Company in May 1929.[257] Gus Pfeiffer assisted Paul and Mary Pfeiffer with incorporating the Piggott Land Company by purchasing 990 beginning shares, or 49.5% interest. Paul also bought 990 shares and Mary owned 20, which gave them a controlling 50.5% portion. Paul and Mary eventually purchased Gus's portion of the company from him in January 1932.

Paul Pfeiffer channeled his farming operations through the Piggott Land Company. He rented office space in the Clay County Bank building in Piggott, hired "Miss Martin from Poplar Bluff"[258] as his secretary to relieve him of detail work, and continued his land transactions from his new offices instead of the study in his home. Gus honored the occasion by sending Paul a roll top desk to use in his new headquarters.[259]

Pfeiffer's association with the Piggott State Bank remained one of his most notable business achievements in the memories of the local people. The Bank of Piggott went "on the blink"[260] in early January 1930. It eventually closed its doors on January 30, 1930, necessitating the need for another local financial establishment.

Paul Pfeiffer and T. W. Leggett of Bald Knob, Arkansas, led an effort to inaugurate the creation of Piggott State Bank. They met with 22 additional community leaders at Reves Drug Store on March 7, 1930 and organized the bank. The group elected Paul Pfeiffer as president, a position he held until approximately 1936.[261] Other beginning officers included H. C. Robbins as vice-president and T. W. Leggett as secretary.[262]

The Piggott State Bank became a corporation on March 10, 1930, with 1000 shares of stock valued at $25 each. Of the $25,000 paid by the stockholders, three directors—Leggett, Pfeiffer, and J. W. Hamilton—invested the most at $12,050, $3,900, and $1,000, respectively. Each of the remaining members of the group contributed $500 or less per person.[263] The new bank opened for business on March 19, 1930. Paul Pfeiffer summarized its first day of business.

> Piggott has organized a new bank. It opened its doors yesterday morning and received over $30,000.00 in deposits the first day. We have a paid up capital and surplus of $27,500.00. They have elected us as president which office, however, we will surrender to younger shoulders as soon as the bank is nicely organized and started. Everybody seems to be pleased in being able to get banking facilities again in Piggott.[264]

Under Pfeiffer's leadership the bank operated in a "conservative manner."[265] They purchased the building of the defunct Bank of Piggott, and Pfeiffer rented a vacant mercantile room next door from the bank for $50 per month "providing the bank would build him a small vault suitable for that purpose necessary for his use."[266]

During the decade of the Great Depression, the Piggott State Bank felt the economic stresses that appeared nationwide; however, it remained solvent throughout those dreadful times. When the daily operations of the local economy felt a financial pinch because of the depression, the bank assisted in ways it deemed necessary to ease the strain. For example, in September 1933, many rural schools in Arkansas, unable to pay the teachers' salaries, failed to open. The board of the Piggott State Bank decided that the bank "should carry school warrants for the Piggott School Districts as far as it seem[ed] practical."[267] The bank maintained a line of credit to the school districts that did not exceed its aggregate loan limit. This action by the bank directors allowed the schools to open and operate throughout the regularly scheduled school term. W. F. Smart, who lived on a Pfeiffer farmstead, attended the one room Pfeiffer School on Pfeiffer Road during most of the Depression era. He recalled that many times Pfeiffer himself paid the teacher's salary when the school did not have adequate funds.[268]

Some local residents who attended Piggott Public School remembered one year when the school ran out of funds to operate for the last two months of the term. Rather than close, the administration decided to charge parents tuition for their children to continue. Families with a large number of children in school could not afford the additional expense. Pfeiffer instructed the school to allow all the students to attend the full term and bill him for the tuition of students whose parents could not pay. As a result, all students completed the school year.

The day after his inauguration President Roosevelt suspended the activity of the Federal Reserve System and all banks during a "banking holiday" that lasted from March 5, 1933, to March 13, 1933. He declared the holiday in order to keep depositors from bankrupting the financial network by withdrawing their money from the banks. The Board of Directors of the Piggott State Bank held a special meeting on March 8, 1933, to discuss the banking holiday. The minutes resulting from the discussion of those assembled stated:

> It was the unanimous opinion of the Board that due to the fact the Bank had an ample supply of cash on hand, the Bank could open...for carrying on of current business. It was thought that we would be within legal requirements of the

order… "to meet the needs of its community for food, feed, medicine, other necessities of life, for the relief of the distress, for the payment of usual salaries and wages, for necessary current expenditures for the purpose of maintaining employment and for other similar essential purposes…"[269]

The bank continued to be successful. It joined the Federal Deposit Insurance Corporation in January 1934. When local farmers began to suffer financial distress caused by deflated prices of surplus crops, the bank granted "quite a number of loans" to those who offered collateral substantial enough to justify their action. The minutes of the April 1933, meeting stated that the board thought it "good business to make a few small loans to good conservative farmers" who offered ample security, such as crops, livestock, and farm implements.[270]

Pfeiffer and the other bank directors determined that the bank's solvency remained the top priority. They regularly discussed the economic situation and continued to operate in a conservative manner by using sound judgment and avoiding high risk loans throughout the remainder of the Depression.[271] They obviously made good decisions regarding the loans they granted because no statements in the minutes during the Depression years mentioned them foreclosing on any farms or forcing any business into bankruptcy.

The Depression brought business in Clay County to almost a standstill; however, the area received many gravel and paved streets with the coming of the Works Progress Administration.[272] Because of the great need for roads in the county, the supervisors of the crews tended to overwork the men, which resulted in many foremen resigning. After the Office of the County Judge assumed the supervision of the work, the community held town meetings to "talk roads." The patrons agreed to pay one-half of the cost of new construction, and the county paid the other half.[273] In many cases when the local people could not afford to pay their share of the cost,

Pfeiffer paid it for them. Matilda Pfeiffer estimated that Pfeiffer paid two-thirds of the local people's share of all the street paving done by the government.[274]

Most local residents benefited from the famous Pfeiffer benevolence in Clay County during the Depression. Others who passed through the area also heard about Paul Pfeiffer's generosity. People who rode the trains knew to go by Pfeiffer's office if they needed food or clothing. Pfeiffer had pre-printed coupons that could be redeemed by local businesses. When someone requested food or clothing from him, he gave them one of the coupons that specified what they needed, and he directed them to a local store or restaurant that honored it. If Pfeiffer ever learned that any business abused the system, he no longer allowed them to redeem the coupons.[275]

Town residents recalled when Piggott held its annual July 4th picnic one year during the Depression. Pfeiffer continually gathered groups of kids throughout the day and bought them ice cream, soda, and popcorn.[276] In the process of treating local children, he also supported the picnic. As a result, the residents of Piggott developed an admiration and affection for him that remained long after his death. Many times the local papers desired to publish an article chronicling Paul Pfeiffer's generosity. He responded, "I did not do it for publicity; please don't print anything about it." Pfeiffer only knew the number and identity of the people whom he assisted, and he preferred for it to remain that way.[277]

Although many relied upon the Pfeiffer generosity during the difficult times of the Depression, the Piggott Land Company suffered financially as well. On May 1, 1929, just a few months before the stock market crash rocked the financial world, Pfeiffer made a major land purchase. The Great Western Land Company completed harvesting the timber from its vast holdings in Clay County and decided to sell the property. Pfeiffer acquired 46,340 acres from them for $24,725, paying 50 cents per acre for the majority of the land.[278] Even though

Pfeiffer purchased the land cheaply, its acquisition practically wiped out the capital remaining in the Piggott Land Company. Mary Pfeiffer described the purchase to her children.

> Your father has purchased several thousand more acres of land. I will not tell you how many, for you would find it hard to believe, but there is now enough to give each of the relatives unto the fourth degree of kindred at least a quarter section. Tell Virginia she may have a town and take her choice between McDougal and Tipperary.[279]

The huge purchase from the Great Western Land Company made the period from 1920 to 1930 Pfeiffer's most active period for acquiring land and erecting farm structures. He put thousands of dollars into land, houses, and barns. The onset of the Depression resulted in deflated land values and record low prices for cotton and corn; consequently, Pfeiffer received no cash flow from his tenants for their crops. In 1929, Mary Pfeiffer stated that their 125[280] tenants "had to be heavily financed this year."[281] Although the Piggott Land Company possessed a large pool of assets, it depleted its operating fund. Mary Pfeiffer summed up the situation:

> We have more acres than ever before. The big land company has not adopted any program as yet in the disposal of its holdings. This is largely due to there being no demand for land. Isn't it strange that the land being the source of all wealth has no value of its own? Millions for luxuries, but nothing for necessities.[282]

Karl Pfeiffer, who still worked for the Richard Hudnut Company in New York, managed to save up several thousand dollars. Paul Pfeiffer asked him to "come back and put it back into the Piggott Land Company because it was broke."[283] Karl and Matilda moved to Piggott in 1932,[284] advanced their capital to the land company, and became business partners with his father. Their combined efforts resulted in the Piggott Land Company becoming profitable during the busiest period of the Pfeiffer farming era in Clay County.

V. Pfeiffer Farm Structures

And the Lord spake…saying…I have filled him with the
spirit of God, in wisdom, and in understanding, and in
knowledge, and in all manner of workmanship, to devise
cunning works…in cutting of stones, to set them, and in
carving of timber, to work in all manner of workmanship.
—Exodus 31:1, 3-5
King James Version

As Paul Pfeiffer had each 40- or 80-acre tract of land cleared and put into cultivation, his construction crew erected farm structures to be utilized by the tenant family. They followed local custom and used wood harvested from the trees on the property to construct the houses and barns. Each Pfeiffer farmstead consisted of a house and an array of outbuildings including a hay barn, mule barn, corn crib, chicken house, outhouse, pump house, and sheds needed to shelter the livestock required to provide the family with meat, eggs, and dairy products and to furnish the mule power for the farming operation.

Pfeiffer's workmen did not follow elaborate plans drawn up by an architect when they built the farm structures. They erected the houses and barns and eventually learned the exact amount of materials needed to complete each project. Pfeiffer set the barns and houses upon concrete piers. According to Bill Leonard, he and his father, residents of Greenway at that time, "hauled all the gravel in the blocks under all the Pfeiffer houses and barns and the Gray brothers made the blocks."[285]

Mules pulled to the building site a wagon loaded with concrete piers used to form the structure's foundation. The men pushed the piers off the wagon at the place where the southwest corner of the building would rest.[286] From that point they relied upon the personal knowledge of Jimmy Underwood, Pfeiffer's main carpenter, to direct the raising of the house or barn.[287]

During the period that Pfeiffer commenced his farming operation, professional architects considered designing traditional structures as unprofitable; therefore, land grant and agricultural colleges and universities assumed the responsibility of providing simple plans to farmers. Since climatic regions dictated housing requirements more than legal or political boundaries, the major changes in the construction of shelters affected primarily the walls and insulation rather than the basic form. Fifteen Midwestern agricultural colleges, working toward greater uniformity in farm management, distributed pamphlets that showed proper building and framing techniques and made other suggestions to prospective builders.[288]

The colleges utilized the knowledge and experience learned by local craftsmen over hundreds of years to illustrate diverse building types suitable for various farming needs. The basic plans included suggestions to remodel old structures and the proper materials to be used. The colleges designed the pamphlets primarily to increase knowledge regarding construction techniques and strongly urged the farmers to "seek competent help before making any major alterations."[289] The "competent help" came from men, such as Jimmy Underwood, who learned the trade through apprenticeships and by trial and error.

The common, everyday structures erected on the Pfeiffer farmsteads, generally known as folk or traditional buildings, fall into the architectural category labeled vernacular. Historian Cary Carson described vernacular architecture as "a term invented by archaeologists to describe buildings that are built according to local custom to meet personal requirements of the individuals for whom they are intended."[290] Some high-style architects who studied folk structures labeled them as "simple, naïve, or primitive dwellings cobbled together by some imaginary oafish, but feisty pioneers."[291] Others, such as Frank Lloyd Wright, looked to vernacular architecture to inspire them to create new designs.[292]

Vernacular Architecture in the Arkansas Delta

Early settlers in the Arkansas Delta erected log barns and cabins with wooden shingled roofs from roughly hewn trees. Often their barns consisted of no more than a pen of logs covered by a roof. Frequently a farmer added sheds on one or both sides of a barn to provide additional storage area for tools and farm implements. Southern farmers rarely provided covering for the livestock because the climate did not require it. When animals needed an outside shelter a roof held up by an arcade of posts, called a "lean-to," sufficed.[293]

Occasionally farmers threw farm buildings together as the mood hit them, resulting in historians unfamiliar with the process judging the arrangement as "a misleading grouping of buildings that do not belong together in any meaningful way."[294] Architect Benjamin H. Latrobe related his humorous observation when he wrote that outbuildings seemed to cluster around southern houses "as a litter of pigs their mother."[295] Fifty years later Emily Burke joked that a southern plantation had "nearly as many roofs as rooms."[296]

Southerners refer to almost any farm structure from a corncrib to a stable as a "barn." The multiple uses of the word probably stemmed from the practice of erecting several out buildings of various sizes and shapes to shelter diverse farm activities. The labels attached to the structures, such as horse barn, mule barn, or hay barn,[297] depended upon their main function and distinguished them from other structures on the farmstead.

Pfeiffer Farm Structures

Alfred Smith, a former tenant farmer for Pfeiffer, called him the "grand-daddy of this part of the country."[298] Although Pfeiffer erected four different styles of houses on his farmsteads for his farm laborers, each structure contained the basic rectangular design attributed to the British. The tenant farmers lived in either a two-story bent house with a gabled roof[299] or a two-story T house with a hip roof. Temporary workers who assisted the tenant farmers during peak farming seasons resided in a four-room bungalow or a two-room shotgun house located on the farmstead close to the cotton fields.

Pfeiffer's builders constructed most of the farm structures from the plentiful and durable cypress trees available on the property. Pfeiffer preferred hardwood as the principle building material to construct the homes and barns for many reasons. Wood is a relatively lightweight, durable, economical, plentiful, and renewable resource. Lumber resisted frost and repelled moisture, desirable characteristics that made the houses and barns easier to heat in the winter and cool in the summer. Also, plank buildings could be altered, remodeled, and repainted easier and less expensively than other exterior facades.[300]

Pfeiffer's houses contained several of the same characteristics regardless of their style. All houses contained tin roofs that extended over the front and back porches. With the exception of the shotgun house, each shelter had a smokehouse located off the back porch behind the kitchen.

Pfeiffer usually paid for all repairs made to the houses with one exception. He initially installed screen doors but found he replaced them more often than he liked. He finally required tenants to furnish them when their houses needed them. When the tenants moved away, he allowed them to take any screen doors they installed.[301]

An unpainted and weathered "lap board siding"[302] covered the exterior of the houses with the rough lumber exposed inside. Those who lived in the Pfeiffer houses concurred that the lack of insulation created very drafty and cold conditions inside the structures during the winter months. Jim Richardson recalled waking up many mornings "worn out" from wrestling throughout the night with the extra quilts needed to shield off the cold air.[303] Others stated that sometimes the wind blew in so strongly through the cracks in the floor that it raised the linoleum rug up off the floor[304] or moved the dust ruffle on the couch.[305]

The back porch became an important venue for various activities for the farm families. Although the homes had outdoor plumbing until around 1940, they all had a pump enclosed in a wooden box with a sink underneath it[306] placed on or near the back porch. The handy location of the pump eliminated the need to carry water a long distance for bathing, cleaning, and cooking purposes. Women found the back porch the most desirable place to can the vegetables from the garden or to do the laundry.

Alfred Smith assembled a makeshift shower on the back porch between the house and smokehouse by hanging from a tall beam a five gallon bucket with holes punched in the bottom. Louise Smith enclosed the "shower area" with a curtain. They filled the bucket with heated water to enjoy a warm shower. When Pfeiffer installed indoor plumbing into the houses, the builders converted the pantry area into a bathroom and relocated the pump into the kitchen.[307]

Two-story Gabled Roof Bent House

In the late nineteenth century rural Arkansans began shedding the traditional balanced housing design in favor for one that displayed more asymmetrical and stylistic features. The new form enclosed a rear shed into a fashionable ell extension underneath a series of gabled roofs. Although local people called it a "prow" house because the central projection resembled a ship's bow, it became commonly known as a "bent" house because its front or side wings often presented an L shaped appearance.[308]

The popularity of the bent houses in Arkansas became associated with the change from sharecropper farming to more affluent operations. The bent house, which reveals Greek Revival influence, evolved from the double pen house form that had been altered to include the front or side projections. The two-storied, gabled roof bent houses with the aesthetic architectural features similar to those that Pfeiffer erected symbolized agrarian prosperity and economic success of local farmers.[309]

Pfeiffer's two-story, gabled roof bent house appeared on the landscape more frequently than the two-story T house with the hip roof. It contained approximately 1,540 total square feet of living space with 915 downstairs and 625 upstairs. The downstairs consisted of a living room, kitchen with large pantry, and bedroom. Three additional rooms located upstairs served as bedrooms; however, some families used one of the upstairs rooms for storage.

Variations existed among the numerous gabled roof bent houses that Pfeiffer built, probably based upon the available materials and personal preferences of the family that occupied the dwelling. For example, some of the houses contained one entrance from the front porch where others had two—one into the living room and the other into the kitchen. Jim and Roma Richardson lived in a house after they married that had one entrance from the front porch, but it also had a second and third entry into the kitchen from the east and south elevations of the house.[310]

The arrangement of the floor plan remained primarily consistent except when the builders reversed the placement of the living room and kitchen. The decision to invert the rooms possibly corresponded to the location of the outbuildings and garden that farmers usually located close to the back door of the house. Chimneys placed over the kitchen provided an escape outlet for smoke emanating from wood burning cook stoves originally used by farmers' wives when preparing meals. Younger farmers, like W. F. and Marguerite Smart, later opted to use the modern Florence coal oil stove for cooking.[311]

The size and placement of windows also varied between the houses. The gabled roof bent house that Alfred and Louise Smith lived in contained double windows in the bedrooms upstairs[312] whereas the one that Dub and Marguerite Smart occupied had single windows.[313] Differences existed in the size of the windows in the pantries and kitchen as well as the placement of windows in the living room.

Pfeiffer allowed the farm families that occupied the homes to finish the inside walls or otherwise make minor changes to the homes that improved their quality of life. Some people purchased rolls of heavy paper that resembled "thin cardboard" or used old newspapers to cover the rough lumber left exposed inside the home.[314] The paper provided a smooth surface on which regular wallpaper could be hung.

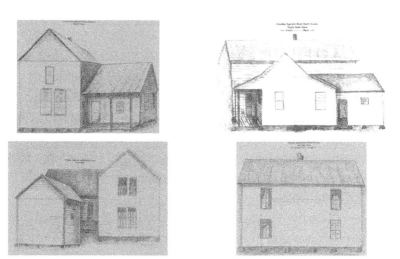

Two Story Gabled Roof Bent House
Based upon a sketch drawn by Jim Richardson.

Upstairs – 625 Sq. Ft.   Downstairs – 915 Sq. Ft.

Two Story Gabled Roof Bent House
Based upon a sketch drawn by Jim Richardson.

Two-story T House with Hip Roof

By the end of the nineteenth century the classic southern I house faded in popularity. The big frame T house evolved by shifting the tall façade of the house to face the entrance, and it eventually replaced the I house. The two-story T house with a hip roof, commonly called a "yankee" house,[315] revealed influences from New England and the Midwest and appeared widely in the upland South.[316] Its interior room arrangements provided comfortable living areas for farm families living in a rural setting.

The T house revealed high-styled influence associated with academic architecture, which lent to its charm in a country setting. It characterized interesting ways that people incorporated fashion into folk buildings. Pfeiffer's decision to erect this house style for his tenants demonstrated his commitment to fit new designs into the rural community. When placed on the architecture scale, the T house ranges between vernacular structures and academic buildings.[317]

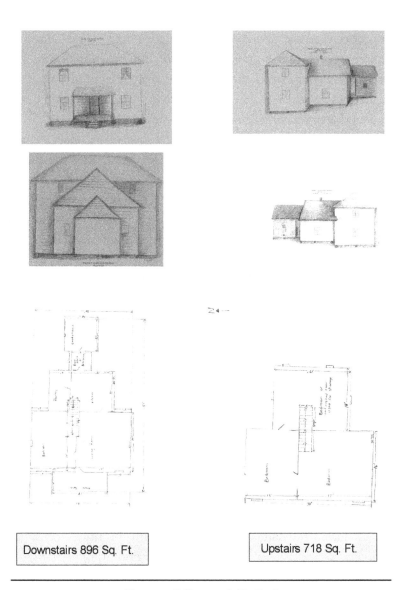

Downstairs 896 Sq. Ft.

Upstairs 718 Sq. Ft.

Two-story T House with Hip Roof

Pfeiffer's two-story T house with the hip roof contained more living space than the gabled roof bent house. It had a total living area of approximately 1,614 square feet with 896 downstairs and 718 upstairs. The floor plan of the T house strongly resembled that of the gabled house with a living room, kitchen with large pantry, and bedroom downstairs and three rooms upstairs.

The T house contained a symmetrical design—its most striking characteristic. The front side of the house with its tall flat façade usually faced the road. The front porch sat centered with the front of the house underneath a separate hip roof. It had two entrances—one from the front porch and one from the back porch. The symmetry extended to the placement of the windows on the front and sides of the house.

The peak of the prominent hip roof rose five feet above the eaves of the house. Although construction crews considered the hip roof more complicated to install, its design eliminated many future roofing problems. It contained no valleys where water could accumulate and cause leakage, and its high angles deflected elements from the weather away from the home. Well-built hip roofs usually withstood high winds better than gable roofs. The high pitch also allowed for extra ventilation in the attic, which reduced moisture buildup that caused molds and mildew to grow.[318]

The Bungalow

The term *bungalow* frequently referred to a small house with wide porches during the late nineteenth and early twentieth centuries. Originally considered a primitive dwelling used temporarily by civilized people, the bungalow eventually evolved into an expansive cottage that contained ornate galleries and roofs.[319]

Pfeiffer's four room bungalow contained some of the same features as the two-story T house, but it included other interesting characteristics that the larger houses lacked. It possessed a high pitched hip roof embellished by a dormer window underneath the peak and centered above the front porch. It also featured a basic symmetrical design. The front porch stretched the entire width of the house. Four strong posts supported the roof that extended over the porch.

The house contained approximately 900 square feet of living space divided into four rooms—two bedrooms, a kitchen with a large pantry, and a living room. A covered back porch spanned the width of the house except for the small area used for pantry space.

The bungalow usually served as shelter for seasonal workers who came from the surrounding hill country to work in the cotton fields during peak seasons. It had a smokehouse attached directly off the back porch behind the kitchen similar to those of the two-story houses. After indoor plumbing reached the area, the building crew installed a bathroom in a corner of the front bedroom.

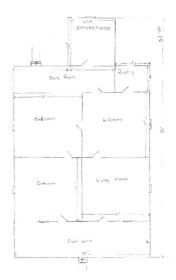

The Bungalow and Floorplan

The Shotgun House

The shotgun house, an architectural form attributed to African-Americans, became a landscape structure associated with southern cotton fields and mill towns. Originally appearing in Louisiana's bayous and sugar plantations, scholars of folk architecture once asserted that its style evolved from Indian dwellings and served as a former prototype of the bungalow.[320]

The shotgun house came to Arkansas from the West Indies via Louisiana. It featured a long, narrow floor plan with a width corresponding to that of one room and a length equivalent to two or more rooms. Symmetrical in form, it contained a gable roof that extended over its front and rear porches.

Many of the Pfeiffer farmsteads contained a shotgun house that housed seasonal hands who worked in the fields. Pfeiffer's shotgun house contained the symmetrical design that resulted in its front and rear views appearing identical. Two posts supported the gable roof that extended out over the front and back porches. Although some shotgun forms often featured one window and one door on either end with a hip roof extending over the porch from the gabled ends, Jim Poole recalled that the Pfeiffer shotgun houses contained a gabled roof that sheltered the porches.[321]

The front and rear views of shotgun houses commonly found in the Delta had a door to one side and a window on the other; however, Pfeiffer's workmen centered the doors between two windows on either end. Also, the roof style over the porches varied from that typically associated with shotgun houses. Pfeiffer's workmen duplicated the same technique for the roof as found on his other house styles by extending the main roof of the house over the front and rear porches.[322]

The change in the building pattern associated with shotgun houses revealed regional architectural features associated with the other structures found on Pfeiffer's farmsteads. Many people commonly considered the shotgun houses in the Delta as shelters for serfs or former slaves. Pfeiffer altered the design of his shotgun houses to demonstrate one of the many differences between his farming operation and others in the Arkansas Delta.

The two rooms, each measuring 10 feet in width and 15 feet in length, contained approximately 300 square feet of living space. Each room had an entrance from the adjacent porch. The house had two windows in the front, rear, and on each side. Houses bearing this design earned the label as "shotgun" house because someone could "fire a gun from one end of the house to the other through the aligned doors."[323]

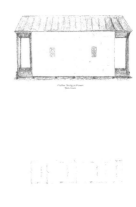

The Shotgun House and Floorplan

Barns in the Arkansas Delta

Farmers often considered their barn, not their house, the most important building on their farm. The barn generally served as the center of activity on a farm, and its upkeep demonstrated the economic success of its owner. The multiple uses of a barn over the years included a place to process and store grain, a shelter for the farmer's livestock and tools, a workshop, and a place for social activities.[324]

A single-crib structure became a typical barn type in the Arkansas Delta, as well as in the upland South and Midwest. It contained a central bay flanked by side sheds on either side. They originally functioned as a small hay barn, corncrib, or wagon shed and featured vertical planking on the outside.[325]

As the farms grew in size, the need for additional barn space increased as well. Practical farmers doubled their single-crib buildings to produce the double-crib barn. If a farmer desired more space, the plan could be doubled again to create a four-crib barn.[326] Initially constructed from logs, the barn with its irregular additions presented a crude appearance. Although they flourished in the early stages of settlement in the South, farmers eventually replaced them with the big frame transverse crib barn.[327] Pfeiffer strongly favored the transverse crib barns and constructed them for hay barns on his farmsteads.

The transverse-crib barn, developed in the upland South and carried to the Midwest by emigrating farmers and carpenters, became typical during the nineteenth century. It contained a central passageway large enough for a loaded wagon to traverse with stables and various cribs and granaries on either side. Usually part of the wide center aisle served as a threshing floor. Stalls on the ground floor sheltered livestock or isolated an injured animal or nursing mother and her young. Other partitioned spaces called bins, cribs, or bays, stored grain during the winter months. The transverse crib barn featured a roof line that ran parallel to the driveway—an arrangement that separated it from other regional barn types.[328]

In addition to providing shelter for livestock, grain, and feed, barns served as workplaces, dance halls, social centers for husking bees and similar activities. Often early settlers built their barn and lived in it while they constructed their home. Children found the barn a warm and friendly shelter to romp in on rainy days. Adults frequently recalled the times their parents "tanned their hides"[329] behind the barn for misbehaving. Many young people attended dances, fall festivals, and social events held in barns to celebrate the end to harvest season. Margaret Bolsterli, who grew up in the Arkansas Delta, related the following description of a barn dance hosted by Arkansas farm families.

> The Duttons had parties that we could hear very well all the way across our orchard and their pasture. Somebody would play a steel guitar for dancing and often, about midnight, when the urge to eat would hit the revelers, we would hear the chickens squawking as they were grabbed off the roost and slaughtered for the skillet.[330]

Pfeiffer Hay Barn

The hay barns that Pfeiffer built all featured a gambrel roof design that the Dutch developed and introduced to America. It contained two slopes on each side of the barn with the lower slope steeper than the upper one. It eventually became the primary roof associated with barns because it provided an increased amount of usable room on the upper floor.[331]

The Pfeiffer barn roofs featured self supporting trusses similar to the Clyde Roof [see Midwest Plan No. 72001, page 104] or the Shawver Roof [see Midwest Plan No. 72002, page 104] truss construction. Both units had to be raised into place after being constructed on the ground. The main difference between the two types rested in the longer and heavier timbers required to form the Shawver Roof. Since the construction of both styles proved to be strong and durable, many farmers preferred the less expensive and less cumbersome Clyde Roof.[332]

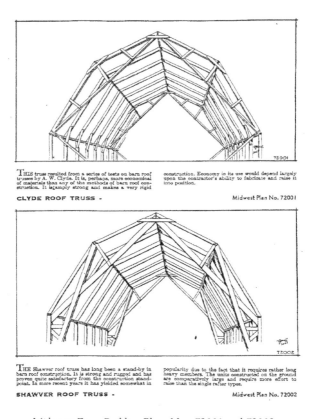

THIS truss resulted from a series of tests on barn roof trusses by A. W. Clyde. It is, perhaps, more economical of materials than any of the methods of barn roof construction. It is simply strong and makes a very rigid construction. Economy in its use would depend largely upon the contractor's ability to fabricate and raise it into position.

CLYDE ROOF TRUSS -   Midwest Plan No. 72001

THE Shawver roof truss has long been a stand-by in barn roof construction. It is strong and rugged and has proven quite satisfactory from the construction standpoint. In more recent years it has yielded somewhat in popularity due to the fact that it requires rather long heavy members. The units constructed on the ground are comparatively large and require more effort to raise than the single rafter types.

SHAWVER ROOF TRUSS -   Midwest Plan No. 72002

Mid-west Farm Building Plans Nos. 72001 and 72002

Pfeiffer chose cypress wood as the principle building material for his barns because of its utility, abundance, and cost-effectiveness. The building crews installed vertical planking on the exterior of the hay barns based upon a common belief that it prevented rainwater from standing on the boards, and, therefore guarded against wood rot. The Pfeiffer barns, similar to most other ones in the Delta, had no decorative symbols or trim on their exterior.

Although Arkansas farmers usually left their outbuildings unpainted, early settlers in other parts of the country produced the traditional red paint associated with barns. They often valued their barns more than their houses and desired an inexpensive coating to preserve the life of the structure. By combining naturally occurring iron oxides, iron filings, lime, and milk, they made a paint, which took a red coloring because of its iron content. Painting barns red has remained a tradition even though the ingredients of the paint have changed.[333] A common home recipe for barn paint that early pioneers formulated follows:

Recipe for Barn Paint[334]

4 pounds or 1/2 gallon of skimmed milk
6 ounces of lime
4 ounces of linseed oil or neatsfoot (cow's hoof glue)
1-1/2 pounds of color (clay mixed with the white of wild turkey eggs)

Most of Pfeiffer's barns remained unpainted unless the individual farmers opted to do so themselves. Pfeiffer used good materials to construct quality barns that served the practical needs of the farmers.

Pfeiffer's hay barns all shared the basic rectangular shape with a wide central wooden walkway flanked on either side by a series of bins, cribs, bay, and stalls. The far left and far right portions of Pfeiffer's hay barns served as "loafing areas"[335] that contained dirt floors and provided a dry shelter for livestock during inclement weather. Tilted and slotted mangers ranging from two-feet to four-feet wide lined the inside partition of the loafing areas. Some farmers built struts from boards and placed them intermittently over the mangers to guide loose hay they tossed down from the hay loft into the feeding troughs. The space between the struts allowed cows enough room to stick their heads through and feed from the mangers.[336] [See Sketch 5.1, page 106]

When changes in farm practices necessitated larger barns, a farmer altered his barn accordingly. Some farmers made hog sheds in the rear of their hay barns, but others preferred to build a sty away from the main building because of the mess created by the pigs.

According to Jim Poole, one of the large side areas of the hay barn located on the farmstead where he lived as a child had been converted into two stalls used for milking cows.[337] Dub Smart used one of the loafing areas of his barn to shelter the rabbits his children raised to show at the local fair.[338]

Pfeiffer's hay barns contained either one or two cribs to store corn raised on the farmstead to feed the livestock. Farmers usually placed the cribs next to an outside wall on either side of the central walkway and at opposite ends from each other. This arrangement permitted farmers to feed the livestock from the crib closest to the feeding area. A large open window located over the cribs allowed farm workers to throw corn into the bins from a loaded wagon outside.[339]

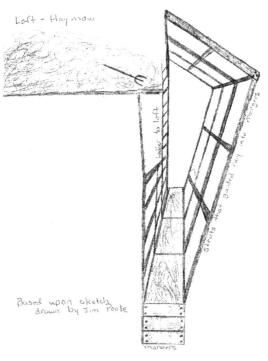

Sketch 5.1

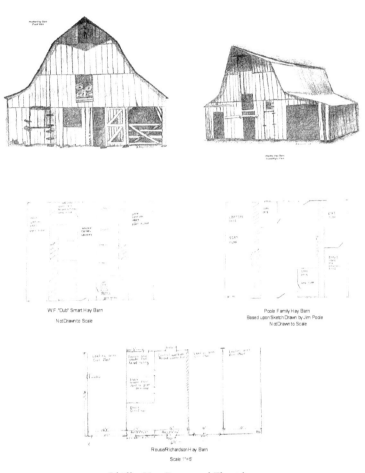

Pfeiffer Hay Barns and Floorplans

The upper floor, called a hayloft or haymow, held hay used as feed for the livestock. A hay hood[340] over the central door housed a track and pulley system containing a two tined fork used to lift hay into the loft from a loaded wagon below. Hoisting hay into the barn loft required three men working together—one on a horse, one in the loft yelling commands to the rider of the horse, and one to hit the trip cord. To operate the contraption they attached a rope to the hay track and to the horse, and then lowered the fork to the wagon containing the hay. After the tines gripped a bunch of hay, the track guided it as the horse pulled it into the loft. When the hay dangled over the desired location, someone hit the trip rope and dropped the hay in the loft. Jim Poole, a young lad when his family used this method to fill the hay loft, recalled that his father usually assigned him the job of hitting the trip cord. Later, when baled hay replaced loose hay, most farmers traded the two tine fork for one with one prong.[341]

Pfeiffer Mule Barn

The mule barn built by Pfeiffer contained many of the same characteristics as the hay barn. Primarily constructed of cypress lumber, it featured an unpainted exterior with vertical planking and a triangular hanging gable with a hay track over the loft. Granary cribs, a wooden threshing floor, and loafing areas with mangers on the far sides formed the interior.

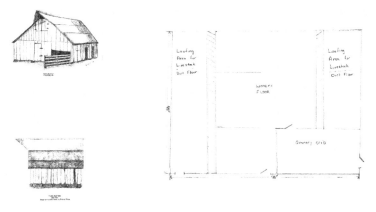

Pfeiffer Mule Barn and Floorplan
Based upon sketch drawn by Rodney Rouse

The floor plan of the mule barn contained a square design with a steep gable roof that gave it a boxy appearance when viewed from the side. The fact that most farmers owned more cattle than mules and needed less space to feed and shelter the mules contributed to its size being dwarfed by that of the hay barn. A series of windows, doors and gates provided various ways to access the barn's interior.

The Corn Crib

In addition to the granary bins located in the hay barns and mule barns, all of the Pfeiffer farmsteads contained an individual double corn crib that the farmers sometimes called the "rent crib."[342] Pfeiffer usually constructed the corn cribs from cypress wood, which resisted the lateral stresses resulting from the weight of the corn it held. The outside planking, whether vertical or horizontal, contained a space of approximately one inch between the slats that allowed air to circulate and dry out the corn and prevent mold and mildew from forming in the cribs. The open area underneath the roof provided extra ventilation.[343]

Two cribs sat on either side of a center dirt driveway wide enough for a loaded wagon to maneuver. The area over the driveway held a loft that farmers used for storage. Stairs located between the cribs on either side of the drive permitted entry into the loft.

Tenant farmers that leased a farmstead from Pfeiffer gave him a portion of the crops they produced. Jim Poole related the method they used to fill the corn cribs proportionately according to the allotted amounts for farm owner and tenant farmer. Since Pfeiffer received one-third of the corn raised on the farm, the farmer usually reserved one section of the corn crib as the "rent crib." When a wagon filled with corn entered the center passage of the corn crib the men, using shovels to unload the wagon, put two scoops of corn in the farmer's crib for every one scoop put in the one reserved for Pfeiffer.[344]

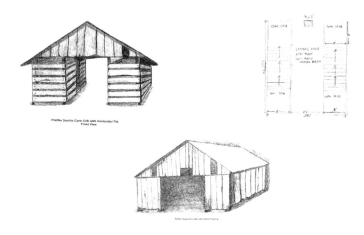

Double Corn Crib

The Smokehouse

Southern farmers valued their smokehouses as much as their barns. Normally a small building, averaging 12 by 14 feet with a gabled roof and placed just a few feet away from the rear kitchen door, it served as an outdoor pantry. To preserve the meat farmers salted slabs of pork and placed them on shelves or benches inside the smokehouses to cure for six weeks. Afterwards they washed the salt off and seasoned the meat with pepper, sage, and other spices, and hung them on hooks from the rafters. A constant, slow burning fire built in the center of the earthen floor with green wood, corncobs, or hickory chips smoked the meat for approximately a week to flavor it. Often other food items, such as onions and sacks of flour or meal, would also be stored in the smokehouse.[345]

The smokehouse held various symbolic meanings for residents of the South. A smokehouse full of hams and sides of bacon symbolized the self-sufficiency of a plantation during pre-Civil War days. It demonstrated a planter's ability to adequately provide for his household as well as his mastery over it. Planters often gave productive workers extra or better cuts of meat as a way to inspire others to work harder. Ironically, slaves frequently plundered the contents of a plantation's smokehouse to strike back at the planter's authority they associated with it.[346]

The planter also used the smokehouse as a symbol of his control in other ways. After a failed escape attempt Major Freeland, a Missouri plantation owner, took his slave, William Wells Brown, to his smokehouse, hung him by the wrists from the collar beams, and severely beat him. To further show Brown that Freeland considered him no more than a piece of meat, Freeland made a fire of tobacco stems underneath the place where he hung and "smoked" him.[347]

Documented accounts of similar smokehouse punishments of slaves attest to the fact that they occurred regularly in the South. One of the songs that slaves sang after learning of their emancipation referred to the smokehouse.[348]

> De oberseer he make us trouble,
> An' he dribe us round a spell;
> We lock him up in de smokehouse cellar,
> Wid de key trown in de well.[349]

The Pfeiffer Smokehouse

With the exception of the shotgun house, all of the Pfeiffer houses had a smokehouse located off the back porch behind the kitchen. It measured 10 1/2 feet wide by 12 feet long. Most of the smokehouses contained an entrance from the back porch, but occasionally one had a rear entrance.[350] It also had two windows centered in its longer sides.

A shelf 30 inches wide used to hold the meat while it cured ran along the interior walls of the smokehouse. A round pit approximately three feet in diameter and 18 inches deep dug in the dirt floor contained the fire used to smoke the meat. Dub and Marguerite Smart used wet wood to keep a fire burning continually for four or five days to let the meat smoke. They preferred to use hickory and pecan wood, and even pecan hulls, to feed the fire because it gave the meat a good taste.[351]

Most farmers eventually found other uses for the smokehouses. The Poole family generally smoked their meat elsewhere but hung it in the smokehouse until they used it for food. After electricity came to the area, they converted the smokehouse into a laundry room. Soon after Maytag marketed gas-operated washing machines, they purchased one, put it in the smoke house, and ran the exhaust through the floor.[352]

Louise Smith used the smokehouse as a laundry room also. Alfred placed a wood stove in the fire pit of their smokehouse and provided Louise with a warm place to do the laundry during the cold months. Others increased the living area of their homes by turning it into a den[353] or a dining room.[354]

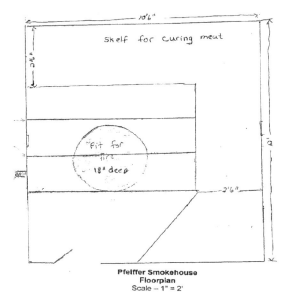

Pfeiffer Smokehouse
Floorplan
Scale — 1" = 2'

The Smokehouse

Other Outbuildings

Some older Pfeiffer farmsteads contained additional outbuildings, such as a chicken house or outhouse. After rural electrification and sewage treatment programs reached the area, Pfeiffer installed the modern conveniences into the farmhouses. Indoor plumbing replaced the standard double-seated outhouses and pump houses.

The Pfeiffer chicken houses measured approximately five feet high in the rear and eight feet in the front. Erected to take advantage of drainage and sunlight, farmers usually located them near the outhouse and facing south. The inside area of the poultry house contained beams for the chickens to roost during the night time and nesting areas for hens to lay eggs and nest, away from drafty areas. Well-maintained chicken houses meant healthier chickens that produced more eggs and chickens for the farm family.

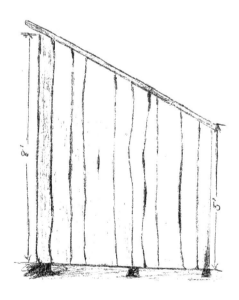

<<< Front ---------- Rear >>>
Chicken House – Side View

Fencing

Most rural landscapes where farming and agricultural activities occur contain various types of fencing. In Arkansas, fences containing three or four rows of inexpensive barbed wire typically outline important boundaries. Most Pfeiffer farmers seldom fenced their cotton or corn fields but constructed a barbed wire fence around the pastures and wood lots to keep livestock within the grazing area. Farmers who raise hogs or sheep used stronger means of restraint, such as a woven wire or board.

The Layout of the Farmstead

No strict rules governed the location of the buildings in reference to the farmhouse, but the right barn in the right spot is crucial to the success of the agricultural operation.[355] A family farmstead, complete with "house, barns, and a scattering of outbuildings"[356] often defined the boundary of the property, denoted the corners of the yard, or separated the residential space from adjacent fields.

Other factors considered in the placement of outbuildings included the location of roads, topography of the land, soil conditions, and the type of farming to be performed. Ultimately weather played a major factor in planning the placement of barns for the health and comfort of the animals and to prevent rain from causing damage to barn timbers and stored grain.[357]

Southerners typically placed the corners of their barns pointing in the four cardinal directions, but prevailing winds always ruled the position of the buildings. For example, the long slant of a saltbox barn[358] faced north and the lowest edge reached within one or two feet to the ground. During winter months farmers placed a mixture of leaves, hay, cornstalks, and sod in that space to allow snow to accrue. A blanket of snow on the long roof and against the shallow wall insulated the barn and prevented wind from reaching its interior.[359]

Farmers desired to place out buildings a comfortable distance from the farmhouse so odors and drainage from the barnlot did not infiltrate the home environment. Locating the farmstead on a slope carried excess surface water away from the buildings and yards and ensured dry pathways between buildings during periods of inclement weather.[360] Stock barns set windward of the house allowed summer breezes to carry unpleasant odors in the opposite direction.

The placement of the barns on the Pfeiffer farmsteads varied depending upon the circumstances of each individual farm. Usually the lay of the land dictated the location of the structures with the outbuildings set on the elevated areas of the property. Often the openings in the barn hayloft faced south to prevent rain from blowing in through it.[361] Generally the farmer placed the barn in a central location to provide a short distance between structures during periods of inclement weather.

W. F. "Dub" Smart, who lived on a Pfeiffer farmstead from the age of five, stated that Pfeiffer generally situated the two-story farm house on the most desirable location on the farm. Since the larger farms required additional farm laborers during the busiest periods, Pfeiffer provided additional structures to shelter them. He located the houses for seasonal farm laborers one-fourth to one-half mile beyond the main house.[362] According to Jim Poole, entire families sometimes lived in the limited space of the bungalows and shotgun houses while working on the farm.[363]

Jim Poole recalled that most of the Pfeiffer farmsteads in Clay County, if not identical, strongly resembled the one his family occupied.[364] The houses generally faced a road, all had large gardens usually behind the house, and the set of outbuildings included a large hay barn, mule barn, corn crib, and sometimes a chicken house. The older Pfeiffer farmsteads had outhouses, but once indoor plumbing became available in the region, Pfeiffer added indoor bathrooms to the houses.

W. F. "Dub" and Marguerite Smart Farmstead
Not Drawn to Scale

Rouse Family Farmstead
Based upon Sketch Drawn by Rodney Rouse
Not Drawn to Scale

Luther and Ida Glasglow Farmstead
Not Drawn to Scale

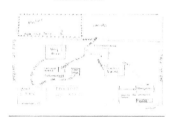

Poole Family Farmstead
Based upon Sketch Drawn by Jim Poole
Not Drawn to Scale

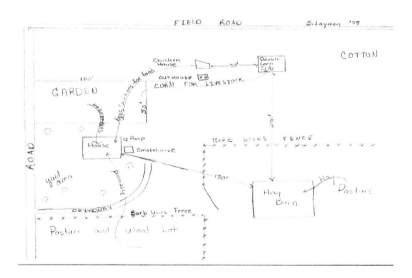

Jim and Roma Richardson Farmstead
Based upon Sketch Drawn by Jim Richardson
Not Drawn to Scale

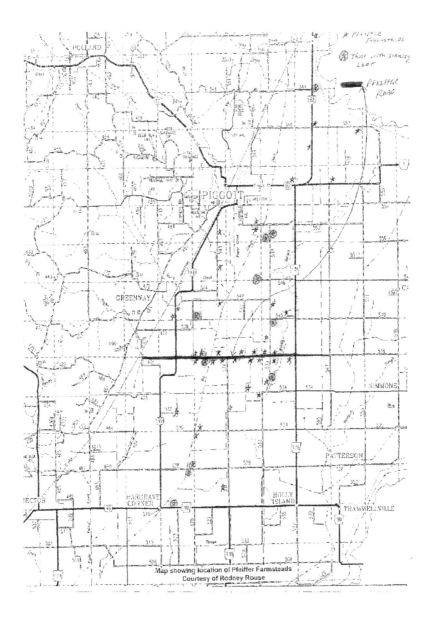

Map showing location of Pfeiffer Farmsteads
Courtesy of Rodney Rouse

Although the farmers raised various crops, cotton became a standard crop on every Pfeiffer farmstead. They grew the maximum amount of cotton that the government allowed and sowed the remaining acreage in soybeans, milo, wheat, and corn; however, they only raised enough corn to feed the livestock, which seldom consumed more than five acres of land.[365] Part of the land that contained a wood lot also served as a pasture for the livestock.

Alfred Smith became the envy of the neighborhood when he purchased the first cotton picker to be used in the area around 1950.[366] Afterwards the farms became more mechanized, and the need for additional laborers required to chop and pick cotton decreased. As a result, the smaller houses on the farms sat vacant or became hangouts for the children in the neighborhood.

When Paul Pfeiffer first purchased land in Clay County in 1902 he set an agricultural example whereby he and his tenants prospered. He provided a high standard of living for his farmers. Pfeiffer initially hired good farmers to cultivate his crops, and he accommodated their desires in addition to their needs, which encouraged them to stay with him for many years.

Pfeiffer distanced himself from other Delta planters who treated their sharecroppers and tenants as lower class citizens. He brought to Clay County his Midwestern beliefs and traditions, which he incorporated into his business activities, farming operation, and farm structures. The landscape reflected the regional changes in architecture that Pfeiffer brought to the area. Instead of rundown shanties commonly associated with sharecropper and tenant farming, Pfeiffer erected quality and fashionable houses for his farmers. He also altered typical architectural features in the buildings to distinguish his attitude and philosophy regarding tenant farming from the stereotype associated with other arrangements located in the Delta.

Numerous residents around Piggott credit Pfeiffer for the quality of life they experienced during a period and in a place where poverty lingered. Only a few of Pfeiffer's houses and barns remain standing, but the memories of the people who lived and worked on the farmsteads are forever seared in their minds.

VI. Pfeiffer Farming Operations

The fertile Mississippi Valley is the greatest food producing center in the world. Here food is raised sufficient for all…in fact, more than sufficient, for farmers are being paid to curtail crops…[367]

G. A. Pfeiffer, 1939

After Paul Pfeiffer purchased a substantial piece of land, he immediately proceeded to clear and drain it. He hired a crew of men to cut down any remaining trees and burn the residue of saplings and underbrush. When a sizable portion had been improved, he divided it into farmsteads of 40- or 80-acre tracts to be occupied by tenant farmers. Pfeiffer leased these lands to grow cotton; however, the system he implemented and his relationships with his farmers differed greatly from comparable arrangements utilized by other planters throughout the Arkansas Delta.

During the period from 1901 to 1945, small farmers primarily participated in the sharecropping and tenant farming system in Arkansas. The "share" farming system provided planters with sufficient labor and croppers with food, shelter, and clothing. Sharecroppers furnished the labor of the entire family in return for a portion of the crop they grew. Additionally, they usually paid for half the cost of the seed, poison, and fertilizer. Tenant farmers supplied their work stock, tools, and seed and typically paid 25% of their cotton and 33% of their corn to the landlord.[368]

After the planter marketed the cotton crop, he settled with the tenants and croppers. Planters owned commissaries on their land where tenants and sharecroppers charged their "furnish"[369] during the year at inflated prices. On "settlement day"[370] planters paid tenants their due after charging interest ranging from 10% to 60% for commissary purchases, a 10% fee for supervision and management, and 10 cents per acre farmed for use of roads and ditches.[371] Most croppers and tenants earned only a few dollars for a whole year of labor. Others never recovered from the amount of debt owed to the planter.[372]

Croppers and tenant farmers in the Arkansas Delta who relied upon cotton for their livelihood lived in an endless cycle of poverty. Meals consisted of cornbread, molasses, and fatback. Malaria,[373] pellagra,[374] pneumonia, and other diseases constantly plagued them because they could not afford, or in many cases, locate medical care. Doctors refused to treat sharecroppers and tenant farmers in the Delta unless the croppers presented to them a note from the landowner guaranteeing that the bill would be paid.

Landowners provided cabins on their property where tenant farmers and sharecroppers lived; however, the planter insisted that the farmers plant cotton on every inch of available ground, even up to the porches and doorsteps of the croppers' houses. Two visitors to the Arkansas Delta on separate occasions during this period made similar statements about the housing for sharecroppers. A government agent described the croppers' homes as "unspeakable."

> [They consisted] of only one room and with no sanitary facilities either indoors or out, they were hastily constructed, often out of green timber, unpainted, prone to warping and leaking, and presenting a bare and uninviting appearance. It is in these cabins, that families, sometimes large ones, with the added company of several dogs, live. Many landowners discouraged garden plots, urging or compelling their croppers and tenants to maximize the acreage and time devoted to cash-producing cotton.[375]

Naomi Mitchison from Britain observed:

> Never have I seen such an untidy countryside ... [Sharecropper shacks are] worse than any rural housing I

have ever seen in Europe, except some pre-Revolutionary
peasants' huts near Leningrad which were about to be pulled
down in 1932.[376]

Often visitors to the Arkansas Delta compared the tenant farming
system to the feudal systems in Europe where lower classed peasants
toiled for members of the nobility. Margaret Bolsterli, a native of the
Arkansas Delta, called it "a caste system…as complex and rigid as that
of medieval Europe, and white landowners were at the top of the
hierarchy."[377] The movement of tenants and sharecroppers from
plantation to plantation, seeking "a little better break," enabled
landless farmers to maintain some control over their lives.[378]

Paul Pfeiffer, a "sun-browned man, fond of old work clothes and
old-fashioned work," based the success of his tenant farming
arrangement upon his policy of picking good farmers and keeping
them for a long time. For the system to work it required a stable
workforce that managed the soil well and maintained a good supply of
livestock. Sharecropping encouraged landless farmers to raise cash
crops that provided for their basic needs another year. Because they
constantly relocated, croppers had no interest in farming techniques,
such as crop rotation, that replenished the nutrients in the soil.[379]

When questioned about his style of plantation farming, Pfeiffer stated:

> If it thrives at all, a plantation thrives on tenant loyalty…Why
> try to make tenants into serfs? All matters of scruples and
> honor aside, it would be the worst business in the world, a
> very nasty way of cutting one's own throat.[380]

Pfeiffer's farming operations differed from other systems in the
Arkansas Delta in various ways. Pfeiffer stressed that his tenants
practice good land management and cultivate a variety of crops
instead of growing cotton only. Rather than keeping his extensive

land holdings as a single plantation worked by sharecroppers, he divided it into 40- or 80-acre farmsteads where individual tenant families lived and produced their own crops. He did not operate a store or commissary where he required tenants to purchase needed items and thus become indebted to him. Pfeiffer also owned and operated a local cotton gin where his tenants deseeded their cotton at discounted rates.[381]

Each farmstead contained a wooded area that provided farmers with shade and firewood, but Pfeiffer did prohibit them from selling the wood for their personal benefit. He also provided quality housing for his farm families that contrasted significantly to the sharecropper shanties that dotted the countryside.[382]

Each farm included a "very substantial"[383] two-story house for the farmer's family with an attached smokehouse, supplemented by a series of additional buildings based upon each farmer's specific needs. Other farm structures included a double-crib corn barn, hay barn, mule barn, and a chicken house.

Pfeiffer usually provided seed, mules, and tools for renters to produce their crops during their first year with him. He also paid the real estate and drainage taxes on the property and maintained the roads for the farmers. When harvest season ended, they gave him one-third of their gross yield as rent. Pfeiffer did not require his tenants to sign written contracts. He based the agreements he made with his tenants on their word and goodwill.[384]

Unlike other Delta planters, Pfeiffer permitted farmers "at least an acre of good land"[385] for a home garden to grow plenty of food for their own family and enough land to grow hay and corn for their livestock. They raised items such as Irish potatoes, sweet potatoes, onions, cabbage, beans, peas, tomatoes, cucumbers, and squash in the garden. Most of them raised hogs, chickens, geese, and ducks for food as well.[386] They only had to buy items like sugar and salt that could not be produced on the farm at local stores.[387]

Before electrification reached rural areas, farm wives used an "outside" method called "cold packing" to preserve the food they raised. They placed a metal rack in a cast iron washpot filled with water and kept a fire burning under it until the water boiled. Meanwhile they heated jars filled with food in empty lard cans on top of a woodstove to prevent the jars from breaking when placed in the boiling water. When the jars reached the appropriate temperature, the women transferred them to the rack in the wash pot and allowed them to boil an additional three hours to properly preserve their contents. By completing this process twice in one day, they usually canned 60 quarts by quitting time. They also used this method to preserve chicken and sausage after they cooked the meat.[388]

Farmers kept potatoes, onions, and turnips all winter by burying them in the ground below the frost line. They dug a large hole about 18 inches deep and lined it with a layer of straw, hay, or leaves to aerate it. After placing the surplus food items in the "cache," they spread the dirt over the food products to provide additional insulation. Sometimes they covered it with a tarpaulin to keep the rain out. Their storage process allowed them to enjoy fresh vegetables throughout the winter months.[389]

Most farmers raised livestock for food as well as work animals. During the fall months, after it turned cool, several families would bring their fattened hogs to one location for the annual hog killing. Jim Poole recalled how four families of his mother's relatives joined together and processed six to eight hogs by the day's end. When the group completed the tasks, they had ground meat into sausage, rendered lard,[390] collected cracklings[391] for cornbread, and separated the meat into bacon, shoulders, ribs, and hams to be smoked, seasoned, and cured in their smokehouses.[392]

When Pfeiffer hired tenants, they only had to move in and start working the land.[393] Pfeiffer used some local farmers as tenants, but he recruited others from the Midwestern states of Illinois, Indiana, Iowa,

Missouri, and Michigan.[394] By providing the best circumstances possible for them, he required their finest efforts in return. He investigated their history of farming but also invited them to inspect his operation and question his management style. After Pfeiffer hired the tenants, they farmed for him on a trial basis for a year. Those who pleased him during the probationary period usually became permanent residents on Pfeiffer's property.[395]

Most farmers who rented from Pfeiffer for an extended period eventually purchased the implements, livestock, and equipment they needed to work their land. They maintained an independent farming enterprise after they paid one-third of their gross yields to Pfeiffer for rent. Most hired share tenants to assist them with cultivating and harvesting the crops and considered it "a blessing" to work for him. They made a "good living" and many of their children attended college,[396] uncommon of other tenant farmers and sharecroppers in the Arkansas Delta. They considered Pfeiffer to be fair with them, and if they produced and did "right by him, he stayed with them to the limit;"[397] otherwise, they did not last.

Leonard Bell, the son of an early Pfeiffer tenant, began making his own crop at the youthful age of 20. By the time he turned 25, Bell used a team of mules and a tractor to farm 80 acres of corn, 50 of cotton, 17 of soybeans, and 15 of wheat. He also owned 100 hogs.[398]

Pfeiffer provided the seed, farm implements, and livestock that Sam Blake needed to make his first crop. In time Blake paid his debt to Pfeiffer and increased the acreage that he farmed. Eventually Blake accumulated enough cash to purchase his own farm implements, tractors, and purebred livestock. He used two tractors and 10 mules to cultivate 520 acres and raise 200 hogs and 50 head of cattle. Blake also possessed something few tenant farmers had—a bank account.[399]

Although Blake earned enough to purchase the farm outright from Pfeiffer, he preferred to rent it. He paid Pfeiffer one-third of his gross yield in rent, which freed him from the worry of paying drainage taxes and upkeep on the roads. Blake credited "a square-dealing landlord and good land" for the success he enjoyed as a tenant.[400]

On occasions when tenants desired to move, they informed Pfeiffer of their decision during the growing season and moved the following January. Pfeiffer refused to allow tenants to leave empty-handed. He provided farmers who owned no livestock or implements with a team of mules and a cow to make a new start.[401]

Pfeiffer financed farmers to make the crop, but sometimes the funds did not last, especially when unexpected circumstances arose. Louise Smith's father, Luther Glasgow, farmed 120 acres in "Pfeiffer Country" for 20 years. Glasgow became sick one year, and the family needed additional funds. Smith's mother explained the situation to Pfeiffer and requested more money. He asked her how much she needed and gave her that exact amount.[402]

By 1923 the size of Pfeiffer's farming operation expanded to the point that Pfeiffer needed a manager to assist him with the daily needs of the tenants. During his search for someone to fill the position, he requested recommendations of several agricultural students from the University of Missouri in Columbia. In March 1923 Pfeiffer hired Don Richardson, a 22-year-old senior from Campbell, Missouri, who knew the area well.[403]

The college allowed Richardson, who made above average grades, to leave school early during his last semester and begin working for Pfeiffer. He returned to the university in June 1923 to graduate. Richardson worked for the Piggott Land Company from 1923 until it liquidated in February 1954. He subsequently operated Karl Pfeiffer's cotton gin until 1964.[404]

Richardson oversaw the farming operations and acted as a "go-between" for Pfeiffer and the tenants. When he started working for Pfeiffer, much of the land still contained a lot of timber. Richardson habitually carried kitchen matches with him to set rotted stumps afire as he came across them on the property. Tenants learned that where smoke arose from a place, Richardson could be located nearby.[405]

Richardson often hired individual sawmill owners to help clear timbered tracts of land that Pfeiffer purchased. Albert and Floyd Milburn's grandfather moved to Boydsville around 1878 and started a sawmill business. They helped their dad and grandfather clear some of Pfeiffer's land. Milburn placed his portable sawmill powered by a steam engine on the property, cut the timber, and sold it to lumber companies. Pfeiffer collected five percent of Milburn's profit as payment for the timber.[406]

In addition to cutting the timber off Pfeiffer's property, the Milburns removed stumps by several methods. Usually they pulled the smaller ones out of the ground with a team of horses or mules. They burned others, but the larger and more stubborn stumps, some measuring 42 inches or more in diameter, had to be dynamited.[407]

Richardson helped tenants improve cropping practices as well as managed the daily farming operations. If any of the tenants needed to see Pfeiffer personally, they stopped by the office he maintained in downtown Piggott when they came to town on Saturdays.[408] He kept several farming implements and tools in his workplace that he allowed renters to use occasionally. He only required them to not make a habit of it and return them as clean as they found them.[409]

Pfeiffer sometimes encountered legal problems in the process of purchasing land from various owners. In most instances he tried to settle with the individuals out of court. Lavonia Couch filed such a lawsuit in Eastern District Clay County Chancery Court on September 24, 1920. Lavonia's grandmother, S. C. Brandon, originally owned 120 acres that she left to her seven children when she died in 1906. One of the seven children and Lavonia's mother, Izzie, preceded her mother in death in 1902. As a result, Lavonia never received her portion of the proceeds when a relative sold the entire parcel to Paul Pfeiffer in or about 1912.[410]

According to Couch's complaint, timber valued at $3,000 had been harvested and the land put into cultivation in 1912. She sued for her legal portion (one-fourteenth share) of the proceeds from the timber and rents of $10 per acre for eight years, totaling $3,200. The case never went to trial, but in October 1920 Pfeiffer purchased her interest in the property for $125.[411]

In October 1923 Jennie Jones, Vera Travis, and R. E. Hibbs filed separate lawsuits against Pfeiffer and D. R. Stanley[412] who "negligently, knowingly, and willfully"[413] constructed a dam across White Creek that resulted in their homes and property becoming flooded. From additional court documents attached to these lawsuits, it appeared that the levee and dam referred to by the plaintiffs had been erected by the St. Francis Drainage District, and it retained the authority to make the final determination of the action. In the end, Pfeiffer stood exonerated of any wrongdoing.

As the 1920s progressed, the price of cotton gradually rebounded after the disappointing crop of 1920 brought only 15.89 cents per pound. From 1922 through 1928 the price remained at or above 20.0 cents per pound with the exception of 1926 when it dipped to 12.5 cents.[414] Even though cotton prices improved during the decade, things remained difficult for farm families in Clay County. Paul Pfeiffer sent frequent "cotton wires"[415] inquiring about the price and occasionally attended cotton conferences in Memphis regarding the unstable cotton market.[416] Pauline Pfeiffer observed the dismal financial circumstances in Piggott.

> Both agronomy and the grocery business are flat. Nobody has any money. No money has been seen here for months. Anyone who wants money writes to Uncle Gus.[417]

After the harvesting season ended, the many necessities for the following year consumed the only cash most farmers received all year. The traveling tent shows, carnivals, circuses, and country music groups scheduled their appearances during the cotton harvesting seasons and assisted the local population with the disposal of any unspent funds. In 1926 the circus entertainment in Piggott consisted of "two rings, an adding horse, a fat tight rope lady, two clowns (both in the late 60s) and THE OLDEST BUCKING HORSE IN THE WORLD…17 years old."[418]

The country experienced changes in various arenas during the 1920s. The ratification of the Nineteenth Amendment gave women the right to vote and opened other political doors for them. Mrs. W. H. Felton of Georgia became the first woman Senator when the governor appointed her to fill a seat vacated mid-term. The state of Wyoming, forefront in the women's suffrage movement, elected Nellie Tayloe Ross its first female governor. Radio technology advanced, and the general population listened to the first broadcasts of the World Series and presidential speeches. Knee length skirts became fashionable and approximately 25% of the people owned cars.[419]

Regardless of the advancements in popular culture made on the national scene, most rural Arkansans remained undaunted by them. Many, being illiterate, never read of the progress being made in other parts of the country. Furthermore, the lack of funds locally forced people to focus on the necessities of survival and pushed any desire for cultural and technological advancements into the background.[420]

The residents of Clay County, who rarely traveled beyond a 25-mile radius of their home,[421] tended to create their own entertainment and socialize with their neighbors. Children romped together in the barns with other youngsters and adopted pets from the young animals raised on the farm. Young couples intermingled at gatherings hosted by local families at homes, schools, or churches. Some of the popular get-togethers of the youth included pie suppers and cake walks held to raise funds for school or church events.

The girls baked pies and expected their beaus to purchase them during the auction. Others attending the event facetiously bid against each young man in order to inflate the price of the pie. Albert and Pauline Milburn recalled that a pie once sold for $18.75. Those who contributed to pie auctions also participated in cake walks. The host for the event marked a section of the floor with numbers. As music played the ones involved circulated in the numbered area. When the music stopped playing, the one closest to a number pulled from a hat received his or her choice of the cakes brought for the occasion.[422]

Women of the local churches organized auxiliary groups to raise funds for charity events, community affairs, church and school needs. Most of them participated in quilting bees as a favorite fundraiser. They met at the church once weekly and quilted all day. In addition to the many quilts they produced, they made cotton mattresses by putting a roll of cotton into a bed ticking and sewing the edges together. The sought-after cotton mattresses, measuring six to eight inches thick, sold well among local people who desired them to replace straw bedding. Though the mattresses flattened out after a period of use, once placed in the sunshine, the warm rays fluffed the cotton out again.[423]

Besides the frequent socials with neighbors and friends, pranks often lightened the monotonous routine of the farming community. Some local boys once stole a buggy belonging to a local farmer, Homer Miller, who later found it on top of a neighbor's house.[424]

Local pranksters also victimized Richard and Tommy Dotson, who owned one of the few cars in town. Their neighbor, Dan Woods, took the seats out of the car and replaced them with buckets. After a week or so Woods put the seats back but removed another part. Richard once responded, "There's somebody stealing my car a piece at a time and making them one of their own."[425]

When the weather prevented the farmers from working in the fields, they often flocked to streams or forested areas for a day of recreation. Mary Pfeiffer noted, "The main industries of a large part of our population are hunting and fishing…"[426] Sometimes the entire family carried a basket packed with food and spent several hours on the river banks or in the woods. If their efforts proved productive, they occasionally camped at the site overnight. Mary fretted when the fishing obsession interfered with her social plans.

> The fishing season is now on and the fishers go in droves from the homes of the natives. It is often difficult to get a foursome for a bridge game. I had two guests for a month that didn't play bridge. I surely felt out of it.[427]

Mary Pfeiffer's social engagements centered upon the bridge parties and family gatherings she hosted. Although she and Paul occasionally attended the picture shows, carnivals, and circuses that came to town, the entertainment did not compare to what she experienced in St. Louis. As the harvest season approached, she eagerly anticipated the annual trip to Arizona. She wrote to Ernest Hemingway, "I am always ready to leave Piggott in the fall before it is time to go…"[428]

Before Mary and Paul left for Arizona in 1929, she hosted a Pfeiffer reunion at her home the first week in October. By the middle of September Mary started planning three menus a day for 14 guests. She admitted that it worried her, but she expected "some help along that line from Aunt Sophia."[429] Mary wrote to Mrs. Linke [in St. Louis] for a "consignment of fruits and things that I can't get here and asked her for suggestions along the line of eats."[430] Although all the children—seven brothers and one sister—came and pronounced the event a success, Mary presented a different perspective.

> …many things…upset my well laid plans. The first was the going out of…my electric refrigerator…just as I had placed in it a large consignment of fruits and other perishable foods from St. Louis. By the time that was straightened out, with the installment of another refrigerator, much good food had gone the way of all flesh.[431]

After family members departed her company at the end of an extended visit, Mary Pfeiffer expressed that she felt "lonesome"[432] and experienced a "let down feeling."[433] She probably wondered how the local people stayed content in such an uneventful place. Mary described its lackluster to Pauline in a letter. "There is not much news in the old town. Doubtless will be tomorrow—being the day after…"[434]

The local people, lacking the financial means to travel extensively and live glamorously, made do with their simple way of life and local forms of entertainment. When Pfeiffer's tenant farmers compared their lifestyles to those of other tenants throughout the Delta region, they considered themselves fortunate. In contrast, Mary Pfeiffer, having experienced Shakespeare's dramas, the World's Fair, and large cities such as St. Louis and New York, sometimes found life in Piggott mundane.

Although the Pfeiffers' and their tenant farmers' backgrounds differed, the weather and crop production concerned them both. The summer and fall of 1928 produced extensive rainfall, and the St. Francis River, threatening to overflow its banks, upset the annual Independence Day picnic in Piggott.[435] Furthermore, 10 additional inches of rain fell that fall and sent cotton prices up a dollar a bale.[436] A "nasty winter" delayed field preparation in the spring of 1929.[437]

By the end of March 1929, the "farm tenants [displayed the] best spirits for the last three years" as they busied themselves getting ready to plant "in the bosom of Mother Earth, whose bounty is never-ending."[438] Paul and Mary Pfeiffer both regarded the weather throughout the summer and into the fall as "favorable"[439] for the crops. Mary kept Pauline updated on the progress of the crops at home. On 17 August 1929, she wrote:

> There has been too much rain for a bumper cotton crop but the prospects are somewhat above the average…the cotton leaf worm has begun operations to the south of us. We have to hold ourselves in readiness with plenty of poison and squirt guns.[440]

By September the crop "deteriorated some," but the price remained "pretty good." Mary remained hopeful that "the majority of the tenants pay out...."[441] During the height of cotton harvesting season the speculation about the quality of the crop varied to the point that Mary could not "tell if it is a good crop, a fair crop, or a poor one."[442]

Cotton prices that fall averaged a respectable 16.78 cents per pound.[443] Meanwhile, Paul Pfeiffer accumulated an additional 46,340 acres from the Great Western Land Company and 1,758 acres from individuals and sold 172 acres.[444] His land holdings in Clay County at the end of 1929 totaled 55,765 acres. For Pfeiffer the year of 1929 ended on a profitable note and he remained optimistic about the future, as stated in his letter to Ernest Hemingway.

> Last week was our most busy week in the cotton game. With rents and accounts, we collected a little over $10,000.00. Last Saturday was our biggest day, on which day we purchased in the neighborhood of $9,000.00 worth of cotton in the seed. A good many of the tenants will make a little money this year and pay up their accumulated old debts, which of course gives us great pleasure. I really believe that the farm condition is a little on the mend and look for a steady though a small improvement in the grower's condition during the next few years.[445]

Unbeknownst to Paul Pfeiffer, Black Thursday—October 24, 1929—loomed on the horizon. On this date the New York Stock Market crashed, initiating the Great Depression. The national incomes statistics showed that 60% of American citizens earned incomes of less than $2,000 during 1929, the least amount on which a family could eke out a living.[446]

The Great Depression Era, New Deal Politics, and the Drought

The spring of 1930 brought "delightful weather," and the farmers made "good progress with their farm work."[447] But June and July registered the lowest rainfall amounts ever recorded in the state. In Clay County the July temperatures reached 107 degrees, and they soared to 110 degrees in August. The extreme heat not only wilted the crops but dried up many wells.[448] Mary Pfeiffer provided the following description of the miserable situation.

> Old Sol continues to pour down his blazing rays and all nature is scorching and drying up with no relief in sight. The surplus of production is going to be done away with…Your father is very busy building bridges. I think he is trying to ignore the things that grow and don't grow on the land…I have never felt the heat so much, and it is wearing to have it day after day for months with but little respite, and then on the side to have it burning up the prospective food products. Of course it will be a big advantage to get rid of the surplus…[449]

The drought created the most critical agricultural situation that the state faced in many years. The heat caused the cotton bolls to open early and produce lower quality cotton. It also devastated the entire corn and soybean crops and resulted in no seed being produced for spring planting in 1931.[450]

As the drought lingered, the situation for Arkansas farmers became more dismal. Food crops failed to provide adequate staples for the people, and lack of money prevented employers from hiring idle laborers. Surplus crops from previous years deflated the prices received for any goods produced. The bleak situation continued indefinitely with no end in sight. The corn that they raised became the primary food staple in most households. They hauled it to the mill to be ground and made corn bread out of it. Pauline Milburn stated that her family ate cornbread three times a day for lack of anything else to eat.[451]

During the difficult times, the people existed on what little provisions they had. Children owned two sets of clothes—usually cotton overalls. They wore one pair for a couple of days and then changed into the second pair while their mother laundered the first pair. The warm summer temperatures seldom required them to wear a shirt underneath the overalls, thus eliminating an additional clothing expense. Mothers patched and passed all wearable clothing items that older children outgrew down to smaller kids to wear and sewed dresses for the girls from flour sacks.[452]

Families only needed footwear in the winter time and usually purchased one pair of shoes or knee boots in the fall with money they earned picking cotton. The Milburns recalled riding to Corning on top of a wagonload of cotton that they sold to the gin. After getting paid for their crop, they went to Jim Oliver's store where each purchased a pair of shoes that lasted until the next harvest season.[453]

The scarcity of money during the depression years resulted in few land transactions being performed by the Piggott Land Company. From 1930 until 1935 Pfeiffer only sold 160 acres and three lots. No property sales occurred during three years during that period—1930, 1932, and 1933. The situation began improving in 1935, a trend that continued until Pfeiffer's business returned to normal in 1938.[454] [See Appendix VIII, page 225]

During these distressful times, many residents of Clay County attributed their survival to the generosity of Paul Pfeiffer. Several tenant farmers also requested assistance from Don Richardson on various occasions. Pfeiffer and Richardson, knowing the tenants' financial situations, practiced the policy of granting loans to them based upon their needs and ability to repay their debts. One tenant requested a $50 crop loan from Richardson, who trying to prevent the man from overextending himself, asked him if he could manage on $40 or $45.[455]

W. F. Smart, who lived on Pfieffer farms his entire life, recalled a particular instance when a neighboring farmer faced difficult times during the Great Depression. The farmer told Pfeiffer that he saw no way possible to keep the payments up on the farm that Pfeiffer sold him. Rather than "taking the farm back," as the man suggested, Pfeiffer allowed him to continue farming the land as a tenant and pay Pfeiffer rent from the proceeds. When the farmer's financial situation improved a short time later, he resumed making payments on the farm.[456] Jim Richardson, son of Pfeiffer's farm manager Don Richardson, stated, "Mr. Pfeiffer never foreclosed on anyone. He always said, 'There'll be next year.'"[457]

The generosity of Pfeiffer did not stop at making loans to people. Many homeless people "squatted" on his property even though they did not get his permission to camp there. Using a broadax, they carved railroad ties from the trees on the property and sold them to the many tie yards situated near the railroad tracks. Pfeiffer allowed them to continue doing this without charging them for the timber because he knew they had children. At least they worked for the money they received, and Pfeiffer benefited in return by getting the land cleared inexpensively. Had Pfeiffer forced the families off the land many of them "would have starved to death."[458]

The limited amount of cash available and the great number of people needing it dictated that difficult decisions be made based upon the needs of the entire community. Pfeiffer portrayed the circumstances as follows:

> The farmers and small towns won't have much cash to spend this fall at the present farm crops prices, which are at the lowest in 30 years. Practically all credit has flown which necessitates living within our income…We have so far had a delightful season, showers as needed, all fields well cultivated and clean, and the present crop and fruit prospects very good. Cotton acreage in Clay County reduced fully 20 percent, but corn, wheat, and oats all show large increased acreage.[459]

The wonderful season and increased acreage to which Pfeiffer referred repeated itself many times across the nation. The government released its agricultural forecasts for the new crop on August 10, 1931. Bumper cotton crops in Texas, Arkansas, and Oklahoma yielded two million bales more than those states produced in 1930. The cotton prices ranked their lowest since January 1905. Southern farmers debated whether harvesting the crop merited the effort it required.[460]

People who suffered through the depression years managed the best they could with what they had. They took advantage of every opportunity available to earn money. One employment agency in the United States reported 52 applicants for every white collar job advertised in September 1931, in comparison to three per job ad published in 1929.[461]

When the chance to obtain cash in hand presented itself to a Pfeiffer tenant farmer, he responded so hastily that he actually undercut his profit. The Underwood Commission in East St. Louis operated cattle sales. Local farmers shipped livestock by train to them for sale in the national stock yards. Underwood contacted Don Richardson and requested a specific number of quality cattle that the Pfeiffer farmer raised. Richardson asked the farmer to ship the exact number needed. The farmer, who owned more cattle than the number desired, shipped the entire herd, assuming that more cattle would bring more money. Because the farmer oversupplied cattle, he reaped a smaller profit than if he had sent the specified number.[462]

When Paul and Mary Pfeiffer returned home from Arizona in March 1932, "…the first news that greeted us was that the fruit crop is completely ruined…" A warm spell advanced "everything to an abnormal stage for this time of the year"[463] prior to an arctic blast of cold air that appeared in the late spring. Even though that news normally dampened farmers' spirits, they welcomed anything that promised to reduce the abundance of farm products.

The combination of many factors, including unfavorable weather and the appearance of the boll weevil, sent cotton prices up to 8.45 cents by October. Furthermore, drought destroyed much of India's and Egypt's cotton crops and the Japanese-Chinese tensions[464] stimulated these nations' need for imported cotton. Cotton exports jumped 99% and wheat exports increased 77% over the same period in 1931, and combined, totaled 20% of the entire exports from the United States in 1932. The stock market enjoyed a brief bull market that gave everyone hope that improvements in the financial world waited on the horizon. "Hysterically jubilant" financial commentators predicted an "apparent turn for the better."[465]

The improved outlook only lasted for a short period. Harvest season revealed a bumper wheat crop that sent prices sharply downward. High shipping and storage prices eroded any profit farmers made from their crops. Textiles, grains, and cattle prices reached record lows worldwide. The country, fed up with Herbert Hoover's inability to remedy the situation, elected Franklin Delano Roosevelt as President by a landslide in 1932.

Roosevelt assumed office on March 4, 1933, and wasted no time in reforming the financial system. He declared a "banking holiday" that lasted from March 5 to March 13, 1933. After closing the federal banks, he devalued the dollar and called in all gold being circulated. Banks rapidly joined the federal system implemented by Roosevelt, but the dollar fluctuated wildly on the world scene as it attempted to establish its true value as a medium of exchange.[466]

The United States followed England's example and officially left the gold standard on April 19, 1933, causing the bond market to respond erratically. Businesses also reacted quickly to stockpile inventories before the weakened dollar further deflated in value. The Roosevelt Administration established the Civilian Conservation Corps (CCC), a New Deal Agency that provided employment to people who took part in a national reforestation campaign.[467]

On the local front the spring of 1933 brought "excessive moisture" that spurred rapid growth of the newly planted crops. Paul Pfeiffer "...following our dynamic President"[468] commenced reforestation projects of his own that provided employment for the local people. He hired some men to plant 100 catalpa trees[469] for two purposes. Because the wood resisted decay they made excellent fence posts. Also, the catalpa worms that infested the trees supplied local fishermen with an abundance of catfish bait.[470] He also hired three men to work as gardeners in his yard, or as Mary Pfeiffer put it, "at least they are on the lawn."[471]

The wet spring resulted in much of the region becoming flooded again. Karl Pfeiffer referred to the highway as being "14 inches under water" in one place and another spot where "it was 27 inches deep [and] the state had a big Mack [truck] to pull us through."[472] When summer arrived it brought plenty of hot and dry air that eliminated much of the flooding problems. By the middle of June 1933, Clay County only received three-eights of an inch of rain "in the last nine weeks"[473] and "no rain since the 12th of May."[474] The hot, dry weather damaged all the crops, except cotton, "quite badly."[475]

Mary Pfeiffer observed that "Roosevelt and Dame Nature working together are going to solve the surplus problem..."[476] The Roosevelt Administration implemented a crop reduction program to rid the nation of surplus products and reduce current production to a level where farmers earned profits for their crops. [See document,[477] page 140] Another New Deal organization, the Agricultural Adjustment Agency (AAA), oversaw the program and paid farmers a subsidy for their fallow acreage.[478] In June 1933, Paul Pfeiffer offered his opinion of the program in a letter to Ernest Hemingway.

The cotton reduction plan has been a God-send to us cotton growers. Clay County will abandon about 17,000 acres which is considerably more than their quota. The Piggott Land Company will plow up 1,328 acres, or about 40% of our total

cotton acreage. We chose the option plan on every acre and
as the price went up about $6 a bale last week, we were lucky
in our choice as the cotton at present prices will net us about
$30 an acre, besides getting the chance at a nice lot of late
corn and hay crops, saving on further cultivation, hauling,
and picking, and the option prices have been double of what
it was last year at this time.[479]

Although the farmers embraced the idea of finally earning a
decent price for their crops, the thought of plowing up their fields after
they toiled many hours to produce the crops proved difficult for them.
Moreover, the mules balked when farmers tried to get them to walk on
the ridge and plow up the crops after training them otherwise. Floyd
Milburn's dad instructed him to plow up part of their corn, but the
mule refused to move out of his tracks.

After making several attempts to get the mule to cooperate,
Milburn piled some corn stalks underneath him and set them on fire.
After the hairs on his belly began to singe, the mule finally changed
his mind. The mule, later named "Dynamite" by Milburn, never
balked afterwards when they used him for plowing fields.[480]

As cotton harvesting season arrived it dumped "considerable
rain"[481] on the crops. Farmers welcomed it for their pastures, late
gardens, and late corn, but cotton, being "a dry weather plant and
loveth not the rain," suffered damage from the excess moisture.
Pfeiffer calculated that the heavy fall rains ruined approximately 20%
of the cotton. The price of cotton increased to above $9 per bale by
September 1933. Paul Pfeiffer received a remarkable $149,400 from
his cotton alone, and many of his tenants earned enough to pay up
their accounts "in full."[482]

As true to tradition when a bountiful season ended, the shows and
carnivals appeared to collect a portion of the profits. Piggott did not
escape the usual cheap entertainment that made the circuits that year.
Some of the attractions booked their appearance several weeks in

advance.[483] The whole town, not just the cotton pickers, enjoyed the amusements. After they experienced several desperate years, the entire population welcomed the opportunity to relax and be entertained before returning to their normal routine and facing the unpredictable future.

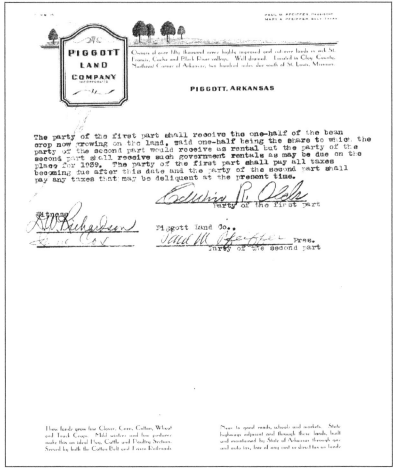

This document on Piggott Land Company letterhead outlined a typical agreement between Pfeiffer and his tenants. Pfeiffer referenced the government subsidy payments implemented by the Roosevelt Administration.

At the end of 1933 after numerous attempts, scientists successfully developed a hybrid seed corn that produced higher yields, resisted disease, and grew more vigorously.[484] The parent stocks of hybrid corn could not transmit their attributes to their offspring, so a new crop of seeds had to be produced each year. The improved yields of the hybrids, ranging from 25 to 50 percent, adequately compensated for the additional cost of the seed. Don Richardson obtained a few sacks of the hybrid seed corn and gave it to some of the "better farmers" to try out. Their success with the new seed influenced the majority of Clay County farmers to use them.[485]

During the mid-1930s cotton prices remained stable, and the surplus grain products decreased. Farm income of large landowners and commercial farmers grew by 50% between 1933 and 1937 largely due to the assistance of the AAA.[486] Sharecroppers and tenant farmers elsewhere in the Arkansas Delta still suffered unmercifully. Since the government instituted programs that reduced cotton production, their landowners no longer required their services, but they hesitated to plow up their crops for fear of being displaced from the land—their source of survival.

Landlords cut off or reduced merchandise and cash credit to croppers and tenants at their commissaries. This action made the croppers feel as though the landlords had mistreated them. Planters physically harmed and threatened to remove sharecroppers who protested. Distrust and resentment between croppers and landowners increased. The farm problems continued, and croppers and tenants remained powerless to amend the situation by themselves.[487]

In July 1934, H. L. Mitchell and Clay East, business owners in the small Arkansas Delta town of Tyronza, organized local sharecroppers into the Southern Tenant Farmers Union (STFU), a labor union created to resist the injustices that sharecroppers suffered at the hands of the landlords. The government agencies and courts consistently sided with the planters when the STFU brought issues before them.

As a result the landlords grew bolder in performing violent acts against the croppers.

They employed "nightriders" to terrorize tenant farmers and sharecroppers who belonged to the STFU. Their tactics included shooting into homes of STFU members, breaking up union meetings, evicting STFU members from their property, and beating many people. This "reign of terror" lasted two and one-half months.[488]

In 1935 a successful strike organized by the STFU among cotton pickers resulted in an increase in wages to 75 cents per 100 pounds. The planters responded by evicting families involved in union activities the last week in December and circulated blacklists of people not to be hired. Streets were lined with "more than 100 sharecroppers camped in snow drifts in below freezing weather, without food, adequate clothing, shelter, or firewood ... in one of the most extensive ... infractions of the Bill of Rights in American history."[489]

The sharecroppers in the Arkansas Delta benefited very little from the relief programs that the Roosevelt Administration continued to create. The STFU persistently applied pressure to the government officials and kept the media informed of its concerns. Its membership increased substantially to 30,000 in several states across the nation by 1937. The efforts of the STFU improved the sharecroppers' plight only temporarily, if at all, but their dismal living conditions persisted until the system eventually collapsed.

To escape the dire situation many African American sharecroppers in the Delta migrated to northern states and gained employment in factories located in Chicago and Detroit. With the decreased labor supply, planters relied more upon day laborers trucked in from the hill country and surrounding areas to work in their cotton fields during peak planting and harvesting seasons.

Regardless of the planter/sharecropper conflicts that transpired in the Delta, Paul Pfeiffer experienced little controversy from his tenant farmers. He applied a policy of generosity and kindness toward them, and they rewarded him with loyalty and hard work. The major concern that Pfeiffer faced in his farming operation rested in the weather. In July 1934, Mary Pfeiffer wrote "…we are all in high spirits over the descent of a much needed rain…Crop prospects are excellent and your father is in high glee."[490] The following December Pfeiffer summed up the harvest season.

> "The tenants have gathered all crops and have liquidated fully 95% of what they owed the Piggott Land Company, for which we are indeed grateful. Some had not cleaned the slate for the last five years, so you may see that the Bankhead Cotton Control Bill[491] was a great practical aid to the whole South, and especially the cotton growers."[492]

Considering the times and events, the farming years of 1935 and 1936 remained average. The prices of cotton stayed constant with that of the previous two years. The spring rains of 1935 delayed the planting season for two weeks but stopped in time for Clay County farmers to make their crops."[493] Karl Pfeiffer called it a "tough farming year" after the fall rains delayed harvesting for a period and caused the crops to produce below their usual yields. But all things considered they got "fine prices for what we have and that helps."[494]

The summer of 1936, as usual, brought sweltering temperatures to Piggott. Mary Pfeiffer implemented her own system of air conditioning by opening up the windows early in the morning and "catching the cool air." In the afternoon when the temperatures started rising, she closed the house "tight like a drum" to prevent the cool air from escaping.[495]

The spring of 1937 brought another major flood to the Arkansas Delta, prompting many people who lived through the flood of 1927 to forecast that it "floods on the sevens." (Their predictions appeared accurate because another hit the area in 1947.) In 1937 the water in Clay County almost reached Corning, but instead of leaving their homes, most people "just stayed with it."[496] They had to take care of their livestock, a source of their livelihood if the crops failed them. Pauline Milburn remembered having to put a sow with a litter of baby pigs in a crib to keep them out of the water."[497] Although Clay County residents experienced problems from the 1937 floods, they "escaped the big floods in [the] lower Mississippi Valley." The previous planning and drainage efforts made by Pfeiffer and the St. Francis Drainage District proved worthwhile because their "levees held."[498]

The extraordinary weather conditions that accompanied the 1930s decade, including the drought, Dust Bowl, extreme heat, and constant flooding prompted Ernest Hemingway to tell Mary Pfeiffer,

> "...If there was such a thing as Mother Nature I'll bet she was...crazy and wicked tempered...I'd like to see you put in as Mother Nature for a while and let there be a little honest, realistic, gentle reasonableness to the weather. You could blow up once in a while and give us a good moderate cloudburst, but none of these insane female tantrums we get from the present occupant."[499]

Regardless of the wet conditions, the spring of 1937 brought an "ideal" harvest season that approached "with a rush."[500] Based upon the bountiful production that year all farm products, but especially cotton and corn, "took a nosedive downward." At the beginning of the harvest season Mary contemplated a profitable year for everyone in the farming business.

> Some people have quite a bit of money and everyone has a little. Even I have something over six dollars in change in my pocket book. Haven't had a tramp for about two weeks now.[501]

Paul Pfeiffer held a different opinion after calculating his slim profits when his cotton only fetched 8.41 cents per pound. He wrote, "So, prosperity ain't for us—perhaps it is just around the corner."[502] Despite Pfeiffer's unwavering optimism prosperity did not come from the cotton crops for the remainder of the decade. The cotton prices hovered below 10 cents per pound until 1941. Mary Pfeiffer adequately described the future when she wrote, "Abundant harvest but low prices bring small profits."[503]

Despite the hardships many endured during the Depression, Paul Pfeiffer noted how the land and farmers benefited from it. The marginal cotton prices allowed thousands of acres of cotton-weary land to replenish the nutrients from the natural grasses that emerged instead. Also, a stronger bond materialized between landlord and tenants who realized their mutual existence depended upon the success of the other.[504]

The Pfeiffers accepted the circumstances in the farming operations as they came and looked forward to a better season the following year. They did not permit the deflated prices and fickle weather patterns to dampen their spirits or affect their generosity. Pauline Hemingway visited her parents in September 1938, and she noted their healthy state of body and mind.

> "...Mother and Papa were never better. Papa looks the best he has in years, and Mother...is completely devoid of physical ills...Although Mother is 71 and Papa 70, I find them much younger than most of my friends, with a fresher point of view, and much much saner. And so tolerant and generous and kind..."[505]

With Pfeiffer's extended background and experience in agriculture, he knew that things changed after a period. The markets had rebounded before and he anticipated them doing so in the near future. They did. In 1941 the value of cotton almost doubled what it brought in 1940 and continued to increase.

Unfortunately for Paul Pfeiffer, his health began to deteriorate. In 1940, he became "quite feeble"[506] and developed a fever that registered 104 degrees. When he became semi-conscious, his family hospitalized him in St. Bernard's Hospital in Jonesboro. He recovered enough to realize that he could no longer farm as actively as he had. He started selling his farmsteads to the tenants soon afterwards.

VII. Liquidation of Pfeiffer Farms

To every thing there is a season,
And a time to every purpose under the heaven:
…A time to plant, and a time to pluck up that which is planted;
A time to get…a time to keep, and a time to cast away;
…A time to be born and a time to die…

—Ecclesiastes 3: 1, 2, 6
King James Version

From 1936 until 1945 war raged across the European and Asian continents. The conflicts included the Spanish Civil War (1936-1939), the Chinese-Japanese War (1937-1945), and the German aggression toward European countries (1938-1944). The entry of the United States into World War II after Japan bombed Pearl Harbor in December 1941 affected the circumstances on the home front in various ways.

The increased demand for food, supplies, and materials needed by the military created shortages at home. As a result, the government rationed items such as sugar, coffee, dairy products, meat, canned foods, fabrics, gasoline, tin, rubber, and metal. Local people assisted in the war effort by donating household items that contained materials that could be recycled to produce equipment used by the troops. Many farmers, including those who worked for Paul Pfeiffer, grew a surplus of fruits and vegetables and canned these items to ensure that their families had an adequate supply of food to last the entire year.

Southern farmers and other employers across the nation faced an acute labor shortage resulting from the enlistment of so many men, and some women, in the military. African American tenant farmers and sharecroppers, enticed by better paying jobs in factories, left the South in droves. Larger farms and plantations in Arkansas eventually used German prisoners of war and temporary workers to cultivate and harvest their crops.

Paul Pfeiffer did not face the critical labor shortages experienced by other large planters in the Arkansas Delta during the war era because he sold most of his farmland before America entered the war. After he recuperated from his illness in 1940, Pfeiffer realized that his health prevented him from keeping the same rigorous work schedule. Although he remained the primary decision maker for the Piggott Land Company, he delegated most of the farming responsibilities to his son, Karl, and his farm manager, Don Richardson.

Realizing his physical limitations, Pfeiffer decided to sell his farmsteads to the tenant farmers who occupied them at that time. From 1939 until 1943 he sold 45,018 acres, or 81% of his land holdings, for $439,756 at an average price of $9.77 per acre. [See Appendix IX, page 226] He completed most of his transactions in 1941 when he liquidated 35% of his land holdings. Of those families who purchased property 29% paid in full at the time of purchase. The Piggott Land Company financed approximately three-fourths of the farmers who purchased acreage from Pfeiffer, 90% of whom paid their mortgages off within three years of the sale. Buyers who purchased larger and more expensive tracts of land represented approximately 1% of the total land sales and required their payments spread out over a period ranging from five to 10 years.[507]

Pfeiffer presented the buyers with either a Warranty Deed[508] or a Special Warranty Deed[509] when they made the initial transaction. In most cases he issued a Special Warranty Deed to the people who paid the full price at the time of purchase. The two documents appeared identical except the Warranty Deed included additional lines that contained the payment arrangements agreed to by the parties. The front page of both included the names of the buyers, the total amount paid for the property, payment details, legal description of the real estate, and the date on which the transaction occurred.

The reverse side had an acknowledgment section where a notary public, usually Irene Cox,[510] authenticated the land transaction. The Circuit Clerk of Clay County completed a Certificate of Record portion giving the record book and page number where the legal deed had been recorded. When the buyers made the final payment on the property, Pfeiffer provided them with a Deed of Release[511] or Quitclaim Deed.[512]

When farmers financed their land purchases through the Piggott Land Company, Pfeiffer often allowed them to dictate the payment schedule. According to the deeds, most of the buyers paid one-third of the total price down when they initiated the transaction and paid the balance in equal payments distributed over a two year period at 6% interest rate per annum. They paid the total amount due each year in one payment, usually in November, to coincide with the cotton harvest season.

The payment schedules that Pfeiffer allowed illustrated his customary kindness and leniency toward people. Table 7.1 contains some typical arrangements that emanated from Pfeiffer's land transactions during September 1941.[513] The financing terms that Pfeiffer allowed for H. A. and Julia Hommel demonstrated his willingness to accommodate the buyers' financial situation. The Hommels purchased 15.42 acres for $107.94 in December 1941. [See copy of Warranty Deed,[514] pages 151] They paid $1.00 down on the property and divided the balance in two equal payments of $53.47 due in November of 1942 and 1943.[515]

Pfeiffer demonstrated his faith in the survival of the small farm system when he divided the largest portion of his immense land holdings into 40- and 80-acre parcels and sold them to his tenants. He assisted farmers whose work ethic verified their willingness to clear, drain, and cultivate the land. Without his help many would never have become landowners. Although Pfeiffer did not dole out land free to charity cases, he made at least five transactions where the buyer paid $1 down on the land and many others that included down payments of $10 or $25. Pfeiffer conveyed his interest in a parcel of land to a church, school, or public organization several times for the total sum of $1.[516]

Table 7.1 Typical Payment Terms of Pfeiffer Land Sales

Name	Acreage	Total Price	Down Payment	Terms of Balance and Date Due
Cate, Van and Ethel	20	$140	$40	$50 due 11/42 and 11/43
Chiles, J. O and Bertha	40	$280	$30	$125 due 11/42 and 11/43
Cate, T. L. and Nora	29	$203	$50	$75 due 11/42, $78 due 11/43
Woodard, Sam and Elsie	20	$140	$50	$45 due 11/42 and 11/43
Cate, N. L. and Arietta	22	$151	$50	$50 due 11/42, $51 due 11/43

Pfeiffer accommodated anyone who seriously desired to own property by selling them land reasonably at terms they could afford. Even though it appeared that he sold the land "dirt cheap," he received a rate comparable to that collected by other Delta landowners for similar property during that particular time.[517] When Pfeiffer paid workers to clear and drain a parcel of land, he sold that piece of property at a price that reflected those improvements. The lenient method of financing that Pfeiffer provided for his buyers corroborated his reputation locally as a kind and generous man.

WARRANTY DEED

(CORPORATION WITH LIEN)

KNOW ALL MEN BY THESE PRESENTS:

That_____Piggott Land Company_____

a corporation organized under and by virtue of the laws of the State of Arkansas, duly authorized and empowered hereto by proper resolution of its board of directors, for the consideration of the sum of___One Hundred Seven and 94/100_____Dollars,

paid and to be paid by__H. A. Hommel and Julia Hommel, Husband and wife_____

as follows, to-wit: One and No/100_____Dollars,

cash in hand (the receipt of which is hereby acknowledged), and _the balance of $106.94 evidenced by two promissory notes of even date herewith as follows:

1 note due on or before November 1,1942, principal amount of $53.47

1 note due on or before November 1,1943, principal amount of $53.47

bearing interest from date until paid, at the rate of Six_____per cent per annum, do hereby grant, bargain, and sell unto the said___H. A. Hommel and Julia Hommel,_

____Husband and wife_____ and unto their____heirs and assigns forever,

the following lands lying in the County of____Clay_____and State of Arkansas, to-wit:
The south 15.42 acres of the W½ of the NE¼ of the NW¼, Section
Eight (8) Township Twenty-one (21) North, Range Seven (7) East,
containing 15.42 acres, more or less, according to U. S. Government
survey. Located in the Eastern District of Clay County, Arkansas.
Subject to all road and ditch rights of way as now laid out.

To have and to hold the same unto the said_____
____H. A. Hommel and Julia Hommel, Husband and wife_____

and unto their____heirs and assigns forever, with all appurtenances thereunto belonging.

And_____we__hereby covenant with the said____H. A. Hommel and Julia Hommel,_

___Husband and wife_____that____we____will forever warrant and defend

the title to said lands against all claims whatever, and that said lands are free from all liens and incumbrances. It being herein expressly understood that a lien is hereby retained upon said lot____ of parcel____ of land to secure the payment of residue of the purchase money hereinbefore mentioned.

IN TESTIMONY WHEREOF, The name of the grantor is hereunto affixed by its President

Hommel Warranty Deed Page One

ACKNOWLEDGMENT

State of ...Arkansas...........................⎫
                                              ⎬ss.
County of ....Clay..................⎭

On this ....5th......... day of ..December....................,1941....., before me..Irene Cox.., a Notary Public, duly commissioned, qualified and acting, within and for the said County and State, appeared in person the within named..Paul M. Pfeiffer..............and..Karl G. Pfeiffer...................... to me personally well known, who stated that they were the..President........and.Asst-Secy.......... of the ....Piggott Land Company.. a corporation, and were duly authorized in their respective capacities to execute the foregoing instrument for and in the name and behalf of said corporation, and further stated and acknowledged that they had so signed, executed and delivered said foregoing instrument for the consideration, uses and purposes therein mentioned and set forth.

IN TESTIMONY WHEREOF, I, have hereunto set my hand and official seal this ...5th............day of..December,..................., 19..41..

                                                              ....
                                                                      Notary Public.

My commission expires...September 5,1943.....

CERTIFICATE OF RECORD

STATE OF ARKANSAS,   ⎫
                                               ⎬ss.
County of ....⎭

I,...Circuit Clerk and Ex-Officio Recorder for the County aforesaid, do hereby certify that the annexed and foregoing instrument of writing was filed for record in my office on the........day of...................A. D. 19......., at ....o'clock............M., and the same is now duly recorded, with the acknowledgments and certificates thereon, in "Record Book..................," Page................ .

IN WITNESS WHEREOF, I have hereunto set my hand and affixed the seal of said Court, this ....day of......................................, 19.........

                                                              ....
                                                       Circuit Clerk and Ex-Officio Recorder.
                                                 By..

Hommel Warranty Deed Page Two

Pfeiffer made a profit from the land sales since he paid approximately 50¢ for each of the 46,340 acres he purchased from the Great Western Land Company in 1929. Additionally, Pfeiffer received a regular income from the land during the many years that tenant farmers worked it for him. With the passage of time Pfeiffer could have reaped a larger profit from his real estate transactions, but his primary objective remained to reward the landless farmers who worked for him many years with their own farmsteads and to do so at a fair price to both parties involved.

Vivian Pentecost recalled the kindheartedness of Paul Pfeiffer when her husband, Sterling, first purchased their farm from Pfeiffer in 1941. They had just married and lived with his parents in Marmaduke, Arkansas.[518] Pentecost and some family members went on an overnight hunting trip in the lowlands when he recognized the fertility of the soil. He selected a parcel of land located between the No. 1 and No. 10 ditches in Clay County that he wanted to buy. After learning that Pfeiffer owned the land, Pentecost went to Pfeiffer's office and discussed the matter with him.[519]

Although Pentecost had no money to pay Pfeiffer for the property at the time of their visit, Pfeiffer agreed to hold the property for him until he harvested his cotton crop that fall. Pentecost asked Pfeiffer whether he would sell the land if another interested buyer appeared with the money first. To reassure Pentecost of his sincerity, Pfeiffer wrote their agreement down on a piece of paper and gave it to him.[520]

Shortly afterwards the Pentecosts relocated to East Chicago, Indiana, where Sterling worked as a pipe fitter and welder; however, Pentecost carried the paper in his wallet until he made a down payment on the land. After he sold his cotton crop, he hitchhiked to Piggott to finalize the transaction.[521]

Timber covered most of the 109 acres that Pentecost purchased from Pfeiffer and knee-deep water stood in the low places on the property. Sterling dynamited a ditch in the property to drain off the water before they harvested the timber. Vivian remembered how the water "swooshed" when the blasts occurred. After the water drained from the property, it revealed an almost perfect "V-shaped ditch approximately five feet deep and three feet wide" left where they placed the sticks of dynamite in the ground.[522]

Although the Pentecosts never worked the land themselves, they constantly received income from the property. They first sold the wild grasses as hay and harvested the hardwood for lumber. After clearing it they leased the land to a tenant farmer who paid them a portion of the income from the crops he produced. Vivian still owns that first parcel of land that she and her husband purchased from Pfeiffer in addition to approximately 600 acres in Clay County that they bought through the years.[523]

The Clay County Courthouse–Eastern District in Piggott, Arkansas, contains 1,138 records of land transactions carried out by Paul Pfeiffer and the Piggott Land Company from 1902 until 1954. Pfeiffer's business agreements that generated the most paperwork included his purchase of 46,340 acres from the Great Western Land Company that resulted in 131 property title transfers in 1929, his 99 sales of farmland in 1940, followed by 296 in 1941, and finally 102 transactions in 1942. Pfeiffer carried out only 25 land deals from 1930 until 1938 during the depression years, his slowest period of activity.

The largest portion of the deeds contains routine information relating to the transfer of the properties. Paul Pfeiffer, being a very private person, did not leave a paper trail of personal documents regarding his business relationships; however, some of the deeds that Pfeiffer kept for his records contained notes concerning details about the transactions that he consummated.

Often the surveys that Pfeiffer ordered on the tracts of land that he sold did not agree with the acreage specified in the Warranty Deeds. When cases of this nature arose, Pfeiffer always rectified the inaccuracy as soon as possible. According to their Warranty Deed,

Pfeiffer sold Claude and Nettie Misenhamer 45 acres for $450 on June 11, 1937. When a survey of the property revealed only 44 acres, Pfeiffer immediately credited them $10 for the phantom acre.[524] [See copy of note below]

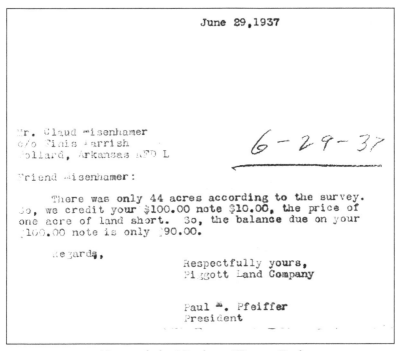

Note attached to Misenhamer Warranty Deed

Often squatters[525] settled on Pfeiffer's property and even cut and sold the timber off the property for personal income.[526] Although Pfeiffer knew about the squatters, he allowed them to continue camping on his property until he sold it. Occasionally the new owners told the squatters to move, but often Pfeiffer assumed the responsibility of dealing with them.

Pfeiffer sold 20 acres jointly to E. C. McElvain and G. McElvain in May 1941. Two families of "squatters named Chappel and Woods" had camped on the property long enough for Pfeiffer to learn their names. The McElvains agreed to "take care of" the squatters located on the property at the time they completed the land transaction with Pfeiffer.[527]

Sometimes the new property owners preferred for Pfeiffer to remove the unlawful tenants from the property. Obviously Pfeiffer had no knowledge of a squatter camped on part of the 430 acres he sold to A. L. Neel in 1942. A note attached to Neel's Warranty Deed stated that "Oscar Payne reports…squatter on part of land sold A. L. Neel." They settled the matter in the fall when Neel fenced around the squatter and Pfeiffer paid the squatter $25 to move. A handwritten postscript at the bottom of the note stated that on June 8, 1942, Pfeiffer "paid $35.00 to A. L. Neel today, settlement in full" regarding the squatter issue.[528] [See copy of note below]

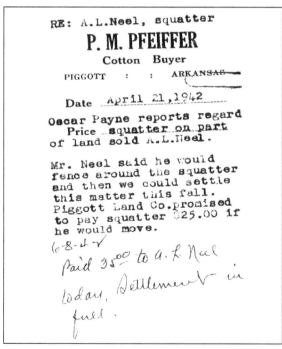

Note attached to Neel Warranty Deed

Pfeiffer tried to prevent disagreements from arising between property owners whose tracts joined the ones he sold. When disputes arose regarding the legal property lines, Pfeiffer had the land surveyed to settle the matter. J. A. and Tina E. Kirby purchased 80 acres from Pfeiffer in 1942. The neighbor enclosed part of the Kirby's land inside his fence before they bought the parcel. Pfeiffer had the land surveyed but agreed to pay the Kirbys $7 per acre for the land under the fence if the other owner refused to move it.[529] [See copy of note, page 158]

Pfeiffer avoided one particular situation regarding a disputed property line that arose from the sale of one of his farms. On May 6, 1936, Pfeiffer sold 80 acres that had been previously surveyed to Pearl and Cleo Huckabay. Pearl Huckabay wrote Pfeiffer a letter stating "...the people who have land joining us were not satisfied with your survey...they are trying to move the county line 300 feet north of the present location..."[530] After Pfeiffer investigated the matter he stated in a letter to the Huckabays, "We note we sold this land to you over five years ago, and it will be up to you folks to protect yourselves."[531]

Pfeiffer extended his generosity when necessary to accommodate the interest of the public. He contributed land free of charge to schools and churches in Clay County. Pfeiffer donated two acres to the Happy Home Pentecost Church in May 1939, "so long as used for church purposes, otherwise this land reverts back to the Piggott Land Company."[532]

Another example of Pfeiffer's willingness to accommodate the public interest rested in a request made by Joseph Sellmeyer, owner of Sellmeyer Mercantile Company in Knobel, Arkansas, and a Commissioner of the Big Gum Drainage District. In a letter[533] dated March 28, 1940, Sellmeyer offered Pfeiffer $25 for 2.3 acres that the drainage district needed to change the flow of water underneath a Missouri-Pacific Railroad bridge. Pfeiffer responded promptly by delivering a Quitclaim Deed to the Big Gum Drainage District on March 30, 1940.[534]

```
          Address: Kennett, Mo. RFD 1
                               Piggott, Ark.
                               May 18,1942
     Received from J. A. Kirby and Tina L.Kirby,
     Husband and wife, $100.00 cash, towards the
        purchase of the SW of NE & NW of SE, Section
     27-20-5, containing 80 acres, more or less.

     Survey necessary.

     Price $550.00 cash,

     Piggott Land Company to furnish abstract.

     Deed to be made as soon as survey is completed.


     If owner joining this tract of lands does not
     agree to move fence on this tract of land,
     the Piggott Land Company will pay Mr. Kirby
     $7.00 per acre for land under fence.




                    Piggott Land Company

               By
```

Note attached to Kirby Warranty Deed

Paul Pfeiffer demonstrated honesty and integrity in his business deals and developed a reputation in Clay County as being a man of his word. If a disagreement arose from any of his actions, he always tried to resolve it. He absorbed losses when necessary to work out problems. Pfeiffer also took much pleasure in providing others with quality land at a reasonable price. A letter from Pfeiffer to Charley L. Palmer demonstrated the satisfaction he received by presenting a "nice new abstract" and "mighty fine title" to Palmer following their land transaction.[535] [See copy of letter, page 159]

Paul Pfeiffer's personal involvement in the Piggott Land Company ended with his death on January 26, 1944.[536] According to the terms of his Last Will and Testament [See Appendix XIII, page 228] that he made on September 20, 1940, he designated his son, Karl, as executor of his estate. Except for the home he and Mary occupied in Piggott, he directed Karl to sell all his real property at "public or private sale, for cash or credit, as in his discretion... and distribute the net proceeds" to his wife and surviving children within the 10-year period following his death.[537]

After Pfeiffer's death, Karl became President of the Piggott Land Company and Don Richardson served as its Secretary. Under Karl's management the Piggott Land Company sold 9,232 acres for a total of $510,868 at an average price of $55.34 per acre. Of the 97 land transactions made by Karl, 55% of the buyers paid the full price at the time of the sale.[538] [See Appendix X, page 226]

Mr. Charley L. Palmer
Pollard, Arkansas RFD 1

Friend Palmer:

12-2-36

We herewith enclose a nice new abstract for the NE¼ NW¼ Section 30, Township 21, Range 7 East. The land you purchased from us, all brought down to date.

You will find this is a mighty fine title, as the Great Western Land Company received a decree of confirmation through the Court giving them a good title. You will, also, note that the taxes have all been paid. Also, that the deed from the Piggott Land Company to you is shown in your abstract.

Wishing you good luck.

Respectfully yours,
Piggott Land Company

Paul M. Pfeiffer
President

Letter attached to Palmer Warranty Deed

Karl Pfeiffer and Don Richardson followed the example that Paul Pfeiffer modeled as they liquidated the remaining real estate that Pfeiffer owned at the time of his death. They demonstrated compassion toward Iva Payne and Eliza Bolen when the widows purchased their property from the Piggott Land Company. They sold Iva Payne 20 acres for $3 per acre on January 27, 1945, and Eliza Bolen one acre for $1 on September 14, 1945.[539]

Bolen Warranty Deed, Page One

Pfeiffer and Richardson also allowed the buyers to suggest the worth of a parcel of land under consideration. In a letter to Karl dated July 14, 1949, Roy Barnhill mentioned a price of $150 that Pfeiffer quoted him for 53 acres "some time ago." After Barnhill learned that the "ditch tax"[540] totaled $143.04, he estimated the value of the property equal to $75 and offered Karl that amount for the land.[541] Pfeiffer's response to Barnhill began, "Send us $75 in American Money and tell us how you want the deed made out."[542]

Another example of the kindness that Pfeiffer and Richardson extended to the property buyers involved the case of J. M. Seachrist. Seachrist purchased 40 acres from Piggott Land Company for $120 on February 8, 1950, and agreed to pay for it in 12 monthly payments of $10 each.[543] As of May 31, 1950, Seachrist had made only one $10 payment on the property. In a letter to Seachrist Pfeiffer stated, "If you find that you can't take care of these payments, just say so and we'll refund you your money…"[544] Evidently Seachrist accepted the offer because Pfeiffer sold the property to I. B. Langley and A. R. Winton on June 10, 1950.[545]

Don Richardson bought the last piece of property sold by the Piggott Land Company. The "short 40"—almost, but not quite, 40 acres—contained the catalpa trees that Paul Pfeiffer planted during the depression in response to Roosevelt's reforestation campaign. Pfeiffer planted "row after row" of the trees to be used as fence posts. After Richardson acquired the land, he cut the trees, trimmed them into fence posts, and sold them to people from the surrounding area.[546]

Although Karl Pfeiffer managed the Piggott Land Company and his personal finances well after the death of Paul Pfeiffer, Mary Pfeiffer struggled emotionally with the loss. The grief she suffered caused her to lose her desire to live and her health began to deteriorate.[547] She eventually became confined to her bed, but she remained mentally alert until her death.

Paul and Mary Pfeiffer's adult daughters, Virginia and Pauline, stayed with Mary at her home in Piggott during her final days. On

January 28, 1950, Virginia and Pauline invited Ayleene Spence to dinner in the Pfeiffer home. When they finished eating, they went upstairs to visit with Mary before retiring for the evening. Karl and Matilda, his wife, came by for a short visit after dinner and then left. Even though Mary appeared to be very sick, her spirits remained high. She talked quite a bit and said, "We're having a party." The next morning Virginia called Ayleene and said, "You've had the last party with Mother."[548] Mary Pfeiffer died at her home on January 29, 1950.[549]

Mary continued to give to others after her death through her Last Will and Testament. [See Appendix XIV, page 229] She left a total of $39,150 to her children, grandchildren, nieces, nephews, sister, employees, the Piggott Library, and several Catholic churches, colleges, seminaries, and priests. She named Karl as executor of her estate. The generosity that Paul and Mary Pfeiffer demonstrated to others during their lifetimes kept their memories in the hearts of the people of Piggott, Clay County, Arkansas. One journalist wrote of Paul Pfeiffer:

> The good deeds of his life were his joy—he did these many acts of kindness because he loved his fellowman…through all these years of love and devotion…Pfeiffer asked nothing and wanted nothing in return except the good will of his fellowman…Piggott will never have another Paul M. Pfeiffer.[550]

Changes in Agriculture after Pfeiffer's Death

Agriculture in Clay County changed significantly after Karl Pfeiffer and Don Richardson liquidated Paul Pfeiffer's real estate holdings and the Piggott Land Company. The three primary crops produced in Clay County during the 1950s consisted of cotton, rice, and soybeans,[551] but farmers grew small crops of corn, wheat, and hay for livestock feed and sorghum for molasses.[552] The use of machines gradually replaced draft animals and humans in the fields, and the demand for sharecroppers decreased.

The Mississippi Delta region suffered critical labor shortages during and immediately following World War II. Some plantations used German prisoners of war or migrant workers from Mexico to cultivate and harvest the crops during the labor crisis, but the replacement hands only eased the situation temporarily. After the war ended, the prisoners returned to Germany. Better paying jobs in urban areas attracted former American soldiers away from the farms. Machines replaced sharecropper labor, and the tenancy system of farming collapsed by the middle of the twentieth century.

Small farmers who had no control over the price of their produce could not afford to keep pace with modern farming methods. Eventually larger and more profitable operations consumed them. As the size of American farms increased, their numbers steadily declined. On the national scene farmers decreased from 30 percent of the population in 1940 to less than three percent by 1981.[553]

Meanwhile Paul Pfeiffer divided his extensive real estate holdings in Clay County into individual farms, which he sold to his tenants. The 1940 and 1950 censuses revealed the impact that the sales made on agriculture locally. The 1940 census data, reflecting the number of tenants who purchased farmsteads from Pfeiffer in 1939, showed a 24% increase of farms operated by full owners while the number of farms worked by tenants decreased by 19%.[554] According to the 1950 census acreage placed into farmland in Clay County increased by almost one-third (32%). Substantial growth also occurred in improved land planted in crops and farmed by full owners—97,407 in 1940 and 122,318 in 1950, growing an incredible 208% and 287% respectively since 1930. [See Appendix XI, page 227]

The technological advancements in farming during the post World War II years aided the transformation of what once had been an agricultural society to an industrial and urban one. Even though tractors, combines, and cotton pickers had been invented prior to

World War II, the shortage of materials during the war prevented large scale production of them until after hostilities officially ended.

Manufacturers began marketing mechanical cotton pickers in 1950,[555] and shortly afterwards Alfred Smith became the first[556] of five farmers[557] in Clay County to buy one that year. During the following years, the scene on the countryside changed significantly as more and more planters exchanged their mules for machines. The tractors appearing in the fields increased by 500% from 1940 to 1950 at the same time that the number of mules decreased by 61%. Several local residents also invested in combines, corn pickers, and hay balers. [See Appendix XII, page 227]

Even with the availability of machines to assist the farmers, many could not afford to completely mechanize their farming operations. Local entrepreneurs often purchased equipment and hired themselves out to farmers in the area. According to agricultural historian R. Douglass Hurt, only 30 percent of American farmers owned a tractor in 1945, and draft animals still outnumbered tractors on farms until 1955.[558]

During the last half of the twentieth century, a large number of farmers sold their farms and moved to uraban areas, but recently many people are returning to live in rural communities. Several diverse reasons inspired people in the past to choose to live on a small farm in a country setting. Some of them, like Paul Pfeiffer did many decades earlier, opted for a more relaxed, and in most cases, less convenient, life in uncongested rural communities, which is perhaps the principal motivating factor that prompted Rodney Rouse to purchase a farm once owned by Pfeiffer's farm manager, Don Richardson, in Clay County, Arkansas.

Rouse, a bank executive, desired to preserve the small farm culture that he and many other local residents experienced and then watched almost disappear. He is committed to recreating a Pfeiffer farmstead from the few surviving Pfeiffer houses and farm structures in Clay County to preserve for future generations the small farm heritage practiced by many local families.

Technological advancements changed agriculture dramatically since Paul Pfeiffer sold his farmsteads six decades ago. Mass production by megafarms replaced the output generated by small farmers similar to those that Pfeiffer employed who worked 40- and 80-acre tracts. Even though most farmers welcomed the new technology in agriculture, not all the changes advanced the general purpose of farming. As a result, the family farm, the economic unit that sustained local economies from the founding of the United States, became almost eradicated during the 1970s decade.

Paul Pfeiffer visualized Piggott as a farm community of well-ordered neighborhoods where the people enjoyed good and prosperous lifestyles.[559] His desire to see people own and work their own land as small-scale, family farmers motivated him to spend a major part of his life working to turn that vision into a reality. Pfeiffer first operated a tenant farming system that permitted farm families to live in fashionable homes and work under humane conditions. He then sold farms reasonably to many landless tenants on terms they could afford, which permitted them to realize the American dream of someday owning their own homestead.

Many explanations can be given why Pfeiffer's farming operation escaped the troubles that plagued similar arrangements throughout the Delta during the early twentieth century. He recruited good farmers for his tenants, and most worked for him many years. Because they stayed for extended periods on the same farm, his farmers benefited from practicing better farming techniques that prevented soil erosion and exhaustion.

Pfeiffer initially provided the seed, tools, fertilizers, and livestock that new tenants needed to produce a crop the first year they farmed for him. By the time they harvested their second crops most made a profit. Eventually they became prosperous enough to purchase additional acreage, livestock, and machines. Many of Pfeiffer's farmers even hired their own tenants and/or seasonal laborers to work a portion of their farms.

The quality farm structures that Pfeiffer provided for his farm families motivated them to work for him indefinitely. They only had to compare their two-story bent house or T house to the shotgun shanties in the Delta that most sharecroppers and tenants occupied to appreciate working for a landlord such as Pfeiffer. Furthermore, they appreciated the added bonuses that a one acre garden spot, a wood lot, and an array of farm buildings provided.

Another factor that contributed to the success of Pfeiffer's farm operation rested in the fact that he recruited many of his farmers from the Midwestern states. Although he used many local farmers, Pfeiffer, being a land speculator, often enticed people from Illinois, Indiana, Iowa, Missouri, and Michigan[560] to work for him as tenants. The Midwesterners, with their industrious backgrounds and plentiful work options available in factories,[561] did not settle for the circumstances and deplorable living conditions that the sharecroppers tolerated.[562] They obviously required arrangements such as Pfeiffer provided before they would agree to work for him as tenants.

Perhaps the main reason that Pfeiffer enjoyed a successful farming operation is Paul Pfeiffer himself. He enjoyed a great working relationship with his tenants because he treated them well and expected the same from them. He based his business agreements with his tenants upon their word and goodwill rather than written contracts. As one tenant stated, "If you did right by him, he'd stay with you to the limit."[563]

Paul Pfeiffer was a good, decent human being that respected people, regardless of their wealth or social status. He desired to prosper from his business deals, but more than that, he wanted others around him to reap a profit as well. He possibly could have increased his wealth by changing how he managed his farming operation. For example, he could have operated a commissary where he required his tenants to purchase their goods, but in the long run, he would have suffered the consequences.

Pfeiffer's impact upon the agricultural and economic progress in Clay County remains unquestionable. Because of the volume of real estate that Pfeiffer purchased, improved, and eventually sold, Clay County developed differently from any other county in eastern Arkansas. Pfeiffer did not approve of Delta planters treating sharecroppers as serfs. Even though his farming operation resembled the sharecropping system to some extent, he treated his tenants more as yeomen farmers instead of sharecroppers.

Many years have passed since Pfeiffer lived among the local residents of Clay County, Arkansas. A few of what has become known as "Pfeiffer houses" or "Pfeiffer barns" still remain in places where many that strongly resembled them once stood. The fertile soil still produces the crops that Pfeiffer's tenants raised—corn, wheat, soybeans, and cotton. The existence of Piggott State Bank, St. Francis Drainage District, Piggott Public Library, many roads and several churches verify that Paul and Mary Pfeiffer once took the initiative to improve the quality of life of the local people.

Everywhere in Clay County one observes the evidence of the goodwill of the Pfeiffers, but the one location where the most evidence exists that demonstrates why Pfeiffer is still revered by the local people is in the Clay County Courthouse–Eastern District. It contains 1,138 deeds that attest to the fact that most of the local residents own homes or farms that Paul Pfeiffer once sold to a member of their family for a reasonable price and at terms they could afford.

Notes

1 Although most documentation regarding Paul Pfeiffer's total land holdings in Clay County cite 63,000 acres, research for this work revealed the most acreage Pfeiffer held in the county at any given time was 55,765 acres in 1929.

2 Harry S. Ashmore, *Arkansas*, (New York: W. W. Norton and Company, 1978), xvi. Planters whose families settled in southeastern Arkansas migrated to the area from Virginia, Kentucky, and North Carolina. They ranked among the middle and upper classes in the societies from whence they departed and highly valued the idea of plantation agriculture. These migrants brought and established the Old South mindset with them. They desired to continue the lifestyle they knew and were willing to protect the institution of slavery as quickly as the most ardent Old South Secessionists.

3 Lee A. Dew, *The JLC&E: The History of an Arkansas Railroad*, (State University: Arkansas State University Press, 1968), 7. The railroad companies began laying tracks in Clay County in 1873. Most of the lines passing through the county contained North/South routes, which brought many migrants to Clay County from the Midwestern states of Illinois, Native Americana, Iowa, Missouri, and Michigan. Many Midwestern immigrants settled in the area immediately before or after the Civil War; therefore, they did not possess the strong feelings about slavery or demonstrate a passionate contempt for Southerners that developed in the people who lived in the United States for many years. As a result, many of the people who populated Clay County remained free of the racism that emerged in other parts of the state.

4 "History and Culture of the Lower Mississippi Delta," *Lower Mississippi Delta Region*, 14 March 2001, <http://www.cr.nps.gov/delta/volume2/history.htm#delta>, (15 April 2004). The information in this site is provided by the National Parks Service.

5 "Arkansas: The Geography of Arkansas," *Netstate.com*, July 21, 2005, <http://www.netstate.com/states/geography/ar_geography.htm>, (30 October 2005). This website contains statistical data and basic information about all 50 American states.

6 The term used by archeologists to label the diverse societies of Native Americans who inhabited the fertile river valleys of the Tennessee, Cumberland, and Mississippi Rivers before European explorers reached the Americas.

7 http://www.cr.nps.gov/delta/volume2/history.htm#delta.

8 V. C. Wright, "A History of Brookings, Arkansas," *Clay County Courier*, 18 June 1953.

9 Fred Berry and John Novak, *The History of Arkansas*, (Little Rock: Rose Publishing Company, 1987), 17.

10 http://www.cr.nps.gov/delta/volume2/history.htm#delta.

11 *Hopefield, The County's First Settlement,* (Earle, Arkansas: Crittenden County Museum, n.d.). Hopefield was incorporated on February 8, 1859, by the Arkansas General Assembly. After Memphis fell to Union forces in 1862, Hopefield became a center for considerable military and guerilla activity which incited the Union soldiers to burn the town in February 1863. The town struggled to survive for the next 40 years; however, it finally yielded to the powerful waters of the Mississippi River in the spring of 1912.

12 *The Historic Districts of Marion, Arkansas,* (Marion, Arkansas: Marion Chamber of Commerce, n.d.), 2.

13 Fred Berry and John Novak, 18.

14 http://www.cr.nps.gov/delta/volume2/history.htm#delta.

15 Carmen Borne, "Delta," *Arkansas Natural Regions,* 18 May 1999, <www.scsc.k12.ar.us/BorneC/delta.htm>, (22 April 2004). France ceded the Louisiana Territory to Spain after the French and Native American War. The Spanish renamed Arkansas Post "Ft Charles III." In 1800, Spain returned the territory to France in a secret treaty. In 1803, the United States purchased the property from France.

16 Berry and Novak, 18.

17 Wright, "A History of Brookings, Arkansas."

18 Berry and Novak, 67.

19 Lee A. Dew, *The JLC&E: The History of an Arkansas Railroad,* State University: Arkansas State University Press, 1968, 7.

20 Robert T. Webb, *History and Traditions of Clay County,* (Mountain Home, Arkansas: Shiras Brothers Print Shop, 1933), 8.

21 Dew, 7.

22 O. L. Dalton, "More About St. Francis…," *Piggott Banner,* 30 August 1963.

23 Jake McNabb, *Clay County Courier,* 12 October 1934. Article is untitled.

24 James R. Scurlock, "Memoirs of a Tiemaker Who Came to Piggott, Arkansas in the Year 1885," *Piggott Banner,* 20 January 1928.

25 Webb, 10.

26 Ibid, 9-13.

27 Ibid.

28 Berry and Novak, 264. A discrepancy exists regarding for whom Clay County was named. Berry and Novak state it was for John Clayton, a state senator and brother of Powell Clayton.

29 Webb, 19.

30 Ibid.

31 O. L. Dalton, "Boydsville – For Fifteen Years the Capital of Clay County," *Piggott Banner,* 22 February 1963.

32 O. L. Dalton, "The Boydsville Story – Early Settlers and Families Listed," *Piggott Banner,* 8 March, 1963.

33 O. L. Dalton, "Some Early History of Greenway," *Piggott Banner,* 13 September 1963. Local leadership can be faulted for the lack of development in Greenway and Rector. It has been stated that Greenway lost the county seat issue to Piggott because Piggott offered the county officials free home sites, which Greenway

did not think was necessary. Greenway lost the issue by 32 votes. Also, the Butler County Railroad wanted to extend its tracks from Tipperary through Rector to Kennett, but Rector refused to grant them the right of way they needed. Therefore, they chose an alternate route through Piggott.

34 O. L. Dalton, "Some Memories about Greenway, Clay County," *Piggott Banner,* 6 September 1963.

35 Dew, 46.

36 V. C. Wright, "A History of Brookings, Arkansas." During World War I the Quallmalz Company held many government contracts and constantly needed laborers. They kept a representative at the Hoxie railroad station who contacted passengers seeking work as they disembarked the trains. They hired a man who proved to be an expert machinist and performed his duties well. He eventually became a disgruntled employee and completely destroyed the mill by setting it afire. By the time the company erected a new mill and acquired enough machinery to resume production, the war had ended and the government cancelled its contracts. As a result, lumber prices fell and the company struggled to survive for several years. In 1930, the company liquidated at a huge loss and sold most of its land to its workers to whom it owed salaries.

37 O. L. Dalton, "More About St. Francis…" B. D. Williams abandoned his mill and returned to Kentucky. The J. M. Myers Lumber Company moved to Piggott and later converted it into a stave mill. The owners of the Southwestern stopped operations and left the plant in charge of a caretaker, Herman Anrep, who served as the postmaster of St. Francis for many years.

38 Hubert Dortch, "History of Vincent – 1880 to 1935," *Clay County Democrat,* 23 May 1935.

39 O. L. Dalton, "More About St. Francis…"

40 Dew, 48-49.

41 O. L. Dalton, "Newspaper Romance of Clay County," *Piggott Banner,* 23 August 1963.

42 Webb, 23.

43 Dew, 4.

44 Ibid, 14.

45 Hubert Dortch, "History of Vincent – 1880 to 1935," *Clay County Democrat,* 18 May 1935.

46 V. C. Wright, "A History of Brookings, Arkansas."

47 The first census that reflects Clay County statistics.

48 University of Virginia, "Statistical and Social Sciences Data," *Geospatial and Statistical Data Center,* 4 June 2004, < http://fisher.lib.virginia.edu/cgi-local/censusbin/census/cen/pl>, (6 August 2004). Agricultural data for Clay County on this website can be reached from the homepage by navigating the following tabs: Collections>Statistics and Social Sciences Data>Historical Census Data. Data for states and counties are available from this page.

49 Ibid.

50 All percentages in this work were calculated by the author based upon data taken from the respective censuses or other sources as referenced for the specific years.

51 Whitten, David O. "Depression of 1893." *EH.Net Encyclopedia*, edited by Robert Whaples, 15 August 2001 <http://www.eh.net/encyclopedia/contents/whitten.panic.1893.php>, (9 August 2004). Violent strikes, the Populist Movement, and major changes in national policy, social and intellectual developments accompanied the Depression of 1893, one of the worst in American history. The unemployment rate exceeded ten percent for five or six consecutive years. The only other time this occurred in the history of the US economy was during the Great Depression of the 1930s. Economic decline began in January, 1893, and continued until June, 1894. The economy then grew until December, 1895, when a second recession developed that lasted until June, 1897.

52 Ibid.

53 Poole, Jim, Interview by author, Piggott, Arkansas, 13 February 2004. These workers came down from the hilly areas around Hardy, Greenbrier, and Quitman to work during cotton season and would return after harvest was over.

54 "Educational Materials – A Brief History of Arkansas," *Arkansas Secretary of State Educational Materials*, 2005, <http://www.sos.arkansas.gov/educational_history.html>, (11 February 2005). Arkansas was labeled as the "Land of Opportunity" as early as 1875 when land speculators launched a campaign outside the state to attract new residents to Arkansas. During the next 25 years, the state's population increased over 200% to 1.3 million.

55 Edwin Reed, "Oldster Remembers Rector as Boom Town," *Clay County Genealogy Club Quarterly Newsletter*, Vol. 13, No. 2, ed. Camilla Cox, June, 1994, 381.

56 Laud M. Payne, "Memoirs of Early Days in Clay County, Arkansas," *Piggott Banner*, 1 January 1937.

57 O. L. Dalton, "Newcomers and New Grounds around Liberty Hill," *Piggott Banner*, 7 June 1963.

58 Ibid.

59 Dalton, "Newcomers and New Grounds around Liberty Hill."

60 "Uncle Bill Rogers: Ninety Two Year Old Citizen Dies in Sight of Birth Place," *Jonesboro Daily Tribune*, August 13, 1926, 1. (hereafter cited as "Uncle Bill Rogers.")

61 Dalton, "Newcomers and New Grounds Around Liberty Hill."

62 "Uncle Bill Rogers."

63 Dalton, "Newspaper Romance of Clay County." A puncheon floor was made from a slab of timber and had its face roughly smoothed.

64 O. L. Dalton, "The Boydsville Story – Early Settlers and Families Listed," *Piggott Banner*, 15 March 1963.

65 Ibid.

66 O. L. Dalton, "The Boydsville Story – Early Settlers and Families Listed."

67 Farmers had their cotton "laid by" when it was in the ground, chopped [weeded], and the plants stood high enough to shade out any future weed growth. Once the crops reached this stage, the farmers remained confident of a good harvest as long and the weather held and no insect infestation threatened.

68 Hubert Dortch, "History of Vincent – 1880 to 1935." 18 May 1935.

69 Robert Henry Pfeiffer, "Henry and Annie Pfeiffer," *Bostonia,* April, 1942, Robert Henry Pfeiffer Collection, Harvard School of Divinity Archives, Andover, Massachusetts.

70 Harris Franklin Rall, "Annie Merner Pfeiffer: A Tribute," *Bennett College Bulletin,* Vol. XIX, No. 1, (Greenboro, NC: Bennett College), November, 1947, 9.

71 Gus Pfeiffer, Memoir honoring Henry Pfeiffer on his 80th birthday, 26 February 1937. Mary Fisher Floyd Archives and Special Collections, Pfeiffer University, Misenheimer, North Carolina.

72 Ibid, 9-10.

73 Mary Pfeiffer, Piggott, Arkansas, to Ernest and Pauline Hemingway, Paris, France, 30 March 1929. Patrick Hemingway Collection, Princeton University Libraries.

74 "Paul M. Pfeiffer Buried Saturday," *Piggott Times,* n.d, Located in vertical file, Piggott Public Library, Piggott, Arkansas.

75 Ibid.

76 Ruth Hawkins, "Chapter 1: The Pfeiffers," *A Family Affair: The Hemingway-Pfeiffer Marriage,* Unpublished Manuscript, 2004.

77 "Paul M. Pfeiffer Buried Saturday."

78 Hawkins, "Chapter 1: The Pfeiffers," *A Family Affair: The Hemingway-Pfeiffer Marriage.*

79 Butler County Record of Deeds Book #48, Recorder's Office, Butler County Courthouse, Allison, Iowa. Land transactions not included in this table include a sale of three city lots and buildings to James R. Russell for $3300 in April 1898. Also not included are those where Pfeiffer was one of four partners involved in the transactions.

80 Henry, Gus, and Paul Pfeiffer were well known for their benevolence and generosity to others. Henry and Gus made large financial contributions to schools, churches, and hospitals in the United States and abroad, while Paul's kindness to the people in Clay County earned him a reputation locally as a generous man.

81 Gus Pfeiffer, Memoir honoring Henry Pfeiffer on his 80th birthday.

82 Ibid.

83 Rall, 10.

84 Gus Pfeiffer, Memoir honoring Henry Pfeiffer on his 80th birthday.

85 Ibid.

86 Robert Henry Pfeiffer, "Henry and Annie Pfeiffer."

87 Gus Pfeiffer, Memoir honoring Henry Pfeiffer on his 80th birthday.

88 Robert Henry Pfeiffer, "Henry and Annie Pfeiffer."

89 Jim Richardson, Interview with author, Piggott, Arkansas, 31 January 2004. Richardson recalled his father, Don, visiting Pfeiffer's farm in Iowa that one of his brother's farmed, but Richardson could not remember the brother's name.

90 Gus Pfeiffer, Memoir honoring Henry Pfeiffer on his 80th birthday.

91 Rall, 10.

92 Ibid.

93 Dr. Robert Henry Pfeiffer, son of Paul's brother, George Washington Pfeiffer, was a noted curator, linguist, author, and ordained minister of the

Methodist Church. He attended Universities of Berlin and Tubingen in Germany and received his S. T. B. degree from the University of Geneva in Switzerland. He returned to the United States, obtained his M. A. and PhD degrees from Harvard University, and joined its staff as an instructor of Semitic languages and history from 1922 until 1958. During his tenure at Harvard, he directed the Harvard-Baghdad School Excavations in Nuzi, Iraq. He also became associated with Boston University in 1924.

94 "Annie Merner Pfeiffer Memorial Day," *Bennett College Bulletin*, Vol. XIX, No. 1, (Greenboro, NC: Bennett College), November, 1947, 7.

95 Rall, 8.

96 "Annie Merner Pfeiffer Memorial Day," 4.

97 Robert Henry Pfeiffer, "Henry and Annie Pfeiffer."

98 "Annie Merner Pfeiffer Memorial Day," 4.

99 Ibid, 13-14.

100 Robert Henry Pfeiffer, Eulogy of Gustavus Adolphus Pfeiffer, 25 August 1953, Robert Henry Pfeiffer Collection, Harvard School of Divinity Archives, Andover, Massachusetts.

101 Ibid.

102 E. T. Jaynes, "Recollections and Mementos of G. A. Pfeiffer," 2 December 1990, < http://library.wustl.edu/units/physics/pfeiffer.pdf >, (16 August 2004). Dr. Jaynes was Waymon Crow Professor of Physics at Washington University, St. Louis, Missouri.

103 Ibid.

104 Gus Pfeiffer, New York City, to Robert Henry Pfeiffer, Boston Massachusetts, 11 July 1932.

105 Jaynes, "Recollections and Mementos of G. A. Pfeiffer."

106 "Our Nominee for Citizen of the Week: Mr. Karl Pfeiffer," *Piggott Times*, 14 January 1971.

107 Jaynes, "Recollections and Mementos of G. A. Pfeiffer."

108 "Our Nominee for Citizen of the Week: Mr. Karl Pfeiffer."

109 *Clay County Land Record Book #24*, Clay County Courthouse – Eastern District, Piggott, Arkansas.

110 Noah E. House, Editor, "Extra Edition," *Piggott Banner*, 1895. S. E. Norman came to Arkansas in May, 1895, and purchased the Greenway Hotel. He remodeled and refurnished the entire building and offered "first class accommodations to the traveling public."

111 Matilda Pfeiffer, Interview with Ruth Hawkins, Piggott, Arkansas, 28 March 1997.

112 Webb, 30. Webb spelled the last name as Waggert, but further research suggests that the correct spelling is Weigart.

113 Ibid.

114 Ayleene Spence, Interview with Ruth Hawkins, Piggott, Arkansas, 10 April 1997.

115 Ron Russell, "Chasing Hemingway's Ghost," *Commercial Appeal*, Mid-South Section, August 27, 1978, 2.

116 Jim Richardson, Interview with Ruth Hawkins, Piggott, Arkansas, 23 June 1997.

117 Ron Franscell, "Pfeiffer Barn Stores Many Memories," *Clay County Democrat*, 30 May 1979, 7.

118 Matilda Pfeiffer, 28 March 1997.

119 Based upon Pfeiffer receiving 25% of the yield of one-half bale, or 250 pounds, per acre at the 1903 price of 10.49¢ per pound.

120 USDA-National Agricultural Stats Service, *Track Records United States Crop Production*, April 2003, < http://usda.mannlib.cornell.edu/data-sets/crops/96120/track03a.htm#cotton>, (3 September 2004). The price of cotton for the decade from 1900-1910 averaged 10 cents per pound.

121 *Clay County Land Record Books*, Clay County Courthouse – Eastern District. Piggott, Arkansas. The acquisition included 1100 acres bought from the Becktold Printing and Book Manufacturing Company of St. Louis for $4.09 per acre and 600 acres from Sallie Kopp for $17.50 per acre. The discrepancy in the price per acre depended on the amount cleared, drained, or otherwise improved.

122 Marcia Schnedler, "Hemingway's Piggott Revisited," *Arkansas Democrat Gazette*, July 23, 1995, 7H.

123 Pfeiffer purchased land in 1909 from Sallie Kopp of Piggott; R. J. Gorppinger and George W. McMillian of Los Angeles, CA; Luther and Nelson McLin of North Dakota; Isaac and Edith Cook of St. Louis, MO; James and Jessie Tower of East Prairie, MO; J. E. and Erin Woolf, W. D. and A. J. Woolf, J. T. and Lula Woolf, W. E. and Jennie Watson, O. T. and Alma Payne, Herman, J. A, and O. B. Coats, John and Hollie Sherfield, G. W. and C. Sanders, A. H. and Nancy Hollis, all of Greenway; Nancy Hargraves, John and Lillie Waldron, J. C. and Ethel Rogers, O. H. and Jettie Parrish, Charles W. and Elizabeth Ohwing, W.C. and S. E. Cochran, Anna M. Kile, W. A. and Clars Waddle, Lum Winston, John Yates, E. C. and S. C. Cook, and O. P. and L. A. Cook, whereabouts unknown. He sold land to W. L. Castleberry, T. L. Davis of Piggott, AR; Ernest Pfeiffer (his brother) of Oelwein, IO; and Ira Harlan.

124 http://usda.mannlib.cornell.edu/data-sets/crops/96120/track03a.htm#cotton.

125 Mary Pfeiffer, Piggott, in letter to Ernest Hemingway, Paris, 7 September 1927, Hemingway Collection, John F. Kennedy Library, Boston.

126 Ruth Hawkins, "Chapter 2, Pauline," *A Family Affair: The Hemingway-Pfeiffer Marriage*, Unpublished Manuscript, 2004.

127 Ibid.

128 Based upon two-thirds of his acreage (3946) in cotton yielding 250 pounds per acre at $13.96 per pound, of which Pfeiffer received 25%.

129 "Local Items," *Clay County Courier*, 16 June 1911, 6.

130 "Severe Hail Storm," *Clay County Courier*, 9 June 1911, 8.

131 "Local Items," *Clay County Courier*, 17 March 1911, 5.

132 Deposition of George M. Jackson, *George M. Jackson, et. al. v. J. M. Myers*, Chancery Court of Clay County, Arkansas – Eastern District, 4 October 1900.

133 "G. M. Jackson in bad in East End," *Corning Courier*, 18 October 1912.

134 *George M. Jackson v. Paul M. Pfeiffer*, Clay County Circuit Court – Eastern District, October, 1912.

135 Ibid.

136 "G. M. Jackson in bad in East End."

137 *George M. Jackson v. Paul M. Pfeiffer.*

138 "Fort Jefferson, Kentucky," *Kentucky Atlas & Gazetteer*, n.d. <http://www.uky.edu/KentuckyAtlas/ky-fort-jefferson.html>, (22 September 2004). "Fort Jefferson was a southwestern Ballard County town on the Mississippi River about one mile south of Wickliffe. It was founded in 1858 near the site of George Rogers Clark's 1780 fort, which became known as Clarksville, and was occupied until 1781. The Fort Jefferson post office opened in 1860, but moved to the new town of Wickliffe in 1879. A later Fort Jefferson post office operated from 1891 to 1892. The town is gone and the site is now the home of the Westvaco paper factory."

139 *George M. Jackson, et al. v. J. M. Meyers.*

140 W. S. Bryan, St. Louis, Missouri, to Fannie C. Jackson, St. Francis, Arkansas, 9 July, 1894.

141 W. S. Bryan, St. Louis, Missouri, to George M. Jackson, St. Francis, Arkansas, 12 July, 1894.

142 W. S. Bryan, St. Louis, Missouri, to Fannie C. Jackson, St. Francis, Arkansas, 12 July, 1894.

143 W. S. Bryan, St. Louis, Missouri, to Fannie C. Jackson, St. Francis, Arkansas, 9 July, 1894.

144 Contract between George M. Jackson, W. S. Bryan, and J. M. Myers, 6 January 1887, *George M. Jackson, et al. v. J. M. Meyers*, Exhibit #2.

145 Jackson and Paul Pfeiffer lived in the St. Louis area at the same time and although the possibility exists that they were acquaintances there, this observation cannot be confirmed.

146 *George M. Jackson, et al. v. J. M. Meyers.*

147 Some court cases in the Clay County Circuit and Chancery Courts, Eastern District that involved Jackson included Cases #803—*Jackson v. Mitch Johnson, et. al.*, #995 – *Jackson v. State of Arkansas*, #648 – *Jackson v. J. M. Meyers and Becktold Printing and Book Company*, #959 – *Jackson v. Paul M. Pfeiffer*, #1255 – *State of Arkansas v. Jackson*, #801 – *Jackson v. J. M. Meyers and Becktold Printing Company*, #1337 – *Jackson v. Same Johnson*, #250 – *Jackson v. B. B. Biffle*, and #794 – *State of Arkansas v. Jackson.*

148 *C. E. Blackshare, et. al. v. G. M. Jackson*, Clay County Circuit Court – Eastern District, 4 April 1913.

149 Ibid.

150 Ibid.

151 *George M. Jackson v. Paul M. Pfeiffer.*

152 There is a possibility that Paul Pfeiffer had prior business dealings with George Jackson before their disagreement over the Clay County land transaction. A reference is made in the *Parkersburg Eclipse*, 9 February 1900, that Pfeiffer purchased from "Go. Jackson nearly all the livestock on the farm, nearly 400 head of cattle, 30 head of horses, hogs, etc...."

153 "G. M. Jackson in bad in East End."

154 Ibid.

155 "Local Items," *Clay County Courier,* 24 January 1913, 8.

156 Case #995, Clay County Circuit Court – Eastern District, *Criminal Record Book #3,* pp. 95, 96, & 100.

157 Hawkins, "Chapter 2, Pauline," *A Family Affair: The Hemingway-Pfeiffer Marriage.*

158 Webb, 39-40. A St. Louis man named Timmerman had established a Catholic Church at Peach Orchard around 1891. He purchased many acres of land, built a Catholic Church and a home for the priest, and paid the priest a salary while living in the community. Timmerman later sold parcels of land to immigrants that came in Clay County only to find that he did not hold legal title to the land. As a result, the settlers abandoned the church, priest's home, and the lands involved in the ordeal. The Star Inn later connected the church and house and turned them into a hotel.

159 *Clay County Land Record Books.* In 1911, Pfeiffer purchased land from David Swinney, Harrison and Cora Shannon, Charles and Therese Smith, W. C. and S. E. Cochran, Louis and Ada Hardesty, Samuel Vancil, W. H. and Nancy O'Barr, Eddius Berr, R. W. Turner, et al., George and Grace Olmsted, and J. M. and Ella Myers. He sold land to T. L. Davis, A. J. Alcorn, R. S. Caldwell, Charles G. Stayback, W. H. O'Barr, and W. F. and E. S. Coleman.

160 *Clay County Land Record Books.* Pfeiffer's assumed real estate in 1912 from J. W. Mann of Danville, IL, R. S. Caldwell, George and Emily Hall, H. A. and Gussie Bennett, C. T. and Rosa Swan, W. E. and Mary Spence, W. H. Cooper, George W. Seitz, et al., G. T. Parrott, W. A. Harlan, et al., John J. Patterson, W. L. Castleberry, James Haire, T. K. and Settie Shoulders, W. D. and Mabel Templeton, Henry and Vera Everett, Samuel and Veronica Elbert, and W. D. and Jennie Lasswell. He sold land to R. W. Turner, Daniel Lang, et al., W. L. Castleberry, C. D. Davidson, Dora E. Walker, J. C. Walker, M. Watson, the Campbell Lumber Company, School District #86, and The St. Francis Box and Lumber Company.

161 *Clay County Land Record Book #38,* 29.

162 "Piggott-The Way It Was," *Piggott Times,* 11 November 1976. Located in Geneaology Section of Piggott Public Library.

163 *Clay County Land Books #208,* 39, and #221, 39.

164 "Piggott-The Way It Was."

165 The price per acre was calculated by author using information taken from Pfeiffer's Land Records in the *Clay County Land Books,* Clerk's Office, Clay County Courthouse – Eastern District, Piggott, Arkansas.

166 "Pfeiffers had Impact in Piggott, Clay Co," *The Piggott Times,* 9 April 1997, 11.

167 Schnedler, 7H.

168 Hawkins, "Chapter 2, Pauline."

169 *Clay County Land Record Books.* Pfeiffer purchased land from L. and A. E. Hubbard, M. V. and Ida Morrow, W. R. and Lizzie Wright, Nancy Hargraves, Sallie Kopp, W. D. and Mabel Templeton, Ira Baker, W. H. Cooper, Edward F. Stahl, and E. S. and Eda Coleman. He sold property to John S. Sherfield, J. A. Reed, W. D.

Templeton, W. L. Castleberry, S. B. Mitchell, E. S. Coleman, Lois Simpson, Clay County Fair Association, and the Piggott Power Company.

170 Based upon the estimate that two-thirds of the land [6,973 acres] was planted in cotton, each acre produced 250 pounds, at the 1913 price of 12.47¢ per pound, and Pfeiffer received 25% of the proceeds. Profits from other crops and land sales are not included.

171 Noah E. House, Editor, "Extra Edition," *Piggott Banner,* 1895.

172 Ibid. Noah E. House, Editor, "Extra Edition," *Piggott Banner,* 1895.

173 James R. Scurlock, "Memoirs of a Tie Maker who Came to Piggott, Ark, in the Year 1885," Piggott Banner, 20 January 1928. The Piggott post office was established in February, 1881, at the home of R. Throgmorton, the postmaster. In February, 1882, A. J. Brown bought a lot and built the first store in Piggott. In March, 1883, the post office was moved to the town of Piggott. Although the town of Piggott already existed; it did not incorporate until August, 1891.

174 Maynard H. Potter, "Notes on the Early History of Piggott, Arkansas," *Clay County Genealogy Club Quarterly Newsletter,* Vol. 3, No. 4, ed. Camilla Cox, Piggott, Arkansas, Oct, Nov, Dec, 1987, 36.

175 Scurlock, 20 January 1928.

176 "History of Piggott," *Piggott Banner,* 11 June 1963.

177 Ibid.

178 Ibid.

179 Potter, 36.

180 University of Virginia, "Statistical and Social Sciences Data," *Geospatial and Statistical Data Center,* 4 June 2004, < http://fisher.lib.virginia.edu/cgi-local/censusbin/census/cen/pl>, (6 August 2004).

181 *Historical Appraisal of Extension Work in Clay County 1914 – 1939,* University of Arkansas Cooperative Extension Service Records (MC 1145), Box 3, Special Collections, University of Arkansas Libraries, Fayetteville. Weigert served as the first county agent in Clay County during the period from 1912 to 1913.

182 Potter, 35.

183 Cox, Camilla, "Development of Nimmons, Clay County, Arkansas," *Clay County Genealogical and Historical Society Quarterly Newsletter,* Vol 10, No. 1, March, 1994.

184 O. T. Ward, "White Walnut Creek and Brick Kilns," *Rector Democrat,* 25 January 1962.

185 A yellow, brown, or red mineral consisting of clay and iron oxide that is used as a dye.

186 Ward, "White Walnut Creek and Brick Kilns."

187 Albert and Pauline Milburn, Interview with author and Phil Cate, Corning, Arkansas, 5 June 2004.

188 "Pounded the Preacher," *Clay County Courier,* 31 July 1909, 1. The tradition means giving a welcome gift of a pound in weight.

189 Ibid.

190 Albert and Pauline Milburn, 5 June 2004.

191 Harris Franklin Rall, "Annie Merner Pfeiffer: A Tribute," *Bennett College Bulletin,* Vol. XIX, No. 1, (Greenboro, NC: Bennett College), November, 1947, 9-10.

192 O. L. Dalton, "The Boydsville Story," *Piggott Banner,* 5 April 1963. Reverend W. W. Spence and his wife, Evelyn McNiel Spence of Alabama, came to the Oak Bluff community in 1878, where they pastored a Presbyterian Church and taught school. Their son, W. E. Spence worked as a bookkeeper and salesman for a mercantile firm in Malden, Missouri, and later moved to Boydsville and worked in a comparable position with W. S. Blackshare & Company. He served as County and Circuit Clerk for six years. During this period he studied law under the guidance of attorney Gus Barlow. He passed the bar examination, entered the law practice in the early 1890s, moved to Piggott when the courthouse was moved, and established a partnership with attorney L. Hunter. Later, attorneys W. H. Spiller, Les Castleberry, and his son, Carl, joined the law firm. The law firm of Moore and Spence was the primary law firm in the county. Spence did the court pleadings and Moore handled the paperwork. Spence was twice elected State Senator, but resigned at the beginning of his second term, and his son Raymond was appointed to fill the unexpired term. Louis Spence, brother of Attorney Spence, studied journalism at the University of Arkansas and became owner and publisher of the *Piggott Banner.*

193 *Clay County Record Book #36,* 483, Clay County Courthouse – Eastern District. Piggott, Arkansas.

194 Ayleene Spence, Interview with Ruth Hawkins, Piggott, Arkansas, 10 April 1997.

195 Matilda Pfeiffer, Interview with Ruth Hawkins, Piggott, Arkansas, 29 March 1997.

196 Pauline Pfeiffer, Piggott, Arkansas, to Ernest Hemingway, Paris, France, 29 November 1926, Hemingway Collection, John F. Kennedy Library, Boston.

197 "Piggott Barn Studio Provided Peace, Quiet," *The Piggott Times,* 20 February 1991, 5.

198 *Clay County Miscellaneous Record Book #1,* Piggott, Arkansas. The other stockholders included G. W. Seitz, T. L Davis, C. W. Pollard, R. H. Dudley, J. M. Turner, J. R. Scurlock, W. E. Spence, W. D. Templeton, E. Williams, L. Hubbard, O. R. Winton, J. M. Myers, J. P. Potter, O. H. Parrish, L. Hunter, Joe Gattinger, who purchased 10 shares at $25 each. Paul Pfeiffer bought 40.

199 Ibid.

200 "Our History," *Electric Cooperatives in Arkansas,* n.d, <http://www.ecark.org/>, (22 August 2004). This official Arkansas Electric Cooperatives website provides a variety of information about rural electrification programs in Arkansas, economic development, energy saving tips, school programs and other items useful to the general public.

201 "Paul M. Pfeiffer Buried Saturday," *Piggott Times,* n.d, Located in vertical file, Piggott Public Library, Piggott, Arkansas.

202 Smart, W. F. Interview with author. Piggott, Arkansas, 13 February 2004; Jim Richardson, Interview with author, Piggott, Arkansas, 31 January 2004.

203 Jim Richardson, Interview with author, Piggott, Arkansas, 31 January 2004.

204 *Clay County Land Record Books #47, 49, and 50,* Piggott, Arkansas. On many occasions when Pfeiffer sold land to people who subsequently faced financial difficulties, he repeated this process of dealing with them regarding their debt to him. He only resumed ownership of the property if they were unsatisfactory tenants or made the decision to sell it back to him themselves.

205 Jerry Hendrick, "Highlights of Days Gone By on Greenway Route One," *Piggott Banner,* 13 April, 1956. Jerry Hendrick served as the mail carrier on Greenway Route One for 28 years.

206Ibid.

207 Ibid.

208 Barry, John M. *The Great Influenza.* New York: Penguin Books, 2004, 92-97. Contrary to the assumption that the Spanish flu originated in China or France, Barry stated that "epidemiological evidence" proposed that it first surfaced in Haskell County, located in western Kansas, during early 1918. From there enlisted soldiers carried the virus to Camp Funston, an army base in the eastern part of the state, then to Europe where it mutated and became a worldwide epidemic during World War I. In the first months of 1918, Dr. Loring Minor, a Kansas physician, reported an eruption of "influenza of severe type" in *Public Health Reports,* a journal published weekly that alerted public health officials to outbreaks of communicable diseases. Articles in other medical journals mentioned influenza flare-ups later that spring, but Minor's account was the first and only one issued as a public health warning that suggested a new and dangerous strand of the flu was developing. Minor's report is significant since influenza was not reported as a communicable disease at that time. Minor obviously encountered several cases of a strange influenza in Kansas that troubled him, and therefore, prompted him to alert other medical professionals about it.

209 Worldwide Flu Pandemic Strikes 1918-1919," A *Science Odyssey-People and Discoveries,* 1997, <http://www.pbs.org/wgbh/aso/databank/entries/dm18fl.html>, (4 September 2004). This is the official website of the Public Broadcasting Station and contains educational information about various topics for public use.

210 < http://www.pbs.org/wgbh/aso/databank/entries/dm18fl.html>.

211 "Timeline," *Hemingway-Pfeiffer Museum and Educational Center,* ((hereafter cited as Hemingway-Pfeiffer Museum) n. d., <http://hemingway.astate.edu/timeline.html>, (4 September 2004). The Hemingway-Pfeiffer Timeline gives the details about the Pfeiffers from the time Paul and Mary Pfeiffer married and continues through the recent purchase of their Piggott home by Arkansas State University.

212 <http://hemingway.astate.edu/timeline.html>, (4 September 2004).

213 Ken Wells, Interview with Ruth Hawkins, Piggott, Arkansas, 10 April 1997.

214 Ayleene Spence, 10 April 1997.

215 Ibid.

216 St. Francis Drainage District Book of Minutes, Piggott, Arkansas. The original name for the drainage district was Clay and Greene County Drainage District.

217 Robert T. Webb, *History and Traditions of Clay County,* Mountain Home, Arkansas: Shiras Brothers Print Shop, 1933, 30.

218 Jake McNabb, *Clay County Courier*, 12 October 1934.

219 Paul Avrich, *Sacco and Vanzetti: The Anarchist Background*, (Princeton: Princeton University Press, 1991), 93—103.

220 "Piggott, Clay County" advertisement, *The Arkansas Gazette*, Little Rock, Arkansas, 20 November 1919.

221 Webb, 17.

222 Ibid.

223 < http://fisher.lib.virginia.edu/cgi-local/censusbin/census/cen/pl>, (6 August 2004).

224 O. L. Dalton, "More About St. Francis…," *Piggott Banner*, 30 August 1963.

225 Webb, 58. Waddle was an early organizer of the Ku Klux Klan in Clay County.

226 Webb, 30.

227 C. E. Jewell, Brooksville, Florida, letter to O. L. Dalton, Piggott, Arkansas, 9 September 1963. Printed in *Piggott Banner* 27 September 1963.

228 *Clay County Land Record Books.* During this period Pfeiffer purchased land from Lavonia Couch, W. E. and Emma Tomlinson, George and Effie Belch, F. A. and Grace Wagner, M. and Martha Watson, J. F. and Lula Woolf, Esco and Lucille Alcorn, A. H. and N. A. Hollis, Charles and Sarah Stayback, R. L. and Jennie Lewis, Norris Greer, Jacob and Floria Barr, J. T. and Dora Haden, Glenn and Maud Norred, N. H. and Mary Whitehurst, C. E. Blackshire, et al., Henry and Laura Weiss, H. A. and Pollie Burns, W. L. and Mayme Castelberry, W. C. and Laura McGhee, H. A. and Estella Hardesty, O. A. and Bertha Faeth, J. H. and Viola Boyd, J. H. and Kate Bruce, J. D. and Lucy Cluck, W. F. Dalton, Nancy Ward, Warren Chair Works, W. M. and Etta Harmon, and Royall and Mabel Brandon. He sold land to John a. Schmidt, Henry H. Schmidt, Glenn and Ralph Norred, T. L. Davis, A. A. Armstrong, George Belch, A. H. Hollis, A. O. and Bertha Faeth, Edwin Williamson, H. A. and Polly Burns, Royall and Mabel Brandon, F. V. Hamilton, O. T. and Edna Ward, J. A. Nichols, W. C. McGhee, T. H. Boyd, V. B. and Versa Davidson, and O. O. and S. E. Holifield.

229 W. F. Smart, Interview with author, Piggott, Arkansas, 13 February 2004. Jim Richardson, Interview with author, Piggott, Arkansas, 31 January 2004.

230 Ibid. Percentages calculated by author based upon U. S. Census Data from 1910-1930 for Clay County, Arkansas.

231 <http://hemingway.astate.edu/timeline.html>, (4 September 2004).

232 "Services Held Monday for Karl Pfeiffer," Newspaper article in vertical file, Piggott Public Library, Piggott, Arkansas, 17 December 1981.

233 <http://hemingway.astate.edu/timeline.html>, (4 September 2004).

234 Ayleene Spence, 10 April 1997.

235 Ibid.

236 Matilda Pfeiffer, 28 March 1997.

237 Webb, 38.

238 Pauline Pfeiffer, Piggott, Arkansas, to Ernest Hemingway, Paris, France, 15 October 1926, Hemingway Collection, John F. Kennedy Library, Boston.

239 Pauline Pfeiffer, Piggott, Arkansas, to Ernest Hemingway, Paris France, 22 October 1926, Hemingway Collection, John F. Kennedy Library, Boston.

240 Pauline Pfeiffer, Piggott, Arkansas, to Ernest Hemingway, Paris France, 1 November 1926, Hemingway Collection, John F. Kennedy Library, Boston.

241 Ibid.

242 Mary Pfeiffer, Piggott, Arkansas, to Pauline Hemingway in Paris, France, 5 June 1929, Patrick Hemingway Collection, Princeton University Libraries.

243 Pauline Pfeiffer, Piggott, Arkansas, to Ernest Hemingway, Paris France, 10 December 1926, Hemingway Collection, John F. Kennedy Library, Boston.

244 Mary Pfeiffer, 5 June 1929.

245 Mary Pfeiffer, Piggott, Arkansas, to Pauline Hemingway, Spain, 15 July 1929, Hemingway Collection, John F. Kennedy Library, Boston.

246 Mary Pfeiffer, 5 June 1929.

247 Mary Pfeiffer, Piggott, Arkansas, to Ernest Hemingway, Paris, France, 7 September 1927, Hemingway Collection, John F. Kennedy Library, Boston.

248 Mary Pfeiffer, Piggott, Arkansas, to Pauline Hemingway, Madrid, Spain, 17 August 1929, Patrick Hemingway Collection, Princeton University Libraries.

249 Virginia Pfeiffer, Piggott, Arkansas, to Pauline Hemingway in Wyoming, 20 August 1928, Hemingway Collection, John F. Kennedy Library, Boston.

250 Pauline Pfeiffer, 15 October 1926.

251 Jim Poole, Interview by author, Piggott, Arkansas, 13 February 2004.

252 Paul Pfeiffer, Piggott, Arkansas, to Pauline Hemingway, Kansas City, Kansas, 1 July 1928, Hemingway Collection, John F. Kennedy Library, Boston.

253 Ibid.

254 St. Francis Drainage District Book of Minutes, Piggott, Arkansas. Paul Pfeiffer filled the seat vacated by A. Bertig, who died on 12 December 1926. Pfeiffer was appointed by Governor Tom J. Terral on January 4, 1927, but sworn in on 18 December 1926.

255 Paul Pfeiffer, Piggott, Arkansas, to Ernest Hemingway, Paris, France, 10 July 1929, Hemingway Collection, John F. Kennedy Library, Boston.

256 James W. Alexander and James R. Scurlock, "Resolution of Condolence," *Piggott Times*, 1 February 1944.

257 *Clay County Miscellaneous Record Book #1*, Piggott, Arkansas. Both companies were dissolved after Pfeiffer's death—the Piggott Custom Gin Company on 18 July 1947, and the Piggott Land Company on 12 February 1954.

258 Mary Pfeiffer, Piggott, Arkansas, to Pauline Hemingway, Paris, France, 8 September 1929, Patrick Hemingway Collection, Princeton University Libraries.

259 Ibid.

260 Mary Pfeiffer, Phoenix, Arizona, to Ernest and Pauline Hemingway, Paris, France, 20 January 1930, Hemingway Collection, John F. Kennedy Library, Boston.

261 Poole, Jim, 13 February 2004.

262 "Notice of Result of Election," *Piggott State Bank Board Minutes*, 7 March 1930.

263 *Clay County Miscellaneous and Incorporation Record Book #3*, Clay County Courthouse – Eastern District Piggott, Arkansas. Initial stockholders in Piggott State Bank included J. A. Adkins, B. E. Williams, R. H. Wall, J. W. Hamilton, G. H. Hitt, J. E. McGuire, F. H. Jones, U. L. Fridenburg, L. W. Brannon, H. C. Robbins,

Frank Underwood, R. C. Tucker, Grover Myers, E. C. Johnson, M. E. Taylor, V. C. Wright, Joe Call, E. G. Ward, A. Stallings, Paul M. Pfeiffer, G. Will Reves, James Chappell, T. A. French, and T. W. Leggett.

264 Paul Pfeiffer, Piggott, Arkansas, to Ernest and Pauline Hemingway, Key West, Florida, 20 March 1930, Hemingway Collection, John F. Kennedy Library, Boston.

265 "Proceedings of the Board of Directors," *Piggott State Bank Minutes,* 7 May 1930 and 3 May 1934.

266 Proceedings of the Board of Directors," *Piggott State Bank Minutes,* 24 September 1930.

267 Proceedings of the Board of Directors," *Piggott State Bank Minutes,* 26 September 1933.

268 W. F. Smart, Interview with author, Piggott, Arkansas, 13 February 2004. Smart's father helped Pfeiffer build Pfeiffer Road in 1927 with teams of mules and wagons.

269 Minutes of the Special Meetings of the Board of Directors, Piggott State Bank, 8 March 1933.

270 Proceedings of the Board of Directors," *Piggott State Bank Minutes,* 13 April 1933.

271 Proceedings of the Board of Directors," *Piggott State Bank Minutes,* 16 November 1933.

272 Don Adams and Arlene Goldbard, "New Deal Cultural Programs: Experiments in Cultural Democracy," *Webster's World of Cultural Democracy,* 7 March 2001, <http://www.wwcd.org/policy/US/newdeal.html#WPA>, (12 February 2005). The most extensive employment program associated with President Roosevelt's New Deal Program that commenced in the spring of 1935.

273 Jerry Hendrick, 20 April, 1956.

274 Matilda Pfeiffer, 28 March 1997.

275 Ibid.

276 Jim Poole, Interview with Ruth Hawkins, Piggott, Arkansas, 9 June 1997.

277 "A Tribute," n.d., Newspaper article in vertical file, Piggott Public Library, Piggott, Arkansas.

278 *Clay County Land Record Book #58,* Clay County Courthouse – Eastern District. Piggott, Arkansas.

279 Mary Pfeiffer, Piggott, Arkansas, to Ernest Hemingway, Paris, France, 4 May 1929, Hemingway Collection, John F. Kennedy Library, Boston.

280 Mary Pfeiffer, 5 June 1929.

281 Mary Pfeiffer, 8 September 1929.

282 Mary Pfeiffer, Piggott, Arkansas, to Pauline Hemingway, Spain, 4 July 1929, Hemingway Collection, John F. Kennedy Library, Boston.

283 Jim Poole, 9 June 1997.

284 Ayleene Spence, 10 April 1997.

285 Bill Leonard, "More About Greenway," *Piggott Banner,* 18 October 1963.

286 Jim Richardson, Interview with Ruth Hawkins, Piggott, Arkansas, 23 June 1997.

287 Alfred and Louise Smith, Interview with author, Piggott, Arkansas, 27 October 2004.

288 *Mid-west Farm Building Plan Service*, (Fayetteville: University of Arkansas, 1933), 1. The fifteen colleges included the University of Arkansas – Fayetteville, University of Illinois – Urbana, Purdue University – Lafayette, Indiana, Iowa State College – Ames, Kansas State College – Manhattan, University of Kentucky – Lexington, Michigan State College – East Lansing, University of Minnesota – St. Paul, University of Missouri – Columbia, University of Nebraska – Lincoln, North Dakota Agricultural College – Fargo, Ohio State University – Columbus, Oklahoma A & M College – Stillwater, South Dakota State College – Brookings, and the University of Wisconsin – Madison.

289 Ibid.

290 Howard Marshall, *Folk Architecture in Little Dixie: A Regional Culture in Missouri*, (Columbia: University of Missouri Press, 1981), 19.

291 Marshall, *Folk Architecture in Little Dixie*, x.

292 Elizabeth Gouwens, "Organic Architecture Pathfinder," *Frank Lloyd Wright Foundation*, 2003, <http://www.franklloydwright.org/index.cfm?section=research&action=display&id=80>, (12 March 2005). This website is maintained by The Frank Lloyd Wright Foundation, a non-profit organization "dedicated to conserving the work of Frank Lloyd Wright and advancing the principles of organic architecture."

293 John Michael Vlach, *Back of the Big House*, (Chapel Hill: University of North Carolina Press, 1993), 108-109.

294 Marshall, *Folk Architecture in Little Dixie*, 24.

295 Vlach, *Back of the Big House*, 77.

296 Ibid.

297 Marshall, *Folk Architecture in Little Dixie*, 84-85.

298 Alfred Smith, Interview with author, Piggott, Arkansas, 28 August 2004.

299 Henry Glassie, Conversation with author, Jonesboro, Arkansas, 7 April, 2005. The gabled roof bent house is also called the gabled ell house.

300 "Why Build With Wood," *The Long-Bell Book of Farm Buildings*, (Kansas City: The Long-Bell Lumber Company, 1926), 16.

301 Jim Poole, Interview by author, Piggott, Arkansas, 13 February 2004.

302 Jim Poole, Interview with author, Piggott, Arkansas, 27 October 2004. The boards "overlapped each other to keep the rain out."

303 Jim Richardson, Interview with author, Piggott, Arkansas, 21 October 2004.

304 Poole, 27 October 2004.

305 Rodney Rouse, Interview with author, Piggott, Arkansas, 21 October 2004.

306 Dub and Marguerite Smart, Interview with author, Piggott, Arkansas, 27 October 2004.

307 Smith, 27 October 2004.

308 Sarah Brown, "Folk Architecture in Arkansas," *Arkansas Folklore Resource Book*, (Fayetteville: University of Arkansas Press, 1992), 123-124.

309 Ibid, 120.

310 Richardson, 21 October 2004.

311 Smart, 27 October 2004.

312 Smith, 27 October 2004.

313 Smart, 27 October 2004.

314 Poole, 27 October 2004.

315 Marshall, *Folk Architecture in Little Dixie*, 38.

316 The Upland South geographic area refers to the states of Virginia, North Carolina, Kentucky, Tennessee, and Arkansas. Sometimes Oklahoma and Texas are considered as part of that region, but the former five states are the ones referred to when the Upland South is mentioned in this work.

317 Marshall, *Folk Architecture in Little Dixie*, 36.

318 Patrick Norton, "Roof Designs," *Long Island Home Inspection*, 2003, <http://www.longislandinspection.com/roof-designs.html>, (3 November 2004). This Website is maintained by the Long Island Home Inspection, a company that "provides inspection services" to residents in New York by providing "vital information" to prospective homeowners that assists them in identifying trouble areas before they purchase a home.

319 John Michael Vlach, "The American Bungalow," *Common Places*, (Athens: The University of Georgia Press, 1986), 79-85.

320 John Michael Vlach, "The Shotgun House: An African Architectural Legacy," *Common Places*, (Athens: The University of Georgia Press, 1986), 58-59.

321 Poole, 27 October 2004.

322 Ibid.

323 Deetz, 216.

324 Leslie C. "Skip" [Stewart]-Abernathy, *Barns in the 19th Century: Archaeological Perspectives on Changes in Farming*, Paper presented at the annual meeting of the Northeast Anthropological Association , April 16-19, 1975, SUNY, Potsdam, New York, 1-2.

325 Marshall, *Folk Architecture in Little Dixie*, 76.

326 John Michael Vlach, *Back of the Big House*, 109-110.

327 Marshall, *Folk Architecture in Little Dixie*, 78.

328 Marshall, *Vernacular Architecture in Rural and Small Town Missouri*, 43.

329 Southern slang for "got a whipping".

330 Margaret Bolsterli, *Born in the Delta*, (Knoxville: University of Tennessee Press, 1991), 86. Pauline Milburn, Interview with author and Phil Cate, Corning, Arkansas. 5 June 2004.

331 Nicholas S. Howe, *Barns*, (New York, NY: Michael Friedman Publishing Group, 1996), 18.

332 *Mid-west Farm Building Plan Service*, Plans Nos. 72001 and 72002.

333 Sloane, 55.

334 Ibid, 66. This barn paint recipe was taken from the 1835 Farmers' Almanac.

335 Rodney Rouse, Piggott, Arkansas, Correspondence with author, 30 November 2004. Farm slang referring to an open barn or an open section of a barn. Sometimes the areas have feed troughs or hay mangers and they provide livestock with a covering from inclement weather and/or during feeding times.

336 Poole, 27 October 2004.

337 Ibid.

338 Smart, 27 October 2004.

339 Poole, 27 October 2004.

340 R. Douglas Hurt, *American Farms: Exploring Their History*, Malabar, Florida: Krieger Publishing Company, 1996, 119. Hay hoods, either boxy openings or triangular cones, were attached to barns over the door opening from an outside wall into the hayloft. They provided a shaded workspace during the summer months for individuals pitching hay from the wagon into the hayloft.

341 Poole, 13 February 2004.

342 Poole, 27 October 2004.

343 Ibid.

344 Ibid.

345 Jean Sizemore, *Ozark Vernacular Houses*. (Fayetteville: University of Arkansas Press, 1994), 116.

346 Vlach, *Back of the Big House*, 64.

347 Ibid.

348 Ibid, 65.

349 Ibid.

350 Richardson, 21 October 2004.

351 Smart, 27 October 2004.

352 Poole, 13 February 2004.

353 Smith, 27 October 2004.

354 Rouse, 21 October 2004.

355 Marshall, *Folk Architecture in Little Dixie*, 84-85.

356 [Stewart]-Abernathy, 1.

357 *Planning the Farmstead*, USDA Farmers' Bulletin 1132, U. S. Government Printing Office, 1949, 4.

358 Henry Glassie, *Vernacular Architecture*, Bloomington and Indianapolis: Indiana University Press, 2000, 122; Hurt, *American Farms: Exploring Their History*, 119. The saltbox barn, one of the latest English models, appeared in New England during the early seventeenth century. It received its name from the long descent of its roof. The barn's gabled roof had a short, steep side that faced South and a long, slanted side that reached within one to three feet above the ground. Its design allowed for accumulated snow on the low roof to provide an insulating sheath to help keep livestock warm during winter months.

359 Sloane, 57-59.

360 Furman Mulford, May Cowles, Thomas Gray, and Warren Manning, "Farmstead Planning and Beautification and Painting," *Farm and Village Housing*, University of Maryland, 1932, 97.

361 Rodney Rouse, Interview by author, Piggott, Arkansas, 29 January 2004.

362 W. F. "Dub" Smart, Interview with author, Piggott, Arkansas, 13 February 2004. Smart's granddad paid Pfeiffer $125 per acre for the farm.

363 Poole, 13 February 2004.

364 Ibid.

365 Poole, 27 October 2004.

366 Smith, 27 October 2004.

367 Gus Pfeiffer aboard the Queen Mary to Louise Pfeiffer and Sister Emma, 2 March 1939, Hemingway-Pfeiffer Museum and Educational Center, Piggott, Arkansas.

368 Donald Holley, *The Second Great Emancipation*, Fayetteville: University of Arkansas Press, 2000, 3.

369 Items needed for daily life – salt, pepper, shoes, and other goods that had been charged during the year at the planter's commissary.

370 The day that sharecroppers sold their cotton in the fall and "settled" their accounts with the landlord. Those whose cotton sales exceeded their debt charged at the commissary would be paid the difference, but most either broke even or ended the harvest season indebted to the planters.

371 David Eugene Conrad, *The Forgotten Farmers: The Story of Sharecroppers in the New Deal*, (Westport, CT: Greenwood Publishing Company, 1982), 17.

372 Holley, 10.

373 National Center for Infectious Diseases, "Frequently Asked Questions about Malaria," *Malaria*, 13 August 2004, <http://www.cdc.gov/malaria/faq.htm>, (12 September 2004). This CDC Website provides information about diseases, symptoms, prescriptions drugs, and other medical information. Malaria is a serious, sometimes fatal, disease caused by a parasite. Humans get malaria from the bite of a malaria-infected mosquito. Symptoms of malaria include fever and flu-like illness.

374 "Pellagra Shown to be Dietary disease 1915, *A Science Odyssey: People and Discoveries*. 1998, <http://www.pbs.org/wgbh/aso/databank/entries/dm15pa.html>, (15 April 2004). Pellagra caused skin rashes, mouth sores, diarrhea, and if untreated, mental deterioration. The diet of poor people in the region, consisting of cornbread, molasses, and a little pork fat, caused them to develop the disease. Medical research revealed that Niacin, one of the B vitamins, prevents and cures pellagra.

375 Thomas Jackson Woofter, *Negro Migration: Changes in Rural Organization and Population of the Cotton Belt*, (New York: W. D. Gray, 1920), 88.

376 Carolyn Terry Bashaw, "One Kind of Pioneer Project: Julia F. Allen and the Southern Tenant Farmers' Union College Student Project, 1938," *Arkansas Historical Quarterly*, 55:1 (1966), 7.

377 Margaret Jones Bolsterli, *Born in the Delta*, Knoxville: University of Tennessee Press, 1991, 6.

378 Jeannie Whayne, *A New Plantation South: Land, Labor, and Federal Favor in Twentieth-Century Arkansas*, Charlottesville: University of Virginia, 1996, 7.

379 Charles Morrow Wilson, "Tenantry Comes Forward," *Country Gentleman*, July 1936, Wilson, 13.

380 Ibid.

381 Ibid.

382 Alfred and Louise Smith, Telephone interview with author, 28 August 2004.

383 Matilda Pfeiffer, Interview with Ruth Hawkins, Piggott, Arkansas, 28 March 1997.

384 Wilson, 13.

385 Ibid.

386 Albert, Floyd, and Pauline Milburn, Interview with author and Phil Cate, Corning, Arkansas, 5 June 2004.

387 Jim Richardson, Telephone interview with author, 28 August 2004.

388 Milburn, 5 June 2004.

389 Ibid.

390 W. F. "Dub" and Marguerite Smart, Interview with author, 27 October 2004. Lard was rendered from the hogs' skins. A fire was built underneath a wash kettle filled with water. When the water became hot the skins were placed in and stirred with a paddle until "they were ready to render the lard." The entire contents of the wash kettle were placed in a lard press (a container about the size of a bucket) and the lard would be squeezed out. Some of the lard was mixed with lye to make soap. They used lye soap to take a bath, wash their hair, dishes, and clothes. Lye was strong enough to "eat up the meat" on the hog skins, but was not diluted when applied to the human body or hair.

391 Parcels of pork skins.

392 Jim Poole, Interview with author, Piggott, Arkansas, 27 October 2004. Although some people cleaned the intestines and used them as containers for the sausage, Jim's family used canvas bags that his mother sewed beforehand for this purpose. The bags measured approximately two inches in diameter and 12 inches long.

393 Rodney Rouse, Interview with author, Piggott, Arkansas, 8 September 2003.

394 Information taken from Pfeiffer's collection of deeds located at Hemingway-Pfeiffer Museum and Educational Center, Piggott, Arkansas. Pfeiffer was a land speculator who often brought in acquaintances from the Midwestern states to work for him as tenant farmers. He later sold parcels of land to people who relocated to Piggott from those states.

395 Wilson, 13.

396 Louise Smith, 28 August 2004. For example, Smith grew up on a Pfeiffer farm and attended college. After she married Alfred Smith, they continued farming for Karl Pfeiffer. They have two daughters – one became a CPA and the other a clinical psychologist.

397 Alfred Smith, 28 August 2004.

398 Wilson, 13.

399 Ibid, 42.

400 Ibid.

401 Jim Poole, Interview by author, Piggott, Arkansas, 13 February 2004.

402 Smith, 28 August 2004. Louise Smith is the daughter of Glasgow.

403 Richardson, 28 August 2004.

404 Ibid.

405 Jim Richardson, Interview with Ruth Hawkins, Piggott, Arkansas, 23 June 1997.

406 Milburn, 5 June 2004.

407 Ibid.

408 Richardson, 23 June 1997.

409 Matilda Pfeiffer, 28 March 1997.

410 *Lavonia Couch v. Paul M. Pfeiffer*, Eastern District Clay Chancery Court, November Term, 1920.

411 Ibid.

412 D. R. Stanley purchased three tracts of land totaling 280 acres from Pfeiffer in the spring of 1918. After this lawsuit, Pfeiffer had no more land dealings with Stanley.

413 *Mrs. Vera Travis v. P. M. Pfeiffer and D. R. Stanley; R. E. Hibbs v. Paul M. Pfeiffer and D. R. Stanley; and Mrs. Jennie Jones v. P. M. Pfeiffer and D. R. Stanley*, Clay Circuit Court, Eastern District, October Term, 1923.

414 USDA-National Agricultural Stats Service, *Track Records United States Crop Production*, April 2003, <http://usda.mannlib.cornell.edu/data-sets/crops/96120/track03a.htm#cotton>, (3 September 2004).

415 Pauline Pfeiffer, Piggott, to Ernest Hemingway, Paris, France, 22 October 1926, Hemingway Collection, John F. Kennedy Library, Boston.

416 Pauline Pfeiffer, Piggott, to Ernest Hemingway, Paris, France, 14 October 1926, Hemingway Collection, John F. Kennedy Library, Boston.

417 Pauline Pfeiffer, Piggott, to Ernest Hemingway, Paris, France, 30 November 1926, Hemingway Collection, John F. Kennedy Library, Boston.

418 Pauline Pfeiffer, Piggott, to Ernest Hemingway, Paris, France, 1 November 1926, Hemingway Collection, John F. Kennedy Library, Boston.

419 John W. Hartman Center for Sales, Advertising & Marketing History, Duke University Rare Book, Manuscript, and Special Collections Library, "Timeline," *Ad*Access On-Line Project—Ad #R0108*, 1999, <http://scriptorium.lib.duke.edu/adaccess/>, (13 September 2004). "The Ad*Access Timeline features a chronology of major events and interesting facts in international affairs; United States government and politics; companies, inventions, discoveries and technology; humanities and the arts; entertainment and sports ; and a miscellaneous section. The timelines mainly list events that occurred in or affected the United States to provide general context for the ads in the project, nearly all of which are from U.S. publications."

420 Milburn, 5 June 2004.

421 Ibid.

422 Ibid.

423 Ibid.

424 Ibid.

425 Ibid.

426 Mary Pfeiffer, Piggott, to Ernest Hemingway, Paris, France, 7 September 1927, Hemingway Collection, John F. Kennedy Library, Boston.

427 Mary Pfeiffer, Piggott, to Pauline Hemingway, Paris, France, 5 June 1929, Patrick Hemingway Collection, Princeton University Libraries.

428 Mary Pfeiffer, Piggott, Arkansas, to Ernest Hemingway, Paris, France, 9 October 1929, Hemingway Collection, John F. Kennedy Library, Boston.

429 Aunt Sophia was the wife of Paul's younger brother Ernest Pfeiffer. Ernest Pfeiffer purchased 200 acres in Clay County from Paul Pfeiffer in December 1914. Paul purchased 180 acres back from Ernest and Sophia Pfeiffer in May 1929.

430 Mary Pfeiffer, Piggott, Arkansas, to Pauline Hemingway, Paris, France, 24 September 1929, Patrick Hemingway Collection, Princeton University Libraries.

431 Mary Pfeiffer, 9 October 1929.

432 Mary Pfeiffer, Piggott, Arkansas, to Ernest and Pauline Hemingway, Paris, France, 30 March 1929, Hemingway Collection, John F. Kennedy Library, Boston.

433 Mary Pfeiffer, Piggott, Arkansas, to Ernest and Pauline Hemingway, Spain, 4 July 1929, Patrick Hemingway Collection, Princeton University Libraries.

434 Ibid.

435 Mary Pfeiffer, Piggott, Arkansas, to Ernest Hemingway, Kansas City, Kansas, 1 July 1928, Hemingway Collection, John F. Kennedy Library, Boston.

436 Pauline Pfeiffer, Piggott, to Ernest Hemingway, Oak Park, 12 October 1928, Hemingway Collection, John F. Kennedy Library, Boston.

437 Paul Pfeiffer, Piggott, Arkansas, to Ernest and Pauline Hemingway, Key West, Florida, 10 March 1929, Hemingway Collection, John F. Kennedy Library, Boston.

438 Paul Pfeiffer, Piggott, Arkansas, to Ernest and Pauline Hemingway, Havana, Cuba, 30 March 1929, Hemingway Collection, John F. Kennedy Library, Boston.

439 Paul Pfeiffer, Piggott, to Ernest Hemingway, Paris, France, 10 July 1929, Hemingway Collection, John F. Kennedy Library, Boston.

440 Mary Pfeiffer, Piggott, Arkansas, to Pauline Hemingway, Madrid, Spain, 17 August 1929, Patrick Hemingway Collection, Princeton University Libraries.

441 Mary Pfeiffer, Piggott, Arkansas, to Pauline Hemingway, Paris, France, 8 September 1929, Patrick Hemingway Collection, Princeton University Libraries.

442 Mary Pfeiffer, 9 October 1929.

443 USDA-National Agricultural Stats Service, *Track Records United States Crop Production*, April 2003, <http://usda.mannlib.cornell.edu/data-sets/crops/96120/track03a.htm#cotton>, (3 September 2004).

444 Clay County Land Record Books, Clay County Courthouse – Eastern District, Piggott, Arkansas. In 1929 Pfeiffer purchased land from Ernest and Sophia Pfeiffer, Edna E. Drace, F. V. Hamilton, A. C. and W. N. Read, Edgar and Cora Carrico, Scott Tie Company [Michigan], V. E. and Sarah Jewell, State of Arkansas, St. Francis Drainage District, and S. B. and Maud Mitchell. He sold land to F. V. Hamilton, O. T. Carpenter, W. P. McGeorge, St. Francis Drainage District, Met Life Insurance, Prairie Grove Church of Christ, William and Grace Burton, W. A. Rabon, and McDougal Public School. In 1930 he purchased another 16 acres and sold 81.5 acres, including land purchased from Ballard and Potter Clark and land sold to E. H. and Porter Ballard and the Piggott Land Company.

445 Paul Pfeiffer, Piggott, Arkansas, to Ernest Hemingway, Paris, France, 14 October 1929, Hemingway Collection, John F. Kennedy Library, Boston.

446 John W. Hartman Center for Sales, Advertising & Marketing History, Duke University Rare Book, Manuscript, and Special Collections Library, "Timeline," *Ad*Access On-Line Project—Ad #R0108*, 1999, <http://scriptorium.lib.duke.edu/adaccess/>, (13 September 2004).

447 Paul Pfeiffer, Piggott, Arkansas, to Ernest and Pauline Hemingway, Key West, Florida, 20 March 1930, Hemingway Collection, John F. Kennedy Library, Boston.

448 Roger Lambert, "Hoover and the Red Cross in the Arkansas Drought of 1930," *Arkansas Historical Quarterly*, Vol. 29 (Autumn, 1970), 3.

449 Mary Pfeiffer, Piggott, Arkansas, to Pauline Hemingway, Cooke, Montana, 30 July 1930, Patrick Hemingway Collection, Princeton University Libraries.

450 Old Statehouse Museum, "Drought Threat is Worse Than Flood," *The Arkansas News*, 2003, "<http://www.oldstatehouse.com/educational_programs/classroom/arkansas_news/d etail.asp?id=773&issue_id=37&page=4>, (14 September 2004). This site contains information about the Old Statehouse Museum exhibits and collections, educational programs, newsletters, and other information useful to the general public about Arkansas history.

451 Milburn, 5 June 2004.

452 Ibid.

453 Ibid.

454 Information taken from Paul Pfeiffer's collection of Warranty Deeds located at Hemingway-Pfeiffer Museum and Educational Center, Piggott, Arkansas The following people purchased land from Pfeiffer in 1931 – W. T. Hazelwood and D. H. Shride; in 1934 – E. K. Deal; in 1935 – Flora Seay; in 1936 – Herman and Lora Scheffler, C. H. and Josephine Smith, V. C. Wright, Oscar Bennett, Charley Palmer, and C. O. and Lura Tinsley; in 1937 – J. I. and Willard Burkhead, W. H. and Julia Nicholas, T. C. and Nancy Permenter, Garland and Gladys Rice, Robert Reeves, Maurice and Letha White, A. N. and Ethel Jones, and Charley Palmer; in 1938 – Barnie Gribble, M. D. Byers, George and Lora Woods, Marion and Jessie Dickens, R. E. and Martha Coleman, J. W. and S. E. Foster, George French, and Ray and Margaret Adams.

455 Richardson, 23 June 1997.

456 W. F. "Dub" Smart and Marguerite, Interview with author, Piggott, Arkansas, 13 February 2004.

457 Richardson, 13 February 2004.

458 Milburn, 5 June 2004.

459 Paul Pfeiffer, Piggott, Arkansas, to Ernest and Pauline Hemingway, Spain, 18 June 1931, Hemingway Collection, John F. Kennedy Library, Boston.

460 Dan Blatt, "Descent into the Depths: The Collapse of International Finance," *Futurecast-Online Magazine*, Vol. 3, No. 6., 1 June 2001, <http://www.futurecasts.com/Depression_descent-end-'31.html>, (17 September 2004). "Dan Blatt, Brooklyn College, '59, and Harvard Law School, '62, has 40 years experience working in and writing about the operations of government agencies. He was a financial columnist for several business newspapers, headed by the *Miami Review*, between 1972 and 1984, and author of the spectacularly prescient book, *Dollar Devaluation*, in 1967." *Futurecasts* is an online magazine that contains information about the United States economy, military, and national and international issues. A lot of the information has been taken from past articles that appeared in the *New York Times*.

461 Ibid.

462 Richardson, 23 June 1997.

463 Mary Pfeiffer, Piggott, Arkansas, to Pauline Hemingway, Key West, Florida, 12 March 1932, Hemingway Collection, John F. Kennedy Library, Boston.

464 Kenneth B. Pyle, *The Making of Modern Japan*, (Lexington, Ma: D. C. Heath, 1996), 55-135. Tensions between the Japanese and Chinese remained high, and often resulted in combat, from the 1890s until the middle of the twentieth century. Japanese conflict with China over Korea resulted in the Sino-Japanese War (1894-95). Japan emerged victorious and enacted a policy of dominion over China and the Far East. In the late 1920s China challenged Japan's control over Manchuria's administrative and economic affairs. Japan eventually occupied Manchuria and placed troops in Shanghai. Although war was never officially declared between the countries, tensions continued to mount until hostilities erupted on July 7, 1937. Japan subsequently invaded China, and Thailand, and occupied eastern Asia and its environs. The Allies stripped Japan of its empire after her defeat in World War II and returned China's former territory to the Chinese government.

465 <http://www.futurecasts.com/Depression_descent-end-'31.html>, (17 September 2004).

466 Ibid.

467 http://scriptorium.lib.duke.edu/adaccess/timeline-1931.html.

468 Mary Pfeiffer, Piggott, Arkansas, to Ernest Hemingway, Havana, Cuba, 4 May 1933, Hemingway Collection, John F. Kennedy Library, Boston.

469 Bob Spalding, "Grow Your Own Catalpa Worms," Clemson University Cooperative Extension Service, 7 September 1998, <http://virtual.clemson.edu/groups/FieldOps/CGS/catalpa.htm>, 18 October 2004. This page maintained by Clemson University in cooperation with the U. S. Dept. of Agriculture and South Carolina Counties. Issued in Furtherance of Cooperative Extension Work in Agriculture and Home Economics, Acts of May 8 and June 30, 1914. "Moths appear in early spring. After mating, the females deposit eggs in large masses on leaves, stems, and branches of Catalpa trees. The eggs hatch in a few days and the worms, or larvae, feed for about a month until they reach maturity. The larvae then enter the soil to pupate. Moths emerge from the soil and return to the tree, laying eggs for the second generation. The new larvae feed for about a month before entering the soil to pass the pupal stage in the soil so the cycle can begin again the following spring.

470 Jim Richardson, Interview with author, Piggott, Arkansas, 31 January 2004.

471 Mary Pfeiffer, 4 May 1933.

472 Karl Pfeiffer, Piggott, Arkansas, to Ernest Hemingway, Havana, Cuba, 18 May 1933, Hemingway Collection, John F. Kennedy Library, Boston.

473 Paul Pfeiffer, Piggott, Arkansas, to Ernest and Pauline Hemingway, Key West, Florida, 17 July 1933, Hemingway Collection, John F. Kennedy Library, Boston.

474 Mary Pfeiffer, Piggott, Arkansas, to Ernest and Pauline Hemingway, Key West, Florida, July 1933, Hemingway Collection, John F. Kennedy Library, Boston.

475 Paul Pfeiffer, 17 June 1933.

476 Mary Pfeiffer, July 1933.

477 Part of Paul Pfeiffer's collection of Warranty Deeds, Hemingway-Pfeiffer Museum and Educational Center, Piggott, Arkansas. The caption at the top of the

letterhead states, "Owners of over 50,000 acres highly improved and cut-over land in rich St. Francis, Cache and Black River valleys. Well drained. Located in Clay County, Northeast Corner of Arkansas, 200 miles due south of St. Louis, Missouri." The script at the bottom reads, "These lands grow fine Clover, Corn, Cotton, Wheat and Truck Crops. Mild winters and fine pastures make this an ideal Hog, Cattle and Poultry Section. Served by both the Cotton Belt and Frisco Railroads. Near to good roads, schools and markets. State highways adjacent and through these lands, built and maintained by State of Arkansas through gas and auto tax, free of any cost or direct tax on lands."

478 http://scriptorium.lib.duke.edu/adaccess/timeline-1931.html

479 Paul Pfeiffer, 17 June 1933.

480 Milburn, 5 June 2004.

481 Paul Pfeiffer, Piggott, Arkansas, to Pauline Hemingway, Madrid, Spain, 19 September 1933, Hemingway Collection, John F. Kennedy Collection, Boston.

482 Ibid.

483 Ibid.

484 "A Moment in Time Archives: Hybrid Seed Corn," Vol. 7, No. 51, 22 August 2003, eHistory, 2004, <http://www.ehistory.corn/world/amit/display.cfm.?amit_id=2141>, (10 September 2004). The Department of History at Ohio State University sponsors the website of eHistory.Com. It contains an extensive historical resources base including over "130,000 pages of historical content; 5300 timeline events; 800 battle outlines; 350 biographies; and thousands of images and maps."

485 Richardson, 23 June 1997.

486 'Barnes and Noble Learning Network, "The Great Depression: Stumbling Blocks – The New Deal Fades," *Sparknotes*, 1999-2003, <http://www.sparknotes.com/history/american/depression/section5.rhtml>, 18 September 2004. "SparkNotes.com (the "Service") is an online information, products and communications service provided by SparkNotes LLC ("SparkNotes")."

487 Gilbert Fite, *Cotton Fields No More: Southern Agriculture 1865 – 1980*, Lexington: University Press of Kentucky, 1984.

488 David Eugene Conrad, *The Forgotten Farmers: The Story of Sharecroppers in the New Deal*, Westport, Ct: Greenwood Publishing Company, 1982.

489 Auerbach, 14.

490 Mary Pfeiffer, Piggott, Arkansas, to Ernest and Pauline Hemingway, Key West, Florida, 18 July 1934, Hemingway Collection, John F. Kennedy Library, Boston.

491 Katie Hines, "History in Pickens: The Farmer, the Politician, the Artist, and the Cow," *Pickens' Weekley Webzine*, 19 September 2003, <http://www.datelinepickens.com/historyinpickens/mural.shtml>, 18 October 2004. This website showcases stories about people from Pickens County, Alabama, that make news. John Hollis Bankhead, a U.S. Senator from 1931 to 1946, and his brother, Speaker of the House William Brockman Bankhead, co-authored legislation to assist tenant farmers during the Depression. "The Bankhead Cotton Control Act

of 1934 boosted the price of cotton by limiting the amount a farmer could market. The Bankhead-Jones Farm Tenancy Act in 1937 provided farm tenants with federal loans to purchase land."

492 Paul Pfeiffer, Piggott, Arkansas, to Ernest and Pauline Hemingway, Key West, Florida, 10 December 1934, Hemingway Collection, John F. Kennedy Library, Boston.

493 Karl Pfeiffer, Piggott, Arkansas, to Ernest Hemingway, Key West, Florida, 18 March 1935, Hemingway Collection, John F. Kennedy Library, Boston.

494 Karl Pfeiffer, Piggott, Arkansas, to Ernest Hemingway, Key West, Florida, 28 November 1935, Hemingway Collection, John F. Kennedy Library, Boston.

495 Pauline Pfeiffer, Piggott, Arkansas to Ernest Hemingway, Paris, France, 10 September 1936, Hemingway Collection, John F. Kennedy Library, Boston.

496 Milburn, 5 June 2004.

497 Ibid.

498 Paul Pfeiffer, Phoenix, Arizona, to Ernest and Pauline Hemingway, Key West, Florida, 1 March 1938, Hemingway Collection, John F. Kennedy Library, Boston.

499 Ernest Hemingway, Bahamas, to Mary Pfeiffer, Piggott, Arkansas, 2 August 1937, Patrick Hemingway Collection, Princeton University Libraries.

500 Mary Pfeiffer, Piggott, Arkansas, to Ernest Hemingway, Montana, September 1937, Hemingway Collection, John F. Kennedy Library, Boston.

501 Ibid.

502 Paul Pfeiffer, Piggott, Arkansas, to Ernest Hemingway, Spain, 15 November 1937, Hemingway Collection, John F. Kennedy Library, Boston.

503 Mary Pfeiffer, Piggott, Arkansas, to Pauline Hemingway, Key West, Florida, 30 November 1938, Hemingway Collection, John F. Kennedy Library, Boston.

504 Wilson, 13.

505 Pauline Hemingway, Piggott, Arkansas, to Ernest Hemingway, Paris, France, 17 September 1938, Hemingway Collection, John F. Kennedy Library, Boston.

506 Pauline Hemingway, Key West, Florida, to Ernest Hemingway, Havana, Cuba, 1940, Hemingway Collection, John F. Kennedy Library, Boston.

507 Statistics taken from Paul Pfeiffer's collection of Warranty Deeds located at Hemingway-Pfeiffer Museum and Educational Center, Piggott, Arkansas.

508 "Legal Encyclopedia: Real Property and Landlord/Tenant Issues," *The 'Lectric Law Library's Lexicon*, February 2002, <http://www.lectlaw.com/ref.html>, 6 December 2004. This Website considered by some as "the net's most extensive legal dictionary" is hosted by legal experts and offers explanations of legal words, terms, and phrases. A warranty deed is "a deed in which the grantor [seller] fully warrants good clear title to the property. Used in most real estate deed transfers, a warranty deed offers the greatest protection of any deed."

509 Ibid. A special warranty deed is "a deed in which the grantor [seller] conveys title to the grantee [buyer] and agrees to protect the grantee against title defects or claims asserted by the grantor and those persons whose right to assert a claim against the title arose during the period the grantor held title to the property. In a special warranty deed the grantor guarantees to the grantee that he has done nothing during the time he held title to the property which has or which might in the future, impair the grantee's title."

510 Irene Cox worked for Paul Pfeiffer and the Piggott Land Company for many years. She frequently signed correspondence generated by the Piggott Land Company.

511 <http://www.lectlaw.com/ref.html>. A Deed of Release is "a deed that is evidence of the release of a property from a lien."

512 Ibid. A Quitclaim Deed is "a document transferring title or right or claim to another."

513 Information taken from Paul Pfeiffer's collection of Warranty Deeds, Hemingway-Pfeiffer Museum and Educational Center and Educational Center, Piggott, Arkansas.

514 Deed is part of Paul Pfeiffer's collection of Warranty Deeds, Hemingway-Pfeiffer Museum and Educational Center and Educational Center, Piggott, Arkansas.

515 Ibid.

516 Information taken from Paul Pfeiffer's collection of Warranty Deeds, Hemingway-Pfeiffer Museum and Educational Center, Piggott, Arkansas.

517 Contract between the Board of Commissioners of Beaver Dam Drainage District, Greene and Randolph Counties, Arkansas, and George Padwell, 15 December 1926; Letter from Robert Fuhr, Jonesboro, Arkansas, to T. A. Henson, W. Frankfort, Illinois, 27 July 1925, H. M. Cooley Collection, Archives and Special Collections, Dean B. Ellis Library, Arkansas State University, Jonesboro. Padwell purchased 4200 acres of land from the Beaver Dam Drainage District for $8.80 per acre and Fuhr estimated the value of land in eastern Craighead and Poinsett County, Arkansas, between $15 to $35 per acre. The rates Pfeiffer received for his property is comparable to that referred to in these documents during the same time period that Pfeiffer sold parcels of property.

518 Vivian Pentecost, telephone interview with author, 1 December 2004.

519 Vivian Pentecost, "Share your Hemingway or Pfeiffer Memories," Hemingway-Pfeiffer Museum and Educational Center, Piggott, Arkansas, 16 September 2004. Although her statement recalled 1943 as the year of the purchase, the deed for the transaction is dated 17 January 1941.

520 Ibid.

521 Vivian Pentecost, 1 December 2004.

522 Ibid.

523 Ibid.

524 Note dated 29 June 1937 attached to Claude and Nettie Misenhamer's Warranty Deed. Deed is part of Paul Pfeiffer's collection of Warranty Deeds, Hemingway-Pfeiffer Museum and Educational Center, Piggott, Arkansas.

525 Joseph Schafer, *The Social History of American Agriculture*, (New York: Da Capo Press, 1970), 9. A squatter is "a person who settled on a selected spot, built his cabin, cleared land and raised crops and cattle without bothering to secure in advance any kind of title to the tract he occupied."

526 Albert, Floyd, and Pauline Milburn, Interview with author and Phil Cate, Corning, Arkansas, 5 June 2004.

527 Note dated 24 May 1941 attached to the McElvains' Warranty Deed. Deed is part of Paul Pfeiffer's collection of Warranty Deeds, Hemingway-Pfeiffer Museum and Educational Center, Piggott, Arkansas.

528 Note dated 21 April 1942 attached to A. L. Neel's Warranty Deed. Deed is part of Paul Pfeiffer's collection of Warranty Deeds, Hemingway-Pfeiffer Museum and Educational Center, Piggott, Arkansas.

529 Note dated 18 May 1942 attached to J. A. and Tina E. Kirby Warranty Deed. Deed is part of Paul Pfeiffer's collection of Warranty Deeds, Hemingway-Pfeiffer Museum and Educational Center, Piggott, Arkansas.

530 Note dated 1 December 1941 attached to Pearl and Cleo Huckabay's Warranty Deed. Deed is part of Paul Pfeiffer's collection of Warranty Deeds, Hemingway-Pfeiffer Museum and Educational Center, Piggott, Arkansas.

531 Note dated 6 December 1941 attached to Pearl and Cleo Huckabay's Warranty Deed. Deed is part of Paul Pfeiffer's collection of Warranty Deeds, Hemingway-Pfeiffer Museum and Educational Center, Piggott, Arkansas.

532 Special Warranty Deed given to Happy Home Pentecost Church. Deed is part of Paul Pfeiffer's collection of Warranty Deeds, Hemingway-Pfeiffer Museum and Educational Center, Piggott, Arkansas.

533 Joseph Sellmeyer, Knobel, Arkansas, to Paul Pfeiffer, Piggott, Arkansas, 28 March 1940. Letter is attached to a Quitclaim Deed given to the Big Gum Drainage District dated March 30, 1940. Deed is part of Paul Pfeiffer's collection of Warranty Deeds, Hemingway-Pfeiffer Museum and Educational Center, Piggott, Arkansas.

534 Quitclaim Deed given to the Big Gum Drainage District dated March 30, 1940. Deed is part of Paul Pfeiffer's collection of Warranty Deeds, Hemingway-Pfeiffer Museum and Educational Center, Piggott, Arkansas.

535 Paul Pfeiffer, Piggott, Arkansas, to Charley L. Palmer, Pollard, Arkansas, 2 December 1936. Letter is attached to Palmer's Warranty Deed. Deed is part of Paul Pfeiffer's collection of Warranty Deeds, Hemingway-Pfeiffer Museum and Educational Center, Piggott, Arkansas.

536 "Timeline," *Hemingway-Pfeiffer Museum and Educational Center*, n.d. <http://hemingway.astate.edu/timeline.html>, 9 December 2004).

537 Paul Pfeiffer, Last Will and Testament, Probate Records Book, 90, Clay County Clerk' s Office – Eastern District, Piggott, Arkansas.

538 Statistics taken from Paul Pfeiffer's collection of Warranty Deeds, Hemingway-Pfeiffer Museum and Educational Center, Piggott, Arkansas

539 Details listed on Warranty Deeds given to Iva Payne and Eliza Bolen. Deed is part of Paul Pfeiffer's collection of Warranty Deeds, Hemingway-Pfeiffer Museum and Educational Center, Piggott, Arkansas.

540 Drainage tax.

541 Roy Barnhill, Corning, Arkansas, to Karl Pfeiffer, Piggott, Arkansas, 14 July 1949. Letter is attached to a Quitclaim Deed given to Roy G. Barnhill dated 20 July 1949. Deed is part of Paul Pfeiffer's collection of Warranty Deeds, Hemingway-Pfeiffer Museum and Educational Center, Piggott, Arkansas.

542 Karl Pfeiffer, Piggott, Arkansas, to Roy Barnhill, Corning, Arkansas, 16 July 1949. Letter is attached to a Quitclaim Deed given to Roy G. Barnhill dated 20 July 1949. Deed is part of Paul Pfeiffer's collection of Warranty Deeds, Hemingway-Pfeiffer Museum and Educational Center, Piggott, Arkansas.

543 Note attached to Warranty Deed given to I. B. Langley and A. R. Winton dated 10 June 1950. Deed is part of Paul Pfeiffer's collection of Warranty Deeds, Hemingway-Pfeiffer Museum and Educational Center, Piggott, Arkansas.

544 Karl Pfeiffer, Piggott, Arkansas, to J. M. Seachrist, Knobel, Arkansas, 31 May 1950. Letter is attached to Warranty Deed given to I. B. Langley and A. R. Winton dated 10 June 1950. Deed is part of Paul Pfeiffer's collection of Warranty Deeds, Hemingway-Pfeiffer Museum and Educational Center, Piggott, Arkansas.

545 Warranty Deed given to I. B. Langley and A. R. Winton dated 10 June 1950. Deed is part of Paul Pfeiffer's collection of Warranty Deeds, Hemingway-Pfeiffer Museum and Educational Center, Piggott, Arkansas.

546 Jim Richardson, Interview with author, Piggott, Arkansas, 31 January 2004.

547 "Mrs. Paul M. Pfeiffer Buried Tuesday Morning," *Piggott Times*, n.d. Located in vertical file, Piggott Public Library.

548 Ayleene Spence, Interview with Ruth Hawkins, Piggott, Arkansas, 10 April 1997.

549 "Timeline, *Hemingway-Pfeiffer Museum and Educational Center*, n.d., <http://hemingway.astate.edu/timeline.html>, (9 December 2004).

550 "A Tribute," n. d., Newspaper article located in vertical file of the Piggott Public Library, Piggott, Arkansas.

551 "Quick Stats: Agricultural Statistics Data Base," *USDA National Agricultural Statistics Service*, 22 December 2004, <http://www.nass.usda.gov:81/ipedbcnty/front.htm>, (15 January 2005). This website is a link from the official site of the United States Department of Agriculture (USDA). The home page includes additional links to topics that include Education and Outreach, Food and Nutrition, Laws and Regulations, Marketing and Trade, Research and Science, Rural and Community Development, and Travel and Recreation.

552 Marie Hillyer, "Farming Foundation for City," Located in vertical file, Piggott Public Library.

553 "Timeline of Farming in the U.S.," *Public Broadcasting Service (PBS)*, 2004, <http://www.pbs.org/wgbh/amex/trouble/timeline/index_3.html>, 21 December 2004. This website dates important events in agriculture throughout the history of the nation.

554 University of Virginia, "Statistical and Social Sciences Data," *Geospatial and Statistical Data Center*, 4 June 2004, <http://fisher.lib.virginia.edu/cgi-local/censusbin/census/cen/pl>, (6 August 2004). The statistics in this table only includes data through 1949 since the information from the 1960 census data has not been published.

555 Holley, Donald, "Mechanical Cotton Picker," *EH.Net Encyclopedia*, edited by Robert Whaples, 17 June 2003, <http://eh.net/encyclopedia/?article=holley.cottonpicker>, (19 December 2004).

556 Smith, Alfred and Louise, Interview with author, Piggott, Arkansas, 27 October, 2004.

557 *Clay County Farm & Home Planning for Better Living*, Compiled 1951, Revised January 1954, 6, University of Arkansas Cooperative Extension Service Records (MC 1145), Box 3, Special Collections, University of Arkansas Libraries, Fayetteville.

558 R. Douglas Hurt, *Agricultural Technology in the Twentieth Century*, (Manhattan, Ks: Sunflower University Press, 1991), 24.

559 Charles Morrow Wilson, "Tenantry Comes Forward," *Country Gentleman*, July 1936. 13.

560 Information taken from Pfeiffer's collection of deeds located at the Hemingway-Pfeiffer Museum and Educational Center in Piggott, Arkansas and from oral interviews of former Pfeiffer farmers.

561 Joseph Schafer, *The Social History of American Agriculture*, (New York: The MacMillan Company, 1936), 212-217.

562 The sharecroppers were locked into a cycle of poverty and unable to improve their situations themselves; therefore they had no alternative but to endure the deplorable living conditions the landlords provided for them.

563 Alfred Smith, 28 August 2004.

Bibliography

Unpublished Materials

Barnhill, Roy, Corning, Arkansas, to Karl Pfeiffer, Piggott, Arkansas, 14 July 1949. Paul Pfeiffer's Collection of Deeds, Hemingway-Pfeiffer Museum and Educational Center, Piggott, Arkansas.

Board of Commissioners of Beaver Dam Drainage District, Greene and Randolph Counties, Arkansas, and George Padwell–Contract, 15 December 1926. H. M. Cooley Collection. Archives and Special Collections. Dean B. Ellis Library. Arkansas State University, Jonesboro.

Bryan, W. S. St. Louis, Missouri, to George M. Jackson, St. Francis, Arkansas, 9 July, 1894. *Jackson, George M., et. al. v. J. M. Myers.* Chancery Court of Clay County, Arkansas–Eastern District.

_____. St. Louis, Missouri, to Fannie C. Jackson, St. Francis, Arkansas, 9 July, 1894. *Jackson, George M., et. al. v. J. M. Myers.* Chancery Court of Clay County, Arkansas–Eastern District.

_____. St. Louis, Missouri, to Fannie C. Jackson, St. Francis, Arkansas, 12 July, 1894. *Jackson, George M., et. al. v. J. M. Myers.* Chancery Court of Clay County, Arkansas–Eastern District.

Fuhr, Robert, Jonesboro, Arkansas, to T. A. Henson, W. Frankfort, Illinois, 27 July 1925. H. M. Cooley Collection. Archives and Special Collections. Dean B. Ellis Library. Arkansas State University, Jonesboro.

Hawkins, Ruth. *A Family Affair: The Hemingway-Pfeiffer Marriage.* Unpublished Manuscript, 2004.

Hemingway, Ernest, Bahamas, to Mary Pfeiffer, Piggott, Arkansas. 2 August 1937. Patrick Hemingway Collection, Princeton University Libraries.

"Notice of Result of Election." *Piggott State Bank Board Minutes*, 7 March 1930.

Pentecost, Vivian. "Share your Hemingway or Pfeiffer Memories." Hemingway-Pfeiffer Museum and Educational Center, Piggott, Arkansas, 16 September 2004.

Pfeiffer, Gus, New York City, to Robert Henry Pfeiffer, Boston Massachusetts, 11 July 1932. Robert Henry Pfeiffer Collection. Harvard School of Divinity Archives. Cambridge, Massachusetts.

_____. Memoir honoring Henry Pfeiffer on his 80th birthday, 26 February 1937. Mary Fisher Floyd Archives and Special Collections.Pfeiffer University, Misenheimer, North Carolina.

Pfeiffer, Karl, Piggott, Arkansas, to Roy Barnhill, Corning, Arkansas, 16 July, 1949. Paul Pfeiffer's Collection of Deeds, Hemingway-Pfeiffer Museum and Educational Center, Piggott, Arkansas.

_____. Piggott, Arkansas, to Ernest Hemingway, Havana, Cuba, 18 May 1933, Hemingway Collection, John F. Kennedy Library, Boston.

_____. Piggott, Arkansas, to Ernest Hemingway, Key West, Florida. 18 March 1935. Hemingway Collection, John F. Kennedy Library, Boston.

_____. Piggott, Arkansas, to Ernest Hemingway, Key West, Florida. 28 November 1935. Hemingway Collection, John F. Kennedy Library, Boston.

_____. Piggott, Arkansas, to J. M. Seachrist, Knobel, Arkansas, 31 May 1950. Paul Pfeiffer's Collection of Deeds, Hemingway-Pfeiffer Museum and Educational Center, Piggott, Arkansas.

Pfeiffer, Mary, Piggott, Arkansas, to Ernest Hemingway, Paris, France, 7 September 1927. Hemingway Collection. John F. Kennedy Library. Boston.

_____. Piggott, to Ernest Hemingway, Kansas City, Kansas, 1 July 1928. Hemingway Collection. John F. Kennedy Library. Boston.

_____. Piggott, Arkansas, to Ernest and Pauline Hemingway, Paris, France, 30 March 1929. Hemingway Collection. John F. Kennedy Library. Boston.

_____. Piggott, Arkansas, to Ernest Hemingway, Paris, France, 4 May 1929. Hemingway Collection. John F. Kennedy Library. Boston.

_____. Piggott, Arkansas, to Pauline Hemingway, Paris, France, 5 June 1929. Patrick Hemingway Collection. Princeton University Libraries.

_____.Piggott, Arkansas, to Pauline Hemingway, Spain, 4 July 1929. Patrick Hemingway Collection. Princeton University Libraries.

_____. Piggott, Arkansas, to Pauline Hemingway, Spain, 15 July 1929. Patrick Hemingway Collection, Princeton University Libraries.

_____. Piggott, Arkansas, to Pauline Hemingway, Madrid, Spain, 17 August 1929, Patrick Hemingway Collection, Princeton University Libraries.

_____. Piggott, Arkansas, to Pauline Hemingway, Paris, France, 8 September 1929. Patrick Hemingway Collection, Princeton University Libraries.

_____. Piggott, Arkansas, to Pauline Hemingway, Paris, France. 24 September 1929. Patrick Hemingway Collection, Princeton University Libraries.

_____. Piggott, Arkansas, to Ernest Hemingway, Paris, France. 9 October 1929. Hemingway Collection. John F. Kennedy Library.Boston.

_____. Phoenix, Arizona, to Ernest and Pauline Hemingway, Paris, France, 20 January 1930, Hemingway Collection, John F. Kennedy Library, Boston.

_____. Piggott, Arkansas, to Pauline Hemingway, Cooke, Montana, 30 July 1930, Patrick Hemingway Collection, Princeton University Libraries.

_____. Piggott, Arkansas, to Pauline Hemingway, Key West, Florida. 12 March 1932. Hemingway Collection. John F. Kennedy Library. Boston.

_____. Piggott, Arkansas, to Ernest Hemingway, Havana, Cuba. 4 May 1933. Hemingway Collection. John F. Kennedy Library. Boston.

_____. Piggott, Arkansas, to Ernest and Pauline Hemingway, Key West, Florida. July 1933. Hemingway Collection. John F. Kennedy Library. Boston.

_____. Piggott, Arkansas, to Ernest and Pauline Hemingway, Key West, Florida. 18 July 1934. Hemingway Collection. John F. Kennedy Library. Boston.

_____. Piggott, Arkansas, to Ernest Hemingway, Montana. September 1937. Hemingway Collection. John F. Kennedy Library. Boston.

_____. Piggott, Arkansas, to Pauline Hemingway, Key West, Florida. 30 November 1938. Hemingway Collection. John F. Kennedy Library. Boston.

_____. Last Will and Testament. Probate Records Book, Clay County Clerk's Office–Eastern District, Piggott, Arkansas.

Pfeiffer, Paul, Collection of Warranty Deeds, Hemingway-Pfeiffer Museum and Educational Center, Piggott, Arkansas.

_____. Piggott, to Ernest Hemingway, Paris, France, 14 October 1926, Hemingway Collection. John F. Kennedy Library, Boston.

_____. Piggott, Arkansas, to Pauline Hemingway, Kansas City, Kansas, 1 July 1928. Hemingway Collection. John F. Kennedy Library. Boston.

_____. Piggott, Arkansas, to Ernest and Pauline Hemingway, Key West, Florida. 10 March 1929. Hemingway Collection. John F. Kennedy Library. Boston.

_____. Piggott, Arkansas, to Ernest and Pauline Hemingway, Havana, Cuba, 30 March 1929. Hemingway Collection, John F. Kennedy Library, Boston.

_____. Piggott, Arkansas, to Ernest Hemingway, Paris, France, 10 July 1929. Hemingway Collection, John F. Kennedy Library, Boston.

_____. Piggott, Arkansas, to Ernest Hemingway, Paris, France, 14 October 1929, Hemingway Collection, John F. Kennedy Library, Boston.

_____. Piggott, Arkansas, to Ernest and Pauline Hemingway, Key West, Florida, 20 March 1930. Hemingway Collection, John F. Kennedy Library, Boston.

_____. Piggott, Arkansas, to Ernest and Pauline Hemingway, Spain. 18 June 1931. Hemingway Collection, John F. Kennedy Library, Boston.

_____. Piggott, Arkansas, to Ernest and Pauline Hemingway, Key West, Florida. 17 July 1933. Hemingway Collection, John F. Kennedy Library, Boston.

_____. Piggott, Arkansas, to Pauline Hemingway, Madrid, Spain. 19 September 1933. Hemingway Collection, John F. Kennedy Library, Boston.

_____. Piggott, Arkansas, to Ernest and Pauline Hemingway, Key West, Florida. 10 December 1934. Hemingway Collection. John F. Kennedy Library. Boston.

_____. Piggott, Arkansas, to Ernest Hemingway, Spain. 15 November 1937. Hemingway Collection. John F. Kennedy Library. Boston.

_____. Phoenix, Arizona, to Ernest and Pauline Hemingway, Key West, Florida. 1 March 1938. Hemingway Collection. John F. Kennedy Library. Boston.

Pfeiffer, Pauline, Piggott, Arkansas, to Ernest Hemingway, Paris, France, 15 October 1926. Hemingway Collection. John F. Kennedy Library. Boston.

_____. Piggott, Arkansas, to Ernest Hemingway, Paris France, 22 October 1926. Hemingway Collection. John F. Kennedy Library. Boston.

_____. Piggott, Arkansas, to Ernest Hemingway, Paris France, 1 November 1926. Hemingway Collection. John F. Kennedy Library. Boston.

_____. Piggott, Arkansas, to Ernest Hemingway, Paris, France, 29 November 1926, Hemingway Collection, John F. Kennedy Library, Boston.

_____. Piggott, to Ernest Hemingway, Paris, France, 30 November 1926, Hemingway Collection, John F. Kennedy Library, Boston.

_____. Piggott, Arkansas, to Ernest Hemingway, Paris France, 10 December 1926. Hemingway Collection. John F. Kennedy Library. Boston.

_____. Piggott, Arkansas, to Ernest Hemingway, Oak Park, 12 October 1928, Hemingway Collection. John F. Kennedy Library. Boston.

_____. Piggott, Arkansas, to Ernest Hemingway, Paris, France, 10 September 1936. Hemingway Collection. John F. Kennedy Library. Boston.

_____. Piggott, Arkansas, to Ernest Hemingway, Paris, France. 17 September 1938. Hemingway Collection. John F. Kennedy Library. Boston.

_____. Key West, Florida, to Ernest Hemingway, Havana, Cuba. 1940. Hemingway Collection. John F. Kennedy Library. Boston.

Pfeiffer, Robert Henry. *Annie Merner Pfeiffer Memorial Day Address.* Bennett College. Greensboro, NC, 25 September 1949.

_____. "Henry and Annie Pfeiffer." *Bostonia.* April, 1942. Robert Henry Pfeiffer Collection. Harvard School of Divinity Archives. Cambridge, Massachusetts.

_____. Eulogy of Gustavus Adolphus Pfeiffer. 25 August 1953. Robert
        Henry Pfeiffer Collection. Harvard School of Divinity Archives.
        Cambridge, Massachusetts.

Pfeiffer, Virginia, Piggott, Arkansas, to Pauline Hemingway, Wyoming,
        20 August 1928. Hemingway Collection, John F. Kennedy Library,
        Boston.

Piggott State Bank Board Minutes. Piggott State Bank. Piggott, Arkansas.

Sellmeyer, Joseph, Knobel, Arkansas, to Paul Pfeiffer, Piggott, Arkansas,
        28 March 1940. Paul Pfeiffer's Collection of Warranty Deeds,
        Hemingway-Pfeiffer Museum and Educational Center, Piggott,
        Arkansas.

[Stewart]-Abernathy III, Leslie C. "Skip," *Barns in the 19th Century:
        Archaeological Perspectives on Changes in Farming*, Paper presented
        at the annual meeting of the Northeast Anthropological
        Association, April 16-19, 1975, SUNY, Potsdam, New York.

_____. *The Barns of Rehoboth, Ma*, Anthropology Department, Brown
        University, May 1974.

Oral Interviews and Personal Communications

Milburn, Albert, Floyd and Pauline. Interview with author and Phil Cate,
        Corning, Arkansas. 5 June 2004.

Norris, Elwanda. Interview with author. Jonesboro, Arkansas. March 11,
        2003.

Pentecost, Vivian. Telephone interview with author, 1 December 2004.

Pfeiffer, Matilda. Interview with Ruth Hawkins. Piggott, Arkansas.
        29 March 1997. Hemingway-Pfeiffer Museum and Educational
        Center, Piggott, Arkansas.

Poole, Jim. Interview with author. Piggott, Arkansas, 13 February 2004.

_____. Interview with author. Piggott, Arkansas, 27 October 2004.

Richardson, Jim. Interview with Ruth Hawkins. Piggott, Arkansas, 23 June 1997.

_____. Interview with author. Piggott, Arkansas, 31 January 2004.

_____. Interview with author. Piggott, Arkansas, 28 August 2004.

_____. Interview with author. Piggott, Arkansas, 21 October 2004.

Rouse, Rodney. Interview with author. Piggott, Arkansas, 8 September 2003.

_____. Interview with author. Piggott, Arkansas, 29 January 2004.

_____. Interview with author. Piggott, Arkansas, 21 October 2004.

_____. Email correspondence with author. 30 November 2004.

Smart, W. F. Interview with author. Piggott, Arkansas, 13 February 2004.

Smart, W. F. and Marguerite Smart. Interview with author. Piggott, Arkansas, 27 October 2004.

Smith, Alfred and Louise. Interview with author. Piggott, Arkansas, 28 August 2004.

_____. Interview with author. Piggott, Arkansas, 27 October 2004.

Spence, Ayleene. Interview with Ruth Hawkins. Piggott, Arkansas. 10 April 1997.

Newspapers

"A Tribute." n.d. Newspaper article located in vertical file of the Piggott Public Library. Piggott, Arkansas.

Cummins, Ronnie. "Organic Food Promotes Health & Ethical Choice." *Charleston Gazette (West Virginia)*, 20 April 2003.

Dalton, O. L. "Boydsville—For Fifteen Years the Capital of Clay County." *Piggott Banner*, 22 February 1963.

_____. "The Boydsville Story—Early Settlers and Families Listed." *Piggott Banner*, 8 March, 1963.

_____. "The Boydsville Story—Early Settlers and Families Listed." *Piggott Banner*, 15 March 1963.

_____. "The Boydsville Story—More Family Histories." *Piggott Banner*, 29 March 1963.

_____. "Early Families of Mars Hill and Liberty Hill Community." *Piggott Banner*, 12 April, 1963.

Hillyer, Marie. "Farming Foundation for City." *Piggott Times*. n.d. Located in vertical file, Piggott Public Library.

_____. "Newcomers and New Grounds around Liberty Hill." *Piggott Banner*. 7 June 1963.

_____. "Newspaper Romance of Clay County." *Piggott Banner*, 23 August 1963.

_____. "More About St. Francis . . ." *Piggott Banner*, 30 August 1963.

_____. "Some Memories About Greenway, Clay County." *Piggott Banner*. 6 September 1963.

_____. "Some Early History of Greenway." *Piggott Banner*, 13 September 1963.

Dortch, Hubert. "History of Vincent—1880 to 1935." *Clay County Democrat*, 18 May 1935.

_____. "History of Vincent—1880 to 1935." *Clay County Democrat*, 23 May 1935.

Flaherty, Julie. "Planting the Seeds for a Resurgence of the Small Farm." *The New York Times*, 14 October 2000.

Franscell, Ron. "Pfeiffer Barn Stores Many Memories." *Clay County Democrat*. 30 May 1979.

"G. M. Jackson in bad in East End." *Corning Courier*, 18 October 1912.

Hansbrough, Vivian. "Dr. Piggott's Namesake." *Arkansas Gazette*, Special Features Editorials Section, 28 December 1948.

Hendrick, Jerry. "Highlights of Days Gone By on Greenway Route One." *Piggott Banner*, 13 April, 1956.

_____. "Highlights of Days Gone By on Greenway Route One." *Piggott Banner*, 20 April, 1956

"History of Piggott." *Piggott Banner* 11 June 1963.

House, Noah E., Editor. "Extra Edition." *Piggott Banner*, 1895.

Jewell, C. E. Brooksville, Florida, letter to O. L. Dalton, Piggott, Arkansas, 9 September 1963. *Piggott Banner*, 27 September 1963.

Leonard, Bill. "More About Greenway." *Piggott Banner*, 18 October 1963.

"Local Items." *Clay County Courier*, 17 March 1911.

"Local Items." *Clay County Courier*, 16 June 1911.

"Local Items," *Clay County Courier*, 24 January 1913.

"Mrs. Paul M. Pfeiffer Buried Tuesday Morning." *Piggott Times*, n.d. Located in vertical file, Piggott Public Library.

"Our Nominee for Citizen of the Week: Mr. Karl Pfeiffer," *The Piggott Times*, 14 January 1971.

"Local Eyetems." *Parkersburg Elipse*, 13 December 1900.

"Paul M. Pfeiffer Buried Saturday." *Piggott Times*. n.d. Located in vertical file, Piggott Public Library.

Payne, Laud M. "Memoirs of Early Days in Clay County, Arkansas." *Piggott Banner*. 1 January 1937.

"Pfeiffers had Impact in Piggott, Clay Co." *The Piggott Times*. 9 April 1997.

"Piggott Barn Studio Provided Peace, Quiet," *The Piggott Times*, 20 February 1991.

"Pioneer Jonesboro Priest Dies." *Jonesboro Daily Tribune*. March 5, 1934.

"Pounded the Preacher," *Clay County Courier*, 31 July 1909.

"Rich Americans Aping European Caste Ideas." *Jonesboro Daily Sun*. 13 July 1927.

Russell, Ron. "Chasing Hemingway's Ghost." *Memphis Commercial Appeal*. Mid-South Section, 27 August 1978.

Schnedler, Marcia. "Hemingway's Piggott Revisited." *Arkansas Democrat Gazette*. 23 July 1995.

Scurlock, James. "Memoirs of a Tiemaker Who Came to Piggott, Arkansas in the Year 1885. *Piggott Banner*. 20 January 1928.

"Services Held Monday for Karl Pfeiffer," Newspaper article in vertical file, Piggott Public Library, Piggott, Arkansas, 17 December 1981.

"Severe Hail Storm." *Clay County Courier*, 9 June 1911.

"Uncle Bill Rogers: Ninety Two Year Old Citizen Dies in Sight of Birth Place." *Jonesboro Daily Tribune*. 13 August 1926.

Ward, O. T. "White Walnut Creek and Brick Kilns." *Rector Democrat*, 25 January 1962.

Winchester, Anne. "Matilda Pfeiffer Dies at Home at Age 97." *The Piggott Times*, 6 February 2002.

Wright, V. C. "A History of Brookings, Arkansas." *Clay County Courier*, 18 June 1953.

Yoon, Carol Kaesuk. "A 'Dead Zone' Grows in the Gulf of Mexico." *The New York Times*, 20 January 1998.

Public and Legal Documents

Blackshare, C. E., et. al. v. G. M. Jackson, Clay County Circuit Court–Eastern District, 4 April 1913.

Butler County Record of Deeds Books #42, 47, 48, 51, 52, 54, and 57. Recorder's Office. Butler County Courthouse. Allison, Iowa.

Criminal Record Book #3. Clay County Circuit Court–Eastern District. Piggott, Arkansas.

Clay County Land Record Books. Clay County Courthouse–Eastern District. Piggott, Arkansas.

Clay County Miscellaneous Record Books. Clay County Courthouse–Eastern District. Piggott, Arkansas.

Commission on Geosciences, Environment and Resources. *Wetlands: Characteristics and Boundaries*. Washington, D.C.: National Academy Press, 1995.

Couch, Lavonia v. Paul M. Pfeiffer. Eastern District Clay Chancery Court, November Term, 1920.

Clay County Miscellaneous and Incorporation Record Book #3. Clay County Courthouse–Eastern District. Piggott, Arkansas.

Hibbs, R. E. v. Paul M. Pfeiffer and D. R. Stanley. Clay Circuit Court, Eastern District. October Term, 1923.

Historical Appraisal of Extension Work in Clay County 1914-1939. University of Arkansas Cooperative Extension Service Records (MC 1145), Box 3. Special Collections. University of Arkansas Libraries, Fayetteville.

Hopefield. The County's First Settlement. Earle, Arkansas: Crittenden County Museum, n.d.

Jackson, George M. v. B. B. Biffle, Case #250, Chancery Court of Clay County, Arkansas–Eastern District.

Jackson, George M., et. al. v. J. M. Myers. Chancery Court of Clay County, Arkansas–Eastern District.

Jackson, George M. v. J. M. Meyers and Becktold Printing and Book Company, Case #648, Chancery Court of Clay County, Arkansas–Eastern District.

Jackson v. J. M. Meyers and Becktold Printing and Book Company, Case #801, Chancery Court of Clay County, Arkansas–Eastern District.

Jackson, George M. v. Mitch Johnson, et. al., Case #803, Chancery Court of Clay County, Arkansas–Eastern District.

Jackson, George M. v. Paul M. Pfeiffer, Case #959, Clay County Circuit Court–Eastern District.

Jackson George M. v. Same Johnson, Case #1337, Chancery Court of Clay County, Arkansas–Eastern District.

Jackson, George M. v. State of Arkansas, Case #995, Chancery Court of Clay County, Arkansas–Eastern District.

Jones, Mrs. Jennie Jones v. P. M. Pfeiffer and D. R. Stanley. Clay Circuit Court, Eastern District. October Term, 1923.

Narrative Report of All County Extension Agents and All Extension Home Economists, Clay County, 1 December 1966 to 30 November 1967.University of Arkansas Cooperative Extension Service Records (MC 1145), Box 1. Special Collections. University of Arkansas Libraries, Fayetteville.

Pfeiffer, Mary. *Last Will and Testament.* Probate Records Book. Clay County Clerk' s Office–Eastern District, Piggott, Arkansas.

Pfeiffer, Paul. *Last Will and Testament.* Probate Records Book. Clay County Clerk' s Office–Eastern District, Piggott, Arkansas.

Planning the Farmstead. USDA Farmers' Bulletin 1132. U. S. Government Printing Office, 1949.

"Piggott—The Way It Was," *Piggott Times*, 11 November 1976. Located in Geneaology Section of Piggott Public Library.

Program for Developing Clay County: Agriculture. Family Living, 4-H and Other Youth, Community Resource Development, 1972-1977. University of Arkansas Cooperative Extension Service Records (MC 1145), Box 2. Special Collections. University of Arkansas Libraries, Fayetteville.

State of Arkansas v. George M. Jackson, Case #794, Chancery Court of Clay County, Arkansas–Eastern District.

State of Arkansas v. George M. Jackson, Case #1255, Chancery Court of Clay County, Arkansas–Eastern District.

St. Francis Drainage District Book of Minutes, Piggott, Arkansas.

The Historic Districts of Marion, Arkansas. Marion, Arkansas: Marion Chamber of Commerce, n.d.

Travis, Vera v. P. M. Pfeiffer and D. R. Stanley; Clay Circuit Court, Eastern District. October Term, 1923.

Internet Websites

"A Moment in Time Archives: Hybrid Seed Corn." Vol. 7, No. 51. 22 August 2003. *eHistory,* 2004. <http://www.ehistory.com/world/amit/display.cfm?amit_id=2141>, (10 September 2004).

Adams, Don and Arlene Goldbard. "New Deal Cultural Programs: Experiments in Cultural Democracy." *Webster's World of Cultural Democracy.* 7 March 2001. <http://www.wwcd.org/policy/US/newdeal.html#WPA>. (12 February 2005).

"Agriculture," Microsoft® Encarta® Online Encyclopedia, 2004,
        <http://encarta.msn.com/encyclopedia_761572257/Agriculture.ht
        ml>, (22 December 2004).

Barnes and Noble Learning Network. "The Great Depression: Stumbling
        Blocks—The New Deal Fades." *Sparknotes.* 1999-2003.
        <http://www.sparknotes. com/history/american/depression/
        section5.rhtml>, 18 September 2004.

Blatt, Dan. "Descent into the Depths: The Collapse of International
        Finance." *Futurecast-Online Magazine*, Vol. 3, No. 6. 1 June 2001,
        <http://www.futurecasts.com/Depression_descent-end-'31.html>,
        17 September 2004).

Borne, Carmen. "Delta," *Arkansas Natural Regions.* 18 May 1999.
        <www.scsc.k12.ar.us/BorneC/delta.htm>. (22 April, 2004).

Brassieur, Ray. "The Bootheel Project: An Introduction." *Western Historical
        Manuscript Collection-Columbia.* 1996-2002.
        <http://www.umsystem.edu/whmc/bootint.html>, (May 28, 2004).

"Educational Materials—A Brief History of Arkansas," *Arkansas Secretary of
        State Educational Materials*, 2005,
        <http://www.sos.arkansas.gov/educational_history.html>,
        (11 February 2005).

"Farmers Market Facts," *USDA: AMS Farmers Markets*, n.d.,
        <http://www.ams.usda.gov/farmersmarkets/facts.htm>,
        (27 December 2004).

"Fort Jefferson, Kentucky." *Kentucky Atlas & Gazetteer.* n.d.
        <http://www.uky.edu/ KentuckyAtlas/ky-fort-jefferson.html>,
        (22 September 2004).

Gouwens, Elizabeth. "Organic Architecture Pathfinder." *Frank Lloyd Wright
        Foundation, 2003.* <http://www.franklloydwright.org/index.cfm?
        section=research&action=display&id=80>. (12 March 2005).

Hines, Katie. "History in Pickens: The Farmer, the Politician, the Artist,
        and the Cow." *Pickens' Weekly Webzine*, 19 September 2003,

<http://www.datelinepickens.com/historyinpickens/mural.shtml>.
18 October 2004.

"History and Culture of the Lower Mississippi Delta." *Lower Mississippi Delta Region*, 14 March, 2001, <http://www.cr.nps.gov/delta/volume2/history.htm#delta>, (15 April, 2004).

"How and Why was the Bootheel of Missouri Formed?" *F.A.Q.* Center for Regional History and Culture. Cape Girardeau: Southeast Missouri State University. September 23, 2001. <http://www2.semo.edu/regionalhist/faq.html>, 28 May 2004.

"Industry Comes to Nettleton." <http://nettleton.crsc.k12.ar.us/history/industry.htm>. n.d., 8 May 2004.

Jaynes, E. T. "Recollections and Mementos of G. A. Pfeiffer." 2 December 1990. <http://library.wustl.edu/units/physics/pfeiffer.pdf>, (16 August 2004).

John W. Hartman Center for Sales, Advertising & Marketing History. Duke University Rare Book, Manuscript, and Special Collections Library." Timeline." *Ad*Access On-Line Project—Ad #R0108*, 1999. <http://scriptorium.lib.duke.edu/adaccess/>. (13 September 2004).

Max, Sarah. "Free Land in the Heartland." *CNN Money*. 23 December 2004. <http://money.cnn.com/2004/12/22/real_estate/buying_selling/Thursday_freeland/index.htm?cnn=yes>, (23 December 2004).

Mchie, Benjamin. "Miflin Gibbs, businessman and abolitionist." *The African American Registry*. 2004. <www.aaregistry.com/african_american_history/829/Mifflin_Gibbs_businessman_and_abolitionist>, (15 April, 2004).

National Center for Infectious Diseases. "Frequently Asked Questions aboutMalaria." *Malaria*. 13 August 2004. <http://www.cdc.gov/malaria/faq.htm>. (12 September 2004).

Norton, Patrick. "Roof Designs." *Long Island Home Inspection*, 2003. <http://www.longislandinspection.com/roof-designs.html>, (3 November 2004).

Old Statehouse Museum. "Drought Threat is Worse Than Flood. *The Arkansas News*," 2003. <http://www.oldstatehouse.com/ educational_programs/classroom/arkansas_news/detail.asp?id=773 &issue_id=37&page=4>, (14 September 2004).

"Our History." *Electric Cooperatives in Arkansas*. n.d. <http://www.ecark.org/>, (22 August 2004).

"Pellagra Shown to be Dietary disease 1915, *A Science Odyssey: People and Discoveries*. 1998, <http://www.pbs.org/wgbh/aso/databank/ entries/dm15pa.html>, (15 April 2004).

Piggott, Arkansas," *Webguru*, 2004, <http://www.webguru.com/piggot-arkansas.htm>, (30 August 2004).

"Quick Stats: Agricultural Statistics Data Base," *USDA National Agricultural Statistics Service*, 22 December, 2004, <http://www.nass.usda.gov:81/ipedbcnty/front.htm>, (15 January 2005).

"Small Farm Policy." *Small Farms @ USDA*. 14 May 2004. http://www.usda.gov/ oce/smallfarm/sfpolicy.htm>, (28 December 2004).

Spalding, Bob. "Grow Your Own Catalpa Worms." Clemson University Cooperative Extension Service, 7 September 1998, <http://virtual.clemson.edu/groups/FieldOps/CGS/catalpa.htm>, 18 October 2004.

Tavernier, Edmund M. and Robin G. Brumfield. " The Federal Agricultural Improvement and Reform Act (FAIR) of 1996: The Conservation Title." *Rutgers Cooperative Extension Fact Sheet*, 2003. <http://www.rce.rutgers.edu/pubs/pdfs/fs859.pdf>. (21 December 2004).

"Timeline." *Hemingway-Pfeiffer Museum and Educational Center*. n. d. <http://hemingway.astate.edu/timeline.html>, (4 September 2004).

"Timeline of Farming in the U.S.," *Public Broadcasting Service (PBS)*, 2004.<http://www.pbs.org/wgbh/amex/trouble/timeline/index_3.ht ml>, 21 December 2004.

"Town History." *City of Jacksonport, Arkansas.* n.d.
    <http://www.geocities.com/jacksonport_ar/>, 5 May 2004.

"University of California Small Farm Center." *University of California, Davis.*
    n.d. <http://www.sfc.ucdavis.edu>, (28 December 2004).

University of Virginia, "Statistical and Social Sciences Data," *Geospatial and
    Statistical Data Center,* 4 June 2004,
    <http://fisher.lib.virginia.edu/cgi-local/censusbin/census/cen/pl>,
    (6 August 2004).

Urban Dictionary, 1999-2005, <http://www.urbandictionary.com/define.
    php?term=dirt+cheap&r=f>, 1999-2005, (18 February 2005).

USDA-National Agricultural Stats Service. *Track Records United States Crop
    Production.* April 2003. <http://usda.mannlib.cornell.edu/data-
    sets/crops/96120/track03a.htm#cotton>, (3 September 2004).

Whitten, David O. "Depression of 1893." *EH.Net Encyclopedia,* 15 August
    2001. <http://www.eh.net/encyclopedia/contents/
    whitten.panic.1893.php>, 9 August 2004.

"Width of Railroad Tracks," *Truth or Fiction,* 30 May 2002,
    <http://www.truthorfiction.com/rumors/r/railwidth.htm>,
    (9 May 2004).

Weaver, H. Dwight. "One Last Word: Bootheel Politics, Frontier Style,"
    Missouri Resources Magazine Winter 99-00. 3 May 2004.
    <http://www.dnr.state.mo.us/magazine/1999-00_wint/one-last-
    word.htm>.(28 May 2004).

"Wetlands: Characteristics and Boundaries," *The National Academies Press,*
    1995, <http://books.nap.edu/books/0309051347/html/44.html>,
    (12 May 2004).

"Worldwide Flu Pandemic Strikes 1918-1919." A Science *Odyssey.* 1997,
    <http://www.pbs.org/wgbh/aso/databank/entries/dm18fl.html>,
    (4 September 2004).

Published Books and Articles

Alexander, Donald Crichton. *The Arkansas Plantation 1920-1942*. New Haven: Yale University Press, 1943.

"Annie Merner Pfeiffer Memorial Day." *Bennett College Bulletin*, Vol. XIX, No. 1. Greenboro, NC: Bennett College. November, 1947.

Arakawa, Yoichi. *Blues Guitar Chords and Accompaniment*. Los Angeles: Six Strings Music Publishing, 2003.

Ashmore, Harry S. *Arkansas*. New York: W. W. Norton and Company, 1978.

Auerbach, Jerold S. "Southern Tenant Farmers: Social Critics of the New Deal." *Labor History*, 7:1, 1966.

Avrich, Paul. *Sacco and Vanzetti: The Anarchist Background*. Princeton: Princeton University Press, 1991.

Ayers, Edward L. *The Promise of the New South: Life After Reconstruction*. New York: Oxford University Press, 1992.

Bashaw, Carolyn Terry. "One Kind of Pioneer Project: Julia F. Allen and the Southern Tenant Farmers' Union College Student Project, 1938." *Arkansas Historical Quarterly*, 55:1, 1966.

Berry, Fred and John Novak. *The History of Arkansas*. Little Rock: Rose Publishing Company, 1987.

Bolsterli, Margaret Jones. *Born in the Delta*. Knoxville: University of Tennessee Press, 1991.

Brown, Sarah. "Folk Architecture in Arkansas." *Arkansas Folklore Resource*. Fayetteville: University of Arkansas Press, 1992.

Brundage, W. Fitzhugh. *Where These Memories Grow: History, Memory, and Southern Identity*. Chapel Hill: University of North Carolina Press, 2000.

Campbell, Rex R. A *Revolution in the Heartland: Changes in Rural Culture, Family and Communities 1900-2000*. Columbia: University of Missouri Press, 2004.

Campbell, Will D. *Brother to a Dragonfly*. New York: Continuum International Publishing Group, 2000.

Cash, W. J. *The Mind of the South*. New York: Knopf Publishing Group,1941.

Cobb, James C. *The Most Southern Place on Earth: The Mississippi Delta and the Roots of Regional Identity*. New York: Oxford University Press, 1992.

_____. *Redefining Southern Culture: Mind and Identity in the Modern South*. Athens: University of Georgia Press, 1999.

Coggeshall, John M. and Jo Anne Nast. *Vernacular Architecture in Southern Illinois:The Ethnic Heritage*. Carbondale: Southern Illinois University Press, 1988.

Conrad, David Eugene.*The Forgotten Farmers: The Story of Sharecroppers in the New Deal*. Westport, CT: Greenwood Publishing Company, 1982.

Cox, Camilla. "Development of Nimmons, Clay County, Arkansas." *Clay County Genealogical and Historical Society Quarterly Newsletter*, Vol 10, No. 1, March, 1994.

DeBlack, Thomas. *A Garden in the Wilderness*. Ann Arbor: UMI Dissertation Services, 2002.

Deetz, James. *In Small Things Forgotten*, New York: Bantam Doubleday Dell Publishing Group, Inc., 1997.

Dew, Lee A. *The JLC&E: The History of an Arkansas Railroad*. State University: Arkansas State University Press, 1968.

Ensminger, Robert F. *The Pennsylvania Barn Book*. Baltimore: John Hopkins University Press, 1992.

Fair, James R. *The North Arkansas Line.* Berkeley: Howell, North Books, 1969.

Fite, Gilbert. *Cotton Fields No More: Southern Agriculture 1865-1980.* Lexington: University Press of Kentucky, 1984.

Foster, W. A. and Deane G. Carter. *Farm Buildings.* New York: John Wiley and Sons, 1941.

Glassie, Henry. *Patterns in the Material Folk Culture.* Philadelphia: University of Pennsylvania Press, 1968.

_____. *Material Culture.* Bloomingdale: University of Indiana Press, 1999.

_____. *Vernacular Architecture.* Bloomingdale: University of Indiana Press, 2000.

Gray, L. C. *Farm Ownership and Tenancy,* New York: Arno Press, 1976.

Harris, J. William. *Deep Souths: Delta, Piedmont, and Sea Island in the Age of Segregation.* Baltimore: John Hopkins University Press, 2002.

Hoffmann, Charles. *The Depression of the Nineties: An Economic History.* Westport, Ct: Greenwood Publishing, 1970.

Holley, Donald. *The Second Great Emancipation.* Fayetteville: University of Arkansas Press, 2000.

hooks, bell. *Ain't I A Woman: Black Women and Feminism.* Boston: South End Press, 1981.

Howe, Nicholas S. *Barns.* New York, NY: Michael Friedman Publishing Group, 1996.

Hurt, R. Douglas, *American Farms: Exploring Their History,* Malabar, Florida: Krieger Publishing Company, 1996.

_____. *Agricultural Technology in the Twentieth Century.* Manhattan, Ks:Sunflower University Press, 1991.

_____. *Problems of Plenty.* Chicago: Ivan R. Dee, 2002.

Jacobson, Timothy Curtis and George David Smith, *Cotton Renaissance*, New York: Cambridge University Press, 2001.

Jones, Jacqueline. *Labor of Love, Labor of Sorrow: Black Women, Work,and the Family from Slavery to the Present*. New York: Vintage Books, 1985.

Jones, J. Wayne. "Seeding Chicot: The Issac H. Hilliard Plantation and the Arkansas Delta. *Arkansas Historical Quarterly*. Vol No. 2, Summer, 2000.

Klamkin, Charles. *Barns: Their History, Preservation and Restoration*. New York: Hawthorn Books, 1973.

Lambert, Roger. "Hoover and the Red Cross in the Arkansas Drought of 1930." *Arkansas Historical Quarterly*, Vol. 29 (Autumn, 1970).

Lichtenstein, Alex. "Proletarians or Peasants? Sharecroppers and the Politics of Protest in the Rural South, 1880-1940, *Plantation Society in the Americas*, 5:2-3, 1998.

Manning, Richard. *Against the Grain: How Agriculture has Hijacked Civilization*. New York: North Point Press, 2004.

Marshall, Howard. *Folk Architecture in Little Dixie*. Columbia: University of Missouri Press, 1981.

_____. *Vernacular Architecture in Rural and Small Town Missouri: An Introduction*. Columbia: University of Missouri Extension Publications, 1994.

Mid-west Farm Building Plan Service. Fayetteville: University of Arkansas, 1933.

Muffly-Kipp, Laurie F. "Negro Race History." *Where These Memories Grow: History, Memory, and Southern Identity*. Chapel Hill: University of North Carolina Press, 2000.

Mulford, Furman, May Cowles, Thomas Gray, and Warren Manning. "Farmstead Planning and Beautification and Painting." *Farm and Village Housing*, University of Maryland, 1932.

Noble, Allen G. and Richard K. Cleek. *The Old Barn Book*. New Brunswick, New Jersey: Rutgers University Press, 1996.

Potter, Maynard H. "Notes on the Early History of Piggott, Arkansas," *Clay County Genealogy Club Quarterly Newsletter*, Vol. 3, No. 4, ed. Camilla Cox, Oct, Nov, Dec, 1987.

Pyle, Kenneth B. *The Making of Modern Japan*. Lexington, Ma: D. C. Heath, 1996.

Rall, Harris Franklin. "Annie Merner Pfeiffer: A Tribute." *Bennett College Bulletin*, Vol. XIX, No. 1. Greenboro, NC: Bennett College. November, 1947.

Reed, Edwin. "Oldster Remembers Rector as Boom Town." *Clay County Genealogy Club Quarterly Newsletter*, Vol. 13, No. 2, ed. Camilla Cox, June, 1994.

Ross, George H. "Recalls Memories of the Bygone Days." *Clay County Genealogy Club Quarterly Newsletter*, Vol. 8, No. 3, ed. Una Pollard, September 1992.

Schafer, Joseph. *The Social History of American Agriculture*. New York: The MacMillan Company, 1936.

Sizemore, Jean. *Ozark Vernacular Houses*. Fayetteville: University of Arkansas Press, 1994.

Sloane, Eric. *American Barns & Covered Bridges*. New York: Wilfred Funk, 1954.

Steeples, Douglas, and David Whitten. *Democracy in Desperation: The Depression of 1893*. Westport, Ct: Greenwood Press, 1998.

Stewart-Abernathy, Leslie C. *The Moser Farmstead*. Arkansas Archeological Survey Research Series No. 26, 1986.

Timberlake, Richard. "Panic of 1893." In *Business Cycles and Depressions: An Encyclopedia*, edited by David Glasner. New York: Garland, 1997.

The Columbia Encyclopedia, Sixth Edition. 2001.

Upton, Dell and John Michael Vlach. *Common Places: Readings in American Vernacular Architecture*. Athens: University of Georgia Press, 1986.

Vlach, John Michael. *Back of the Big House*. Chapel Hill: University of North Carolina Press, 1993.

_____. "The Shotgun House: An African Architectural Legacy." *Common Places*. (Athens: The University of Georgia Press, 1986).

_____. "The American Bungalow." *Common Places*. (Athens: The University of Georgia Press, 1986.

Webb, Robert T., *History and Traditions of Clay County*. Mountain Home, Arkansas: Shiras Brothers Print Shop, 1933.

Whayne, Jeannie. *A New Plantation South: Land, Labor, and Federal Favor in Twentieth-Century Arkansas*. Charlottesville: University of Virginia, 1996.

Whayne, Jeannie and Willard Gatewood, Editors. *The Arkansas Delta-Land of Paradox*. Fayetteville: University of Arkansas Press, 1993.

Whayne, Jeannie, Thomas DeBlack, George Sabo III, and Morris Arnold, Editors. *Arkansas: A Narrative History*. Fayetteville: University of Arkansas Press, 2002.

"Why Build With Wood." *The Long-Bell Book of Farm Buildings*. Kansas City: The Long-Bell Lumber Company, 1926.

White, Gerald Taylor. *Years of Transition: The United States and the Problems of Recovery after 1893*. University, AL: University of Alabama Press, 1982.

Wilson, Charles Morrow. "Tenantry Comes Forward." *Country Gentleman*. July, 1936.

Woofter, Thomas Jackson. *Negro Migration: Changes in Rural Organization and Population of the Cotton Belt*. New York: W. D. Gray, 1920.

Appendices

I. Paul Pfeiffer's Land
Transactions in Butler County, Iowa

Year	Acres bought	Amount paid	Avg price per acre	Acres sold	Amount received	Amount per acre
1895	136	$5,200	$38.24	------	------	------
1897	614	$15,750	$25.65	314	$13,082	$41.66
1898	407	$10,280	$25.26	------	------	------
1899	160	$6,400	$40.00	286	$6,600	$23.07
1901	------	------	------	300	$12,000	$40.00
1902	190	$1.00	------	------	------	------
1903	------	------	------	320	$13,760	$43.00
1907	------	------	------	190	$8,550	$45.00
Total	1,507	$37,631	$24.97	1,410	$53,992	$38.29

II. Paul and Gus Pfeiffer's Land
Transactions in Butler County, Iowa

Year	Acres bought	Amount paid	Avg price per acre	Acres sold	Amount received	Amount per acre
1896	340	$6,800	$20.00	------	------	------
1897	934	$17,552	$18.79	278	$7,440	$26.76
1898	280	$8,400	$30.00	------	------	------
1899	240	$6,401	$26.67	190	$8,550	$45.00
1900	640	$23,680	$37.00	276	$12,420	$45.00
1901	------	------	------	960	$54,948	$57.24
Total	2,032	$51,572	$25.38	1,704	$83,358	$32.25

III. Bushels of Crops Produced in Clay County, 1880-1910

Year	Corn	Oats	Wheat	Cotton (bales)
1880	343,836	12,406	13,408	2,307
1890	259,898	29,259	733	------
1900	795,160	15,600	66,870	3,689
1910	278,768	20,748	7,908	12,520

IV. Pfeiffer Land Purchases and Sales, 1914-1919

Year	Acres bought	Avg price paid/acre	Acres sold	Avg price rec'd/acre	Price of cotton/lb.
1914	339.5	$31.81	476.33	$23.52	7.35
1915	40	$25.00	------	------	11.22
1916	40	$25.00	281	$19.24	17.36
1917	------	------	1,532.4	$60.56	27.09
1918	103.15	$.01	1,383.47	$60.21	28.88
1919	103.15	$79.91	1,938.775	$60.94	35.36

V. Pfeiffer Land Transactions, 1920-1928

Year	Acres bought	Avg price paid/acre	Acres sold	Avg price rec'd/acre	Price of cotton/lb.
1920	40	$3.13	513.28	$127.82	15.89¢
1921	683.07	$54.32	120	$89.17	17.00¢
1922	550	$64.10	240	$80.38	22.88¢
1923	169.48	$84.85	------	------	28.69¢
1924	275.79	$66.76	240	$53.33	22.91¢
1925	502.97	$58.75	172.1	$73.91	19.62¢
1926	1,044	$74.05	95.125	$75.00	12.49¢
1927	326.125	$55.04	------	------	20.20¢
1928	304.84	$9.85	46.21	$96.65	17.98¢

VI. Crops in Clay County, 1910-1930

Year	Value all crops	Value cereals	Value grains seeds	Value hay and forage	Value vegetables	Value cotton
1910	2,179,762	671,058	3,563	168,541	106,043	1,154,751
1920	5,606,138	1,493,735	13,263	652,542	341,298	2,964,244
1930	4,051,602	823,170	15,015	297,064	83,722	2,699,273

VII. Farms in Clay County, 1910-1930

Year	Total farms	Avg price per acre	Owner farms	Tenant farms	Sharecropper farms
1910	4,321	$29.24	1,417	1,827	1,177
1920	3,535	$81.56	1,607	1,852	273
1930	3,435	$28.11	940	2,181	2,132

VIII. Pfeiffer's Land Transactions, 1931-1938

Year	Total acres sold	Total amont received	Avg cost per acre
1931	Three lots	$340	------
1934	40	$400	$10.00
1935	120	$1,500	$12.50
1936	343	$3,480	$10.14
1937	324	$3,765	$11.64
1938	2,328	$14,800	$6.35

IX. Paul Pfeiffer Land Sales, 1939-1943

Year	Total acres sold	Total amont received	Avg cost per acre
1939	2,507	$39,708	$15.84
1940	7,073	$87,718	$12.40
1941	19,356	$181,331	$9.37
1942	9,933	$78,192	$7.87
1943	6,149	$52,807	$8.59
Total	45,018	$439,756	$9.77

X. Karl Pfeiffer Land Transactions, 1944-1954

Year	Total acres sold	Total amont received	Avg cost per acre
1944	2,117	$35,354	$16.70
1945	2,063	$17,757	$8.61
1946	628	$21,790	$34.70
1947	769	$99,825	$129.81
1948	403	$1,800	$4.47
1949	237	$720	$3.04
1950	531	$1,321	$2.49
1951	435	$44,801	$103.00
1952	444	$54,047	$121.73
1953	1,398	$205,453	$147.00
1954	207	$28,000	$134.62
Total	9,232	$510,828	$55.34

XI. Farm Statistics in Clay County, 1930-1950

Year	Total acres in farms	Acres in crops of full owners	Total farms of full owners	Total farms of tenants
1930	234,411	31,614	940	2,181
1940	241,424	97,407	1,170	1,760
1950	319,372	122,318	1,328	1,231

XII. Trend Toward Mechanization in Clay County

Year	Tractors	Combines	Cotton pickers	Corn pickers	Hay balers	Draft animals
1940	326	------	------	------	------	4,640
1950	1,924	434	5	56	40	1,822

XIII. Last Will and Testament of Paul Pfeiffer

LAST WILL AND TESTAMENT OF
PAUL M. PFEIFFER

KNOW ALL MEN BY THESE PRESENTS: That I, Paul M. Pfeiffer, being of sound and disposing mind and memory, but realizing the uncertainties of life, do hereby make, publish and declare this to be my Last Will and Testament, hereby revoking any and all other wills or testaments by me at any time heretofore made.

I: I direct that all of my just debts be paid.

II: To my beloved wife, Mary A. Pfeiffer, I give and devise absolutely our home place described as Lots One (1), Two (2), Three (3), Four (4), Five (5) and Six (6) in Block Twelve (12) and Lots Four (4), Five (5) and Six (6) in Block Five (5) of Bare's Second Addition to Piggott, Clay County, Arkansas, together with all appurtenances thereunto belonging and including all household effects and furnishings.

III: As to all other real and personal property, except stocks, bonds and promissory notes, of which I may die seized and possessed, my executor hereinafter named is hereby authorized to sell the same at public or private sale, for cash or credit, as in his discretion seems to be to the best interest of my estate, and distribute the net proceeds to my wife, Mary A. Pfeiffer, and my Children, Pauline Marie Hemingway, Karl Gustavus Pfeiffer and Virginia Ruth Pfeiffer, share and share alike.

IV: Any stocks, bonds and promissory notes which I may own at the time of my death I give and bequeath to Pauline Marie Hemingway, Karl Gustavus Pfeiffer and Virginia Ruth Pfeiffer, as Trustees, to have and to hold the same, in trust, for a term of ten years for the joint use and benefit of my wife and children, with the powers and authority and subject to the terms, conditions and provisions hereinafter set forth:

          My said trustees are hereby authorized and empowered to collect any promissory notes due me or to renew or extend the same as in their discretion seems advisable, but shall annually make distribution of the interest and principal collected in any one year among my wife, Mary A. Pfeiffer, and my children, Pauline Marie Hemingway, Karl Gustavus Pfeiffer and Virginia Ruth Pfeiffer, share and share alike.

          As to stocks and bonds, my trustees are authorized and empowered to collect the interest and, in case of maturing bonds, the principal, as well as all dividends which may be declared on stocks. They shall make distribution of the net amount collected in the same manner and to the same persons as is directed in the preceding paragraph referable to collections from promissory notes.

          Should any of my children predecease me or during said ten year period die, leaving a child or children surviving, then such child or children shall take the deceased parent's part; but should any of my children predecease me, being childless, or die childless during said ten year period, then the part of such deceased child or children shall pass to my wife, Mary A. Pfeiffer, and my surviving children, share and share alike.

          My trustees shall be exempt from giving bond as such. In the event during the term of this trust any one or more of the trustees should die, then the survivors or survivor shall have all of the powers hereby granted to all jointly.

          At the termination of the trust herein provided for such property as shall still remain in the hands of the trustees shall be distributed in equal share to my wife, Mary A. Pfeiffer, and my children, Pauline Marie Hemingway, Karl Gustavus Pfeiffer, and Virginia Ruth Pfeiffer, share and share alike, as set forth in the preceding paragraphs of this item.

V: I hereby name, constitute and appoint my son, Karl Gustavus Pfeiffer, Executor of this my Last Will and Testament, to be exempt from giving bond as such.

          IN TESTIMONY WHEREOF I have hereunto set my hand to this my Last Will and Testament, this 20th day of September, 1940.

                                        Paul M. Pfeiffer

Signed, published and declared by the above named testator, Paul M. Pfeiffer, as and for his Last Will and Testament, in the presence of us, who in his presence, at his request and in the presence of each other, have hereunto subscribed our names as witnesses, this 20th day of September, 1940.

                                        Wm. F. Kirson
                                        F. M. Thornton
                                        Irene Cox

Filed this 1st Day of Dec, 1944.
By J. F. Irby, Co. Clerk
See Page 108 for Proof of Will and Order probating Will and appointing executor.

XIV. Last Will and Testament of Mary Pfeiffer

LAST WILL AND TESTAMENT

I, MARY A. DOWNEY PFEIFFER of Piggott, Clay County, Arkansas, being of sound mind and disposing mind, memory and understanding, do make, publish, and declare this to be my Last Will and Testament, hereby revoking any and all other wills by me at any time made.

1. I direct that all of my just debts be paid.

2. To each of my children, Pauline P. Hemingway of Key West, Florida, Karl G. Pfeiffer of Piggott, Arkansas, and Virginia Ruth Pfeiffer of New York City, and to my daughter-in-law, Matilda Carolyn Pfeiffer of Piggott, Arkansas, I give and bequeath the sum of Five Thousand Dollars ($5,000.00). Should any of them predecease me, leaving a child or children surviving, then such child or children shall take the deceased parent's part.

3. To my sister, Cora Downey of Boulder, Colorado, I give and bequeath the sum of One Thousand Five Hundred Dollars ($1,500.00).

4. To each of the following I give and bequeath the sum of One Thousand Dollars ($1,000.00): My niece, Katherine Geitz of Carroll, Iowa; my niece, Charlette Baldwin of Maryville, Missouri; my niece, Ruth Downey of Norcross, Minnesota; my niece, Dorice Coffin of Council Bluffs, Iowa; my niece, Grace Downey of Boulder, Colorado; my niece, Elita Downey of Wheaton, Minnesota; my niece, Vina Downey of Wheaton, Minnesota; my nephew, Frank Younker of Parkersburg, Iowa; my granddaughter, Barbara Louise Pfeiffer of Piggott, Arkansas; my grandson, Paul Mark Pfeiffer of Piggott, Arkansas; my grandson, Patrick Hemingway of Key West, Florida; and my grandson, Gregory Hemingway of Key West, Florida.

5. To each of the following I give and bequeath the sum of Two Hundred Dollars ($200.00): My grandnephew, Louis Franke of Chicago, Illinois; my niece by adoption, Mary Katherine Downey of Boulder, Colorado; and my niece by adoption Julia Cooney of Houston, Texas.

6. To Don Richardson of Piggott, Arkansas, in appreciation of the many services cheerfully rendered, I give and bequeath the sum of Two Hundred Fifty Dollars ($250.00).

7. To each, Hattie Stallings and Linnie Cole of Piggott, Arkansas, I give and bequeath the sum of One Hundred Fifty Dollars ($150.00).

8. To Little Rock Seminary, Little Rock, Arkansas, for the education of priests to work in Arkansas, I give and bequeath the sum of Five Hundred Dollars ($500.00).

9. To Subiaco College of Subiaco, Arkansas, I give and bequeath the sum of Five Hundred Dollars ($500.00).

10. To the St. Bernard Hospital of Jonesboro, Arkansas, I give and bequeath the sum of Two Hundred Fifty Dollars ($250.00).

11. To the Piggott Library, Piggott, Arkansas, I give and bequeath the sum of Two Hundred Fifty Dollars ($250.00).

Mary Pfeiffer's Will, Page One

12.   To Father Joseph M. Hoflinger of Paragould, Arkansas, I give and bequeath the sum of Five Hundred Dollars ($500.00).

13.   To the Catholic Church of Rector, Arkansas, I give and bequeath the sum of Two Hundred Fifty Dollars ($250.00).

14.   To the Catholic Church of Parkersburg, Iowa, I give and bequeath the sum of Two Hundred Fifty Dollars ($250.00).

15.   To the Catholic Church of Malden, Missouri, I give and bequeath the sum of Two Hundred Fifty Dollars ($250.00).

16.   To St. Mary's Mission House, Techny, Illinois, I give and bequeath the sum of Five Hundred Dollars ($500.00) for masses for the repose of my soul.

17.   To the Catholic Church Extension, 360 North Michigan Avenue, Chicago, Illinois, I give and bequeath the sum of Five Hundred Dollars ($500.00)

18.   To Visitation Sodality of Visitation Convent, Cabanne Avenue, St. Louis, Missouri, I give and bequeath the sum of Two Hundred Fifty Dollars ($250.00).

19.   To the Sisters of Perpetual Adoration of Clyde, Missouri, I give and bequeath the sum of Two Hundred Fifty Dollars ($250.00).

20.   To the Carmalite Nuns of Normany, Missouri, I give and bequeath the sum of Two Hundred Fifty Dollars ($250.00).

21.   Should any of the persons named in the paragraphs subsequent to Paragraph 2 herein predecease me, then the bequests in their favor shall become part of residuary estate and pass to the hereinafter named beneficiaries of said estate.

22.   All the rest, residue, and remainder of my estate, whether real, personal, or mixed and wheresoever situate, I give, devise, and bequeath in equal shares to my three children, Pauline P. Hemmingway, Karl G. Pfeiffer, and Virginia Ruth Pfeiffer, the child or children of any deceased parent to take the parent's share.

23.   I nominate and appoint my son, Karl G. Pfeiffer, Executor of this my Last Will and Testament, and direct that he be permitted to serve as such executor without bond and without accountability to any court.

24.   I authorize and empower my said Executor to sell and convey any and all property--real, personal, or mixed--of which I may die seized or possessed, or which may become part of my estate, at public or private sale, without application to or authority of any court, at such times and upon such terms and conditions as my said Executor shall deem advisable, for any or all of the following purposes; to pay my debts and the expenses of administration of my estate; to pay the bequests herein made; to facilitate devision and prompt distribution of the residue and remainder of my estate; and, in general, to close the administration and make distribution of my estate speedily and effectively.

IN WITNESS WHERE, I, Mary A. Downey Pfeiffer, have to this, my Last Will and Testament, subscribed my name this 15th day of May, 1944.

/s/ Mary A. Downey Pfeiffer

The foregoing instrument, consisting of three typewritten pages, including this page, each of the two preceding pages identified by the signature of the said Mary A. Downey Pfeiffer on the margin thereof, was, on this 15th day of May, 1944, signed, published, and declared by the testatrix, Mary A. Downey Pfeiffer, to be her Last Will and Testament, in the presence of us and each of us, the undersigned, who thereupon, at her request, and in her presence, and in the presence of each other, hereunto subscribed our names as attesting witnesses thereof, on the day and year above written.

/s/ Irene Cox   of Piggott, Arkansas.

/s/ Carl L. Hunter   of Piggott, Arkansas

Filed the 25th day of February, 1950.

Recorded February 27, 1950.

Mary Pfeiffer's Will, Page Two

XV. Sale of Pfeiffer Property by Paul Pfeiffer (Ordered by Date of Purchase)

People who purchased land from Paul Pfeiffer in 1939

January–F. E. and Ada Crawford, Eliphes Morlan, Ted and Bessie Key, Luther and Opal Malin, Oscar and Dora Walker, Cecil and Luecetla Nix, and Tolbert O'Guin,

April–Marion and Jessie Dickens, Central Clay Drainage District, and Jesse and Itha Honeycutt,

May–Happy Home Pentecost Church

June–Olin and Eathel McFarlin

July–Floyd and Agnes Shride

September–Henry and Lillie Dowdy, and Luther and Ida Glasgow

October–Glen and Flora Laws, Lon and Mettie Hanner, and W. F. and Gladys Scheffler

November–Loran and Hugh Holifield, W. P. and Effie Williams, S. N. and Hattie Parrish, John Parker, J. O. and Elsie Holt, W. T. and Gertrude Owen, Marlie and Millie Parrish, and John and Martha Hargate

December–L. R. and Zora Watson, Birdie Morris, and Elmer Coleman and Berylus Cato.

People who purchased land from Paul Pfeiffer in 1940

January–H. B. and Myrtle Satterfield, F. T. and Edith Roberts, Roy and Alice Battle, Marion Dickens, G. M. and Ethel Davidson, and John L. and Madge Denny

February–Andrew and Arizona Tibbs and M. O. Brosely

March–William F. and Daisy Hale, J. C. and Bonnie Higdon, Amos and Fannie May Young, Dewitt and Auda Huckaby, Vergil and Cletis Brown, Jeff and Ruby Morris, A. L. and Lizzie Herring, and Roy Barnhill

April–P. H. and Nellie Nolan, Aubrey and Doris Mansker, Sellmeyer Brothers, and Clyde and Earlene Boyd

May–Jasper and Fannie May Young

June–W. H. and Addie Jackson, Fuson and Stella Crowson, and William and Geneva Walker

August–Orville Hoffner, and Osco and Edith Jackson

September–Foy and Merlie Moseley, R. M. and Minnie Roofe, Clyde and

Cleatis Roofe, C. T. and Mamie Linam, E. W. and Minnie Smart, Odie Huckaby, Otis French, and Maurice Jeffries

October–Clarence and Linnie Kirklin, George French, J. A. Watson, Berylus and Melcenia Cato, L. A. and Julia Johnson, Tom Carter, Silas and Claudean Bolen, Wayne and Lottie Rowton, and Jessie and Ida Green

November–Diamond and Agnes Pemberton, Cecil Chilcutt, H. A. and Julia Rommel, Willie and Artie French, A. C. and Gertie McElyea, John and Lear Johnson, D. E. and Willer Lee Gregory, Clyde and Nancy Sells, Ebert and Dorothy Gatewood, Claud and Verna Bateman, Walter and Nettie Howell, Willie and Estell McElyea, Herman and Floria Page, R. H. and Minnie Hardin, B. L. and Lula Jewell, H. B. and Myrtle Satterfield, Lee and Marie Gunnels, Louis and Georgia Hart, and Sellmeyer Brothers

December–Oscar and Zettie Misenhamer, Virgil and Mirt Cochran, William and Geneva Hollowell, W. P. and Minnie Shepherd, Edwin and Vella Olds, Jeff and Ruby Morris, J. C. O'Bryan, Odie Huckaby, Dewey and Effie Hickerson, Paul and Pansy McLeskey, A. B. and Missie Lucy, G. G. and Edith Carter, G. R. and Ura Carter, Van and Eathel Cate, Thelma Hinklin, Johnie and Gertrue Pruett, G. W. and Mary Ellen Green, S. J. and Ethel Crawford, B. W. and Teula Wells, W. A. and L. D. Ogden, C. S. and Ruby Lunsford, B. F. and Ona Cate, Tw. W. Leggett, John and Pearl Morgan, Charley and Thula Shrum, R. A. and Bessie Adams, Vealus and Hattie Wall, Carrie Sims, Loyd Harley, Edgar and Leopha Harley, Blanche Bell, Elihue and Nina Battles, J. B. and Marguerite Futrell, Earl and Vera Parrish, Louis and Nell Toombs, E. M. and Gurtha Purcell, and L. C. and Bessie Sells.

People who purchased land from Paul Pfeiffer in 1941

January–Roy and Mabel Benson, Burtis and Lydia Tate, R. E. And Ella Davidson, Harvey Craft, Pete and Ellen Kerley, G. R. and Sallie Pierde, A. C. and Girtie McElyea, W. T. and Laura Shannon, F. W. and Amy Hubble, Emmett and Trella Bippus, Charles and Marie Martin, William Raborn, Ray and Veda Crowson, J. W. and Lora Rosson, E. H. and Maggie Rice, J. W. and Bertha Phillips, Dell and Osie Robinson, J. A. and Dora Watson, E. L and Lola Wilson, E. E. and Marie Miller, Harrison and Eva Hays, Iva McCracken, Sterling and Vivian Pentecost, George and Emma Roop, W. O .

Dobbins, Jake and Louisa Groaning, Henry and Leona Pence, J. W. and L. A. McMahan, Tom Carter, Don and Gusta Wilson, Robert and Lois Milburn

February–Robert and Annie Moore, A. e. and Lidy Mae Rice, Charles and Hazel Cate, J. C. O'Bryan, W. L. and Vera Pruett, Bertha Hollis, J. O. and Elsie Holt

March–W. N. and Pearl Johnson, A. L. and Lizzie Herring, Otto and Ethel Carpenter, F. M. O'Neal, H. I. and Lela Renard, Herbert Morrow, A. B. and Missie Lee Lucy, B. F. and Addie McElyea, A. C. and Laymon Harris, W. P. and Minnie Shepherd, Berylus and Melcenia Cato, Robert and W. P. Reeves, W. H. and Ila Myers, Joe and Leona Herring

April–John and Myrtle Ary, Alonzo and Fredonia Parrish, Roger and Barbara Spain, Walter and Dorothy Abbott, Tom and Nellie Kilbreth, Earl and Stella Coomer, Elmer Deniston

May–Ollie Bearden, O. E. and Pauline Dorris, D. C. and Geneva Wyatt, E. C. and R. F. Thomas, H. F. and Cora Whitt, John and Mary Wikoswky, Rube and Ethel Estes, Faber and Lena Gibson, Carl and Helen Graham, Frank and Velma Chappell, Henry and Freeda Duffell, Pfeiffer School, C. C. and Jessie Rowlett, Oba and Thelma Rogers, Louis Phillips, George and Claudia French, W. B. and Jennie White, William Fridenberg, E. C. McElvain, G. and Betty McElvain, Dalton and Eldress Mobley, R. M. Gilliam, Oscar Bennett, V. C. and Nora Wright

June–James and Dottie Beckwith, Claud Hancock, Grady and Bertha Walker, Elmer and Ada Rogers, Paul and Maudie Greene, F. E. and Elsie Parrish, George French, G. R. Watson, Eugene Luttrell, E. O. and Maudie Greene, Oscar and Myrtle Graves, and C. A. and Eula Green

July–J. B. and Marguerite Futrell, Frank Gower, Dean and Estelle Wright, J. S. and R. A. Davis, and T. A. Morgan

August–Sterling and Vivian Pentecost, Louie and Meda Gossett, Ralph Windham, Thomas George, Harry and Lura Watson, J. M. Hooper, Oscar and Effie Hooper, Milbern and Hattie Russell, W. B. and Mary Corder, Elsie Loveless, Claud and Nettie Misenhamer, Homer and Esther Johnson, Otto and Ethel Carpenter, W. M. Graves, Lee and Marie Gunnels, W. R. and Clara Wright, A. D. Foster, G. C. and Ollie Flaningan, O. B. and Sadie Loveless, Ruth Lawrence, and O. W. Powers

September–Denver and Nellie Romine, Raywilson and Murriel Langley, D. F. and Lois Powers, J. S. and R. A. Davis, Ollin and Agnes Billings, Orie and Melda Karnes, D. H. and Belle Shride, Layton and Emma Pollard, Floyd and Mirtle Forrest, Odell and Helen Ray, A. D. Foster, B. H. and Finnie Howell, J. A. Mays, E. H. and Maggie Rice, Orville Hoffner, M. E. and Maurie Taylor, J. H. and Bertha Page, Tom Boyd, Orville and Gertrude Forrest, G. A. and S. C. Toombs, A. A. and Lessie Toombs, John and Paul Morgan, Rollen and Lawanda Dunlap, Arvel Mallard, Tom and Ruby Ervin, Steve and Eva Brown, C. L. and Lennie Lutrell, Van and Eathel Cate, Lee and Betty Downey, C. M. Lamp, J. O. and Bertha Chiles, John and May Garis, T. L. and Nora Cate, B. F. and Ona Cate, M. C. and Willie Chisolm, Sam and Elsie Woodard, H. and Eva Vardell, Albert Bowden, Lawrence and Kate Butler, E. R. and Edna Chisolm, N. L. and Arietta Cate, H. B. and Myrtle Satterfield, Robert and Virnie Payne, Cris and Florence Reithemeyer, Silas and Lizzie Reed, and Garland and Gladys Rice

October–Raymond and Flossie Murphy, W. D. and Jimmie Wood, T. L. and Nora Cate, Frank and Lillie Holcomb, Albert and Lillian Wikosky, A. C. and Girtrude Conly, Henry and Stella Hogan, Jesse and Matilda French, Okley and Delia Wall, A. W. and Christine Pyland, J. L. and Dora Rowton, G. C. and Georgia Parkin, Adrian and Mary McClelland, J. W. Culbertson, Clifford and Bernice Coffee, Aubrey and Marie Ward, Leo Sellmeyer, J. A. and Ethel Nunley, E. L. and Mertie Galyean, Ollie and Girthy Calhoun, Lester and Marie Bettis, Willie and Madge Woods, Otto and Vera Renfro, Odra Carder, Finis and Elizabeth Welty, Henry and Rosa Tolbert, Clarence and Linnie Kirklin, Chester and Edna Cooksey, Will Rogers, T. H. and Minnie Crawford, Luther and Beulah Dobbins, Dempsey Cato, Berylus and Melcenia Cato, Cora and S. G. Cobb, Carlos and Mary Pierce, O. R. and Urra Carter, C. c. Fitzgerald, Earl and Elsie Aud, George and Harley Keller, Denver and Leoma Allen, W. J. Rickman, W. C. Rickman, Weldon Rickman, Roy and Louise Richey, Lacy and Janie Nunnally, W. L. and Eula Burns, O. C. and Callie Shannon, H. L. and Mary Ella Livingston, Edgar Whitehead, Alfred and Ella Allen, Frank Gower, Doyle and Denver Davis, Odis French, E. H. and Maggie Rice, Orris and Winnie Richey, S. P. and Katie Masters, L. S. and Denver Grissom, Orris and Agnes Billings, A. D. Mayfield, Louis Thornberry, Lawrence and Beulah Grayum, Orville Fridenburg,

Perry Thompson, L. S. Grissom, V. C. Wright, H. A. and Julia
Rommel, and George and Ada Nixon

November–Clyde and Opal Watson, C. T. and Sivel Dickerson, Cecil
Mitchell, Guy Robins, Robert Dortch, W. C. and Ruby Byars, J. M.
Custer, Ulyss and Louise Jackson, Clarence and Alpha Thasher, B.
R. And Finnie Howell, William and Georgia Rowton, Paul and
Mary Morrison, W. F. and Edna Irby, Robert and Eugenia Huckaby,
V. C. Wright, Dan and Pearl Phillips, Ora Pemberton, Othel and
Inis Burns, Ollie and Margaret Householder, W. T. and Wretha
Demay, Floyd Burns, and Raymond and Nova Carter

December–G. R. and Maude Norred, H. O. and Nellie Runyon, Loyde
Merrell, W. A. and Alcie Arnold, Jewell and Ruby Vaden, M. E.
and Hazel Claxton, Luther and Ruby Clayton, Odie and Cecil
Hayden, T. C. Justus, H. A. and Julia Rommel, Eliza Bolen, Loyd
and Ruby Hampton, Willie and Mildred Davis, J. A. Purdom,
Edgar and Leopha Harley, J. W. and Lydia Simmons, Coley and
Faye High, Earl and Eva Payne, Elmer and Bessie Guhleman, Eric
and Welda Haley, J. A. and Lela Hill, James Edwards, G. D. and H.
I. Schales, James and Beulah Bowers, Fred and Bessie Ervin, A. C.
and Gertrude Conly, W. W. and Eula Bookout, Claude and Ica
Taylor, Ernest Copelin, James Copelin, Harlin and Geneva
Shepherd, Everett and Rovilla Allman, Cecil and Hazel Nokes, J.
T. and Ozellar Nokes, H. B. and Oma Yates, Carl and Ola Davis,
Lambert and Norene Miller, L. M. Shrum, and J. A. Purdom

People who purchased land from Paul Pfeiffer in 1942

January–Robert and Maxine Chilcutt, J. C. Crowson, J. N. and Helen
Lutrell, Monette Milling Company, John W. and John J. Masters,
John and Alma Phillips, B. F. and Nora Arnold, H. E. and Addie
Arnold, Tom Buxley, M. T. Byrn, A.L. Neel, Sellmeyer Brothers, L.
M. and Esther Shrum, and James and Geneva Childress

February–Sellmeyer Brothers, Bill and Dollie Gregory, W. T. and Rebecca
Pendergrass, G. H. and Edith Ridings, A. N. and Georgia
Warbritton, H. A. and Pearl Walker, J. A. and Beulah Evans,
Robert and Inus Faucett, Ed Henderson, G. A. and Lella Wagner,
Daniel and Ruby Karnes, and Everett and Lillian Beaver

March–Emmett and Trella Bippus, Roland and Helen Baker, Bert and
Thelma Clark, Woodrow and Iramae Garner, Howard and Mae
Crowson, Harold and Arah Maple, O. C. and Callie Shannon, T. J.

and Janie Stubbs, Jim and Bettie Smith, Irene Freytag, W. B. and
      Rosie Fears, Elvis and Maggie Hasten, and Cecil and Lou Nix
April–Walter and Alta Kersey, Pink and Mammie Cruce, Ora Adam,
      Maggie Montgomery, Pearl Hendry, Sally Neal, Buster Orsburn,
      and W. L. and Verneal Shook
May–Sally Neal, E. H. and Van Clifford, Tom Carter, Charlie and Delphia
      Grimes, Orlie and Irene Karnes, E. C. and Pearl McElvain, Walter
      Anders, Harce and Hubert Taylor, William and Edna May
      Thomas, Orville and Flossie Friedenberg, and Sellmeyer Brothers
June–J. A. and Tina Kirby, N. C. and R. G. Matthew, J. P. Miller, and
      Robert Morrow
July–John Crockett, John Holifield, Joseph Stokes, and G. A. and Lella
      Wagner
August–J. D. and Bertran Pittman, Jesse and Flossie Stanley, E. M. and
      Gurtha Pucell, Raymond and Millie Conyers, and William and
      Daisy Hale
September–R. P. and Virnie Payne, L. B. and Elsie Haley, O. S. and Emily
      Lanham, and Norman and Bessie Lee Knowlton
October–Monette Milling Company, Daniel and Ruby Karnes, Vernon and
      Mary Catherine Watson, Steve and Eugene Brown, Steve and Eva
      Brown, Eugene and Juanita Thornberry, Elmer and Goldie Marie
      Cooper, R. E. and Raye Coleman, Noel and Wilma Roach, W. C.
      and Lelah Pearl Hosea, Lula Neel, A. L. Neel, Andrew Buxley, and
      Garland and Gladys Rice
November–J. M. and Belle McCain, J. E. and Lena Langley, Phillip and
      Pauline Sprock, S. C. and Mrytle Lee, T. H. and Minnie Crawford,
      Denzil and Birdie Holifield, Sadie Pence, Ralph and Ora Read, and
      Monette Milling Company
December–George and Ada Nixon, Leo and Jewell Gaulden, Jean and
      Rosalee Craig, and A. P. and A. P. Jr Russell

People who purchased land from Paul Pfeiffer in 1943

January–Everette and Novilla Allman, Jesse Edwards, Luther and Beulah
      Dobbins, Raymond and Mettie Conyers, Hardy and Jewell Brown,
      J. C. and Bonnie Higdon, Joe and Florence Jackson, Anna and
      Faris Smith, Eugene and Carnie Robinson, Walter and Roso Lee,
      Martin and Lerlie Lee, Thomas Lee, and Dock and Ruth Roark
February–L. Carl and Amy Williams, Leah Williams, W. A. and Della
      Bennett, Edward Sellmeyer, and Henry and James Jackson

March–L. H. Champ, L. M. Whitener, B. M. Fowlkes, Grady and Bertha
  Walker, Roy and Ruth Walk, Lester and Bernice Clayton, Willis
  and Laverna Garver, Bryce and Maxine Read, Asa Lamp, and J. D.
  and Itha Honeycutt
April–D. W. and P. Margaret Richardson, Cleo and Sylvia Satterfield, R. E.
  and Marguerite Massey, H. P and Hiddah Craft, Clyde Hardin, J.
  T. Dortch, R. D. Parsons, Raymond and Flora Read, Clifford and
  Cornelia Toombs, and Mabin and Sarah Gardner
May–L. R. James, James Smith, and Buster Orsburn
June–J. R. and Mary Leona Sanders, and Daniel and Ruby Karnes
July–Bill Ray, and Odia and Icie Russell
August–A. C. Read
September–John and Lucille Davenport, Andrew and Belle Holcomb, Roy
  and Laura Dobbins, R. R. and Carrie Hill, and A. L. Neel
October–Joe and Kate Gates, Georgie and Vera Garrett, E. C. and Pearl
  McElvain, and Thelma Hart
November–J. A. Cleveland, George Floyd Anthony, J. W. and Lora Rosson,
  George and Lorene Farrent, Everett and Rovilla Allman, C.E. and
  Stella Rice, and Wallace Graves
December–William and Lena Little, Martin and Nora May Burns, A. L.
  Neel, Perry and Janetta Ermest, and Donald Cunning

XVI. Sale of Pfeiffer Property by Karl Pfeiffer

People who purchased land from Karl Pfeiffer in 1944

January–W. W. and Eula Bookout, and R. C. and Lois Milburn
February–Luther and Opal Malin, and Jess and Ora Lee Lively
March–O. A. and Audrey McKenney, and Therman and Gladys Opal
  Kellar
April–Bill and Birtie Tippy
June–Don Byers
August–Samuel and Lora Seachrist
September–B. H. and Finnie Howell, and Sellmeyer Brothers
October–Charles and Dora Stanley
November–Harold Seachrist, J. R. and Leona Sanders, John and Pearlie
  Spence, W. J. and Viola Wilcoxson, A. L. and Flora Wood, N. S.
  Hoggard, and Melvin Boyd

December–Amos and Mamie Dollins, Robert and Lillie Boyd, Carl and
        Earlene Boyd, Theron Gatewood, and Francis and Irene Lloyd

People who purchased land from Karl Pfeiffer in 1945

January–Ira Payne, J. A. and Bettie Grisham, Charles and Etta Ellis, and A.
        N. and Georgia Warbritton
February–A. N. and Martha Niswonger, Ivan Pinkston, Donald Cunning,
        and James Jackson
March–H. L. Morrow, Thomas Lee, James Jackson, Donald Cunning,
        Ernest Copelin,
June–Charles and Edith Ellis
July–W. O. Barnhart
September–Delbert and Louise Chilcutt, Eliza Bolen, W. H. and Maggie
        Burk, and Conley and Versie Speer
October–Laura Groff, and Ebert and Dorothy Gatewood
November–W. M. and Georgia Rowton, Loyd and Lena Murray, Leonard,
        Leo and Edna Casteel, and Harl and Ruth Burk
December–B. H. and Fannie Howell, and Omer Curtis

People who purchased land from Karl Pfeiffer in 1946

January–Don Byers, and Harrison and Bessie Vallance
July–Paul Oliver
August–Harry Seachrist, and Amos and Martha Niswonger
October–J. A. McNiel, and Leon and Vonigene Gatewood
November–Binford and Mary Stone
December–Samuel and Lora Seachrist, and Calvin and Ada Green

People who purchased land from Karl Pfeiffer in 1947

January–Granville and Olean Speer
February–J. M. and Charles Rouse, and Elton Fluty
April–J. H. and Bertha Page, and Minnie Elizabeth Smart
May–J. L. and Mammaietta Hargrave
September–C. H. Davidson
October–C. E. and Mary Ellen Potts, and Lee Roy and Lela Kegley
December–George and Gurtha Griffith, Dave and Ara Collins, and R. L.
        and Vada Harris

People who purchased land from Karl Pfeiffer in 1948

February–L. C. and Adele Ort
March–W. H. and Ivy Thomas
April–M. U. Sowell
August–C. H. and Odessia Davidson
October–Jesse and Dora Burkhart

People who purchased land from Karl Pfeiffer in 1949

March–Joyce and E. A. Allman
September–Ennis Gatewood
October–Ebert and Dorothy Gatewood, and W. H. and Goldie Hayes

People who purchased land from Karl Pfeiffer in 1950

March–A. R. Winton, and I. B. Langley
June–A. R. Winton, and I. B. Langley
September–Lesley and Agnes Baker

People who purchased land from Karl Pfeiffer in 1951

October–W. F. and Marguerite Smart
November–J. Howard Crowson, Eugene and Lorene McKelvey, and J. T.
and Mary Barnes

People who purchased land from Karl Pfeiffer in 1952

January–J. M. and Charles Rouse, Loyd and Mable Cox, Rual and Maudie
Coomer, and Hudson and Bernice Moore

People who purchased land from Karl Pfeiffer in 1953

January–Grover and Dorothy Snider, and W. E. and Mildred Rouse

People who purchased land from Karl Pfeiffer in 1954

January–W. E. and Mildred Rouse

CPSIA information can be obtained
at www.ICGtesting.com
Printed in the USA
BVHW081149080721
611307BV00001B/59